In Achieving Total Quality, *Wayne Brunetti shares his unique insights into successful TQM implementation, as only someone who has led an organization down the path to world-class excellence can. He has captured the essence of what it takes to institutionalize TQM.*

Jacques Raiman
Chairman, GSI – Générale de Service Informatique

ACHIEVING TOTAL QUALITY

INTEGRATING BUSINESS STRATEGY AND CUSTOMER NEEDS

WAYNE H. BRUNETTI

Most Quality Resources books are available at discount rates when purchased in bulk. For more information contact:

Special Sales Department
Quality Resources
A Division of The Kraus Organization Limited
One Water Street
White Plains, New York 10601
800-247-8519   914-761-9600

Printed in the United States of America

97 96 95 94 93   10 9 8 7 6 5 4 3 2 1

Quality Resources
A Division of The Kraus Organization Limited
One Water Street
White Plains, New York 10601
914-761-9600
800-247-8519

The paper used in this publication meets the minimum requirements of American National Standard for Information Sciences—Permanence of Paper for Printed Library Materials, ANSI Z39.48— 1984.

ISBN 0-527-91724-9

Library of Congress Cataloging-in-Publication Data
Brunetti, Wayne H.
Achieving total quality : integrating business strategy and customer needs / Wayne H. Brunetti.
p. cm.
Includes bibliographical references and index.
ISBN 0-527-91724-9 (acid-free)
1. Total quality management. 2. FPL (Florida : Firm)—Case studies. I. Title.
HD62.15.B78 1993   93-7276
658.5′62—dc20   CIP

To Mollie, for always believing in me,
and for the support and love she has always given me.
This book would not have been possible without her.

Contents

Preface

There are many ways to run a successful company. Every so often a business "genius" appears and produces incredible results. Geniuses do not make up the majority of the population, however, and for those of us who cannot claim that distinction a systematic management process is needed to make our businesses more successful. If, along the way, this process also makes our employees and us a little happier, and work more fun, then so much the better. A "total quality management" (TQM) approach to doing business is such a system: it is a comprehensive management practice that can make a very real difference for your customers, your employees, and your shareholders, and can increase any company's ability to succeed.

A management approach using quality techniques as its base is, unlike many "quick fix" cures, more systematic and thorough. Although adopting this approach takes an initial investment in time, resources, and effort, the results are more significant and more sustainable because this management practice is a long-term investment in your customers and your employees. It has been my long-standing belief that if one can satisfy one's customers with products and services that meet their needs, the business will grow; and if the business process can provide a means to tap the brainpower of the entire workforce instead of a select few, the chances of succeeding will be heightened.

For eight years I was involved in the development and implementation of a quality management system for a major U.S. corporation, Florida Power & Light Company (FPL). I watched and helped nurture the system from its clumsy beginnings and struggled through its most interesting and frustrating stages. I enjoyed the satisfaction of seeing it become a working, integrated approach, and I felt the exhilaration that comes from winning an international prize for quality. From grass roots beginnings through receiving the prestigious Deming Prize, and on through establishing a successful and gratifying consulting practice, I have learned a great deal about quality and its effects.

Through study, trial and error, and cultivated instinct, I have learned what does and does not work in the quest for total quality management. This book offers a working approach—a pragmatic guide—to achieving total quality. It contains practical advice and guidance, including real tools that you can sink your teeth into, to help you and your company manage in a world of intangibles. It can be used as an introduction to "applied" total quality management or as a complement to the advice and guidance your company may receive from in-house experts and outside consultants hired to help implement a quality system.

In the course of learning what does and does not work for companies, I found much truth to the saying that the quest for quality is not merely a destination but a continuing journey. A reward like the renowned Deming Prize is truly a great honor in recognition of a tremendous accomplishment. But one cannot lose sight of the fact that there is always more to learn. The journey should never end. Winning the Deming is akin to obtaining a hoped-for promotion: it is a cause for celebration but you must realize that the real challenge still lies ahead, requiring even more dedication and hard work. Total quality management is based on solid principles, but it is also ever evolving and its techniques are constantly being refined.

Successful managers are supported by other good management and nonmanagement people who are smart, able to motivate the workforce, and good at communicating. I believe that most workers are ready, willing, and able to make major contributions to improving one's business if given the chance. In my experience, employees have great minds and great insights. It is management's job to provide a work environment in which all employees' minds can be exercised.

Management, at all levels, must be willing to take time to *listen*. They must be willing to implement the creative ideas and solutions that employees put forth. They must be willing to put in place methods and systems, and education and training, that allow employees to contribute to the improvement of the organization. The eagerness and ambition of employees will then pay off for everyone. Management must realize that most problems are caused by the existing management *system*; rarely are problems created by workers. This book seeks to address this area and provide ways to improve deficient systems.

I was taught the value of competition—that it provides the vehicle for a company to keep abreast of the marketplace. But I have learned that the competitive spirit is often misapplied in many companies. There is no place for competition when it only creates obstacles between departments or divisions within a company. Customers will bear the ultimate consequences of such misguided management practices. Internal competition has caused artificial barriers to be created within many companies. Instead of valuing internal competition, I have learned the value of cross-functional management and cooperation. Using this and other methods, problems that seem insurmountable can be overcome.

Another key lesson to learn is that problems should be thought of as *opportunities* . . . opportunities to improve. Recognizing problems is the first step toward improvement, and those who identify problems should be applauded, not criticized. I have learned that problems can be your best friend; the more one focuses on them, the more adept one becomes in implementing total quality.

I used to think that having a quality program or system would yield tremendous improvements through one or two breakthrough ideas. Although it is true that major improvements sometimes come from one or two brilliant ideas, this does not happen very often. Most major improvements come from the cumulative effect of thousands of small improvements. Senior management must pay attention to what might otherwise seem like less significant improvements, for there is no such thing as an insignificant improvement. It is important to create an environment in which small improvements are recognized and celebrated. This, in turn, will help develop the conditions for achieving one or two major breakthroughs.

I have also learned that a total quality approach is fairly straightforward, and that far too many companies overcomplicate this basic management theory with unnecessarily exotic methods. This book is directed to senior managers and others in organizations who may be contemplating adopting TQM or who may be struggling with their own or some other approaches. The market today is filled with neatly packaged, catchy-sounding, management techniques, many promoted under the guise of TQM. TQM, however, has only two fundamental parts: establishing priorities and conducting daily work. Everything else being touted is, or should be, in support of these two activities.

This book begins with a synopsis of the history and background of quality – the minimum that every manager should know about quality. Much advice has been given about the importance of senior-management involvement in quality, but little has been written about the exact role it should play. I have tried to fill that void by providing some advice to senior managers about the role they can play in making the management system work. This is practical advice that I hope will be useful.

Chapters One and Two deal with principles and processes of TQM and the role management should play. Chapter Three, Policy Management, covers priority setting, and Chapter Four, Daily Management, discusses methods that can be used to introduce improvement and control activities in daily work. The remainder of the book is devoted to supporting these two business activities. Team activity, vendor quality programs, education and training, problem solving, and suggestion systems are all designed either to improve the daily operations and quality of work life or increase the market share by improving the quality of products and services.

Policy Management and Daily Management are the two principal ways that Japanese companies introduce TQM. Some Japanese companies say that they begin with teams because teams take the longest to implement; but if you ask for a more detailed explanation they will tell you that the teams are structured to support Policy or Daily Management. I believe that too many companies begin with teams as the focal point of their approaches, only to find out that with no direction and priority, team activity alone will and does fail.

Teams, as well as the other support roles, are covered in Chapter Five to give senior managers and their advisors information on what is important and what to avoid. My advice is not foolproof, but I hope that it will assist companies in avoiding repetitive failures. As with any major undertaking, planning often becomes a critical ingredient. Chapters 10 and 11 are devoted to planning—the first focusing on the process of implementation planning and the other on integrating a quality management system into the culture of the company.

I hope that you will find this book a useful companion to assist in undertaking a management practice that will revolutionize your company and revitalize both you and your employees. If I could give senior managers one substantive piece of advice about TQM or about undertaking any management initiative, it is, in a word, *focus*. Whether you are undertaking improvement activities in daily work, Policy Management, team activity, or any other area, *focus* on the most important things that need to be accomplished. Use resources wisely. Use them where they will have the greatest impact on improving the products and services you provide your customers and improving the quality of work life for your employees. TQM, I believe, helps provide that focus.

In writing this book, I would like to acknowledge with gratitude the help of many friends and associates, especially:

My very creative and dedicated partners and associates at Management Systems International (MSI), who gave me their full support during the writing of this book and throughout our work together as we formed our new consulting group.

My clients, who have become my friends and "partners" in the quest for continuous improvement.

My former associates at FPL, who worked beside me to bring total quality management to the electric utility industry—at the beginning and through changing circumstances while facing daunting odds. They never stopped recognizing TQM's tremendous value.

The great teachers, Dr. Tetsuichi Asaka, Dr. Noriaki Kano, Dr. Yoshio Kondo, Dr. Kenji Kurogane, and Dr. Hajime Makabe, from whom I learned so much during FPL's work in TQM and the challenge for the Deming prize, and from whom I am still learning.

The Union of Japanese Scientists and Engineers (JUSE) and the many organizations I was privileged to observe and learn from—in particular, Kansai Electric Company, Yokogawa Hewlett-Packard, Fuji-Xerox, Komatsu Limited, the family of Toyota companies, and NEC Integrated Circuits.

The staff at Quality Resources, and especially my helpful and patient editor, Michael Shally-Jensen.

Organizations everywhere who recognize the need for quality and aren't afraid to go after it.

1

Understanding Total Quality

WHAT IS QUALITY?

In embarking on the quality journey, as with any other worthy undertaking, one must first have a few definitions, rules, and an understanding of the basic philosophy and history of the subject.

Dr. Yoshio Kondo, Professor Emeritus at Kyoto University and Chairman of the Deming Prize Committee, reminds us in his lectures about the history of management and quality that quality, cost, and productivity have been, and still are, fundamental concerns of management. He says that the concept of quality has been around for a very long time (the characters for quality appear in ancient Chinese writings); that quality is the very essence of humanity. The concept of cost, too, has been around for at least 10,000 years, and its beginnings can be traced to the beginning of trade activities and bartering. Productivity, however, has been around for only the past 200 years, with its beginnings identified with the industrial revolution and reinforced with the advent of the Taylor system.

If we evaluate the three management concerns in terms of how they relate to the customer (see Table 1.1), we find that only one of them, quality, is common to both management and the

TABLE 1.1. Concerns of a Company and its Customers

Company	*Customer*
Quality	Quality
Cost	Price
Productivity	After Sales Service

customer.[1] Customers do not think in terms of production costs, they simply do not care about what a company pays for a service or product. They care about price—what they have to pay and whether they are getting good value for their money. Customers also do not think about a company's productivity. What they want is sales service and after-sales follow up. However, both management and customers *do* think about quality. This is Dr. Kondo's reason why companies must put their greatest efforts in quality.

Since the advent of industrial society, the term "quality" has in part related to "adequacy," as in conforming adequately to expectations or the requirements of use. Generally an engineer created a set of specifications and, if a production crew met the engineering specifications, a "quality" product was said to be delivered. For a long time, producing quality goods meant making sure that the product conformed to its specifications. This had some degree of credibility—the product was generally fit for use and the customers were usually more or less satisfied.

At one time the U.S. was thought to produce the highest quality products in the world. This perception emerged after World War II, when U.S. goods were in very high demand, and continued until about the mid-1970s. U.S. products did, in fact, exhibit good quality when compared to products produced elsewhere in the world. This seems impressive until one considers that most of the world's production capacity was destroyed dur-

[1]Source: Dr. Yoshio Kondo

ing the war and what was left was not in very good shape. It is easy to achieve good quality when all that is expected is that the product be generally fit for use and if there is no competition against which to measure it.

In the early 1970s, U.S. manufacturers realized, to their surprise and disbelief, that customers were no longer buying their products. Why were sales dropping off so rapidly when our products were supposed to be the world's best? Had the definition of quality changed? Was the "fitness for use" standard no longer valid? After all, American cars usually got you where you wanted to go, so why were Americans now buying automobiles manufactured abroad?

The answer is that the definition of quality *had* changed, and conformance to specifications or fitness for use were no longer sufficient. Others had changed the definition without telling us. They had defined quality as *meeting customer requirements.*

TOTAL QUALITY

What do customers know about the process of producing high-quality products or services? How can customers determine specifications?

Successful companies have not fundamentally redefined the word quality; they have expanded it to include *design* and *service* quality (i.e., incorporating the requirements of the customer into the product design and service while also retaining "conformance" quality). Incorporating the customer's requirements into the product design and service requires companies to change the way they treat their customers. Companies now need to translate the words and ideas of customers into product and service specifications. This is *total* quality.

In addition, the most widely-used definition of the customer today is that *the customer is the next process.* We often think of customers only in terms of those who pay directly for the product or services we offer. The idea of the customer as the next process expands the classical sense of the customer to include not only those whom we traditionally call customers but also the myriad of *internal* customers (i.e., employees) who may never see the final or end-user customer. This total quality definition includes those whose work-product is an integral part of satisfying the ultimate customer's requirements. The concept of the internal customer helps strengthen cooperation within the organization, helps eliminate internal competition, and helps drive out fear.

However, caution should be exercised when using this modern definition of the "customer." All too often I have seen internal customers taking advantage of it. Internal customers may, under this definition, require conditions to be satisfied that have nothing to do with meeting the ultimate customer's requirements. In these instances, the internal customer is requiring things that may be for their own personal use and serve no other significant purpose. To avoid this situation, as requirements are being established, all requirements should be *validated* to see that the specification requested by the internal customer satisfies the ultimate customer's needs and expectations. One must see past the internal customer's requirement to the customer who pays for the product or service.

Few managers understand what is or should be included in the definition of total quality. Many managers continue to think in terms of traditional conformance quality. They think in terms of basic, tolerably defective, adequately durable, acceptably performing and reliable goods and services.

These quality characteristics are all very important, but managers typically fail to consider them in conjunction with the equally important attributes of safety, cost, and delivery. Safety-related quality characteristics must be met for a product or service to be acceptable. Whether a company is providing food, running an airline, or providing a consumer or industrial product, it must be safe. Cost quality characteristics must be met because consumers must receive value for the products or services they receive, and often the cost of a product or service is directly reflected in the price paid. Delivery quality characteristics must be met because a product or service may have the best quality, price, and safety characteristics, but if it is not received in a timely manner, it loses its value. When managers begin to understand all of these characteristics, they will see what steps are needed to improve their overall product or service.

One must appreciate the broader meaning of quality. One should know the difference between "big *Q*" quality and "little *q*" quality. Big *Q* quality is important because it encompasses cost, delivery, and safety, as well as the traditional view of "conformance" quality.

In addition to including safety, cost, and delivery in the definition of quality, today more and more businesses that have adopted total quality as their management practice will also add corporate-responsibility items to their definition of quality. One such item is environmental protection. For some companies this is an extremely important part of achieving total quality, and it may make the difference in the company's ability to stay in business.

Required Versus "Exciting" Quality

The perception used to be that, as a company improved its ability to conform to its customers' requirements, the level of satisfaction would improve to the point where customers would be extremely satisfied. This is known as single-dimension quality, and is shown in Figure 1.1[2]. Today we know that just meeting the minimum requirements is insufficient to gain high levels of customer satisfaction. Supplementing the idea of big *Q* versus little *q* quality, therefore, is the notion of "required" or "must be" quality versus "unexpected" or "exciting" or "attractive" quality. A product or service cannot attain true "quality" status unless it is fit for use and meets the expectations of the customer. Customers expect certain things from a product or service and, at a minimum, a company must deliver what the customer expects. When you buy an automobile, you expect it to start, to be reliable, to be durable, and to be safe. These are the minimum standards—the required quality—that every company producing automobiles must meet.

Similarly, if you go to a restaurant you expect the food to be palatable and the service to be courteous and efficient. This is the minimum. You do not want to be served bad food or to be

[2]Source: Dr. Noriaki Kano

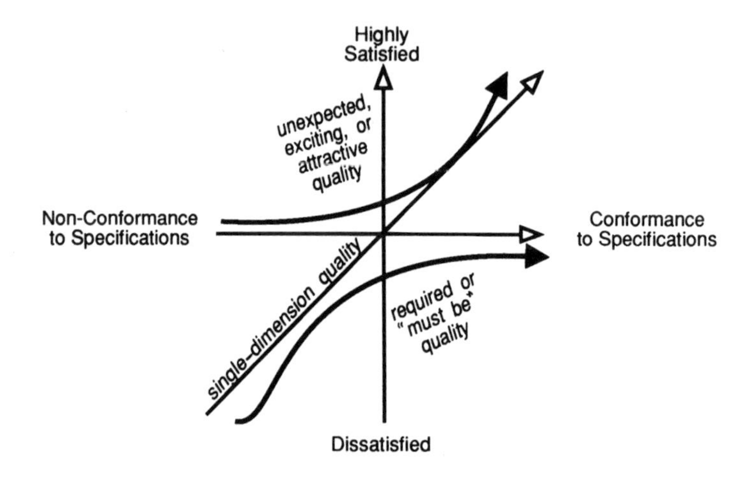

FIGURE 1.1. Kano's Dimensions of Quality

treated rudely. A company cannot achieve basic quality unless it meets the minimum specifications of its customers.

A second dimension or aspect of quality, however, serves to differentiate the truly great companies from the average ones. This is the notion of "attractive quality." This occurs when the level of quality goes *beyond* what the customer expects. It is sometimes referred to as "exciting" or unexpected quality. When you buy an automobile, you do not normally expect the service manager or the dealer to call you periodically to find out how satisfied you are with the car. You do not expect a service repair person to come and pick up your car for periodic maintenance. You do not expect personal notes from the manufacturer. Yet some automobile dealers provide such a level of service. This is "exciting" quality—an unexpected pleasure for the customer.

Unfortunately time can erode "exciting" quality, particularly if a competitor decides to incorporate your current exciting features. If a company or its competitor provides the added features for a long time, customers may become so accustomed to them that those features begin to be expected. In these instances, a company must think of newer and more exciting features to differentiate their product or service from the rest.

COST VERSUS QUALITY

Before one properly understands the concepts and management practices of total quality, it may seem that if a higher level of quality is desired, the consumer will have to pay a lot for it. This, however, is a common misconception.

Dr. W. Edwards Deming, the dean of modern quality control, states that, as quality increases, productivity increases.[3] Deming advises that costs will ultimately *decrease* as quality increases. Another noted U.S. quality consultant, Philip B. Crosby, says in his book *Quality is Free* that the cost of nonconformance to quality requirements is 15 to 20 percent of a company's sales dollar! This, in other words, is the cost of producing defects or the cost of inspection and rework. It is easy to understand that if quality can be increased (e.g., by reducing defects), the cost of quality will be reduced and productivity increased.

As a company begins to implement quality as a way of doing business, it will probably find other examples where the cost of defects is even higher. Cost reduction is an integral part of quality improvement. By improving quality, costs will be reduced. This is apparently hard for some senior managers to accept. But have they ever taken the time to measure the real cost of nonconformance? My experience is that few companies understand the costs they incur for inspection, rework, defects, and lost sales because of quality problems.

Reporters and people from other companies have repeatedly asked me the total cost of Florida Power & Light Company's (FPL's) quality program, and I always, in despair, realize that the questioner has missed the point entirely. In my working career, I have never been asked, for example, "How much does your accounting or purchasing system cost per year?" or "How much does the company's human resource system cost?". Nor have I ever been asked any other question about the costs of the myriad business management systems a company uses. It is hard

[3]W. Edwards Deming, *Out of Crisis*, Massachusetts Institute of Technology, Center for Advanced Engineering Study, Chapter 1.

to put a price tag on a management system. Like other systems, a quality management system becomes part of the corporate culture, part of the way of doing business. So how do you put a price tag on that?

From my experience, the principal incremental cost associated with any quality management system is the cost of training employees and senior management to use the tools and techniques. These costs are not, however, *additional* costs that a company inevitably must incur—they are *substitute* costs. Every company must train its employees to use the business systems that run the organization, but few keep track of this cost. So why not take the positive step of redirecting the training effort to quality-related courses?

A second area of cost for quality improvement is the initial productive time that is lost in getting workplace teams started (see Chapter 5). This cost should be considered training costs. Teams may at first seem to flounder and produce few tangible results. But as management begins to gain an understanding of the power of teams, and as progress is made, costs will eventually be reduced.

A third cost consideration is the management time needed to institute a total quality management system. Implementation cannot be delegated to others; it must be done by senior management. Some senior managers may feel that this task is not their responsibility or that it imposes constraints on their discretionary time. Yet, if there is only one recommendation here that you choose to follow, it should be this one: senior managers must be thoroughly educated and involved in total quality if a company expects good results and lowered costs.

WHY TOTAL QUALITY?

After reaching an understanding of what total quality is, the next question that must be asked is, "Why do *we* need it?" The answer is that the process of change has undergone change. For example, after the fluorescent light bulb was invented, it took 83 years to put the bulb into production. Today ideas are conceived and brought to market in a matter of months or even weeks. Products

FIGURE 1.2. Kano's Basics of TQM

are made obsolete by new and better products in incredibly short time frames. Would we really want to adopt a cellular phone with analog technology when we know that someone else is about to break through with digital technology?

In other words, change tends to produce further change. All businesses must have a method to deal with an environment of ongoing change. Businesses need total quality management because, unlike in the past, when customers had few options and demand generally exceeded supply, customers today have many more options and can select products that offer the highest value. A total quality approach will help any company be more tuned-in to its customers' needs and expectations. If one can successfully respond to customer requirements, the business will likely prosper.

FUNDAMENTALS OF TOTAL QUALITY MANAGEMENT

In his lectures on quality, Dr. Noriaki Kano, professor and department head at Science University of Tokyo, and a member of the Deming Prize Committee, uses a simple picturegram and model to describe the basics of TQM (see Figure 1.2[4]). He ex-

[4]Source: Dr. Noriaki Kano

plains that companies adopting TQM must first have strong foundations. The core foundation is the intrinsic technology that the company possesses; no company can succeed unless it has good technology. Fundamental skills and technology are needed to run even the simplest business. The next critical foundation is some motivation for quality. If the management of the company does not see clearly on this point, no amount of training, tools, or techniques will work. There must be clear agreement among senior management on the need to concentrate on quality.

Dr. Kano's model goes on to explain the three pillars of TQM. The first of these is concepts. In examining those companies that have been successful, there are several fundamental concepts or principles followed.

Putting the customer first or achieving *customer satisfaction* is at the heart of total quality management. This principle supports the traditional notion that the "customer is king." If a company cannot satisfy its customers, another company will. Processes and products must be designed with one thing in mind—satisfying the customer. Companies must move from a "product out" mentality (i.e., pushing a product or service out) to a "customer in" attitude (i.e., providing the product or service that customers expect, or better yet, *beyond* what they expect).

A second principle of TQM is *management by fact*. Management by fact is difficult to institutionalize, however, because everyone has opinions, views, and notions about how things should be done or about what the root cause of a problem is. But facts are far better than opinions. Senior and middle management, supervisors, and employees should all be taught statistical techniques and the importance of *facts* in solving problems. If a poor decision-making process exists, it can only produce poor decisions. Facts can dramatically improve decision-making abilities. Management by fact means solving problems and making decisions based on data.

The *Plan-Do-Check-Act (PDCA) principle* is another essential for implementing a successful quality program. PDCA, also referred to as the "Deming Wheel," is the principle of continuous improvement. Most companies do not have practices in place that force continuous improvement. Following the PDCA principle forces the examination of business processes. It is a check of processes against a relevant standard or stated business objective. Practicing PDCA generates numerous opportunities for further improvement. A systematic process for examining how to improve things is necessary in a successful application of TQM. Because conditions are never as good as they might be in any business, managers should never be satisfied with the status quo. Becoming complacent will allow competitors to win; following the PDCA principle guards against this complacency.

Still another principle is *focus on prevention*. Companies that have mastered TQM realize that solving problems is but a first step in making improvement. Not until methods are instituted to *prevent* the recurrence of problems can long-lasting results be achieved. Companies that do not understand this fundamental principle generally end up solving the same problem over and over. Companies must not only ensure that problems are solved but that there are methods in place to prevent the recurrence of the problems.

Rounding out these four fundamental principles are two others that relate to how people should work together. First there is *employee involvement*, sometimes referred to as *respect for people*. When it comes to brainpower, the more the better. It is lamentable, however, when organizations limit the use of the available brainpower. Most employees have good minds. All that is needed is a process to tap them to discover their often innovative and exciting ideas. Employees know about problems within the business and can help solve them. Successful TQM applications recognize that workers' energy, enthusiasm, and value to the company can be limitless given the proper forum where their ideas can be expressed, and given the proper respect for their abilities.

The last foundational principle is *cross-functional management*. Cross-functional management recognizes that no organizational unit can by itself control every aspect of the business operation to ensure that the customers' requirements are met. Cross-functional management is a method of cooperating across functional organizational boundaries—cooperating with each other to make sure that the product or service meets the quality standards that are established. It took me some time to fully appreciate the power of this principle. Early in my working career, I joined a company that was organized around centrally controlled functional processes. Each local manager worked well in his or her own area of responsibility, but without regard for other departments. It was a kind of an "every person for himself" focus. As long as they got their own job done, to hell with the other guy (or so the feeling ran).

Over time, however, we moved away from this highly centralized functional design to a more decentralized one. Each step of the way, local managers were given more control over the resources necessary to satisfy their local customers. Each step of the way improvements in customer satisfaction and costs were achieved. As we began learning more about TQM, we felt that we clearly understood the meaning and application of cross-functional management.

It was not until we began the process called Policy Deployment, or more properly, Policy Management, that I discovered the full potential of cross-functional activities. Even though at that time I had control over most of the resources necessary to do what my organization and I were responsible for, we quickly realized that there were others whose help we desperately needed if we were going to make major improvements.

One of the quality characteristics that my organization was responsible for was meeting commitments made to our customers by installing new services or changes in service by the negotiated dates. We thought that this was fully under our control; however we soon came to realize that if we were to have good results, we needed the cooperation of others. Purchasing, industrial relations, human resources, accounting, and information services were among the many departments that made major contributions to my own organization's success. As a result of practicing cross-functional management activities, major corporate barriers were broken down. Communication among departments improved dramatically.

Personally, I had never seen this level of cooperation in the 25–plus years that I had worked for the company. I believe that the success of the Japanese in achieving high levels of quality and quick response time to market is largely a result of their success in this area.

Cross-functional management techniques reduce design time, improve product and service quality, and build a sense of mission in a company. It aligns the vectors so that everyone and everything is going in the same direction. No TQM approach can be successful without this important feature.

ADOPTING TOTAL QUALITY: MAJOR PROCESS COMPONENTS

Another pillar used by Dr. Kano to describe TQM is the promotional vehicles used to introduce TQM as a management system. In examining successful applications of TQM principles, there consistently appears to be three major program segments, or distinctive process components, that can be identified as bases for organizing and implementing the principles. These three process components are Policy Management, Daily Management, and Team Activity. For many companies, a fourth major component, Vendor Quality, also appears, because many companies are highly dependent on the quality of their vendors' products and services in ensuring their own success.

In the following sections I will briefly sketch the four major process components, leaving more detailed discussions of each in the chapters to follow.

Policy Management

Policy Management is sometimes called by other names, such as policy deployment, management by policy, or (in Japanese) *Hoshin Kanri*. It is a systematic process used to direct corporate resources toward solving problems and making major improvements in *select high-priority* areas. Policy management is, in my view, the most important element of the four program segments. It is a means of executing overall corporate strategy and realizing the corporate vision. It is a process that involves commitment from senior management and from the entire organization.

Some of the main resources drawn on to identify opportunities for improvement and to develop policies are:

- Customer requirements compared to company performance.
- Internal business problems.
- The external business environment, including competition and changes in technology.

In the case of customer requirements, the Policy Management process usually starts with coming to know and understand customers' requirements and, most importantly, their problems. Identifying customer requirements is no easy task and requires much diligence, but some useful tools include surveys and research, customer contact, warranty performance records, and customer complaint records. One successful method to organize customer requirements and identify gaps in performance is to use a customer needs analysis. This method uses "quality function deployment" techniques and other information readily available within a company (see Chapter 3). This ties in well with Policy Management.

Policy Management also looks at two levels of internal business problems: those that are serious enough to affect the entire corporation, and those that are more local in nature. The first group includes any problems other than those that can be solved by local management and its employees under policy direction and resource allocation provided by top management. Identifying the more broad-based corporate problems can be accomplished in several ways—a "bottom up" approach (where employees target problems), a systematic management review process, or a combination of both.

A third major source of corporate problems or opportunities for improvement is the external business environment, including the competition. Sometimes external problems are among the most difficult to identify and solve. Changes in technology can also be of strategic importance to many companies.

As explained more thoroughly in Chapter 3, after major corporate problems are identified, the list is pared down to five or six of the most critical ones. After the first major corporate problem is resolved, the next most important is attacked, and so forth. Next, establish, revise, or review corporate policies to ensure that the problems being solved (or yet to be solved) are consistent with the strategic direction the company has set for itself.

Once policies are developed, they must then be "deployed" (i.e., circulated) and implemented. Polices must be clear enough that they provide not only the objective but the means to obtain the objective. The policies should be clear enough so that even a new employee can understand what must be accomplished. Every unit in the company that can contribute to resolving a problem is identified and its contribution determined. Local management should have the authority to implement problem-solving techniques and to suggest solutions. Resources are reallocated by top management as appropriate. In addition, a monitoring process is established to check on progress.

Finally, local-level problems that do not generally affect the company as a whole are also identified and targeted for improvement. This is the second level of Policy Management. Several techniques are used to identify and resolve problems at the local level, including the "reason for improvement" worksheet, which explains solutions in terms of the annual business plan, and standard control charts. (For other techniques, see Chapter 8.)

Problem solving and review techniques should in fact be similar for both corporate and local problems. Remember, problems are your best friend! Without problems, things can never really improve. Policy Management provides the means to effect this integration and make the necessary improvements. It is the most important of the four major process components in adopting a total quality approach to business management.

Daily Management

While a company is working on major improvements, the daily operations of the company go on. The minimum specifications or standards that have already been established for a product or a service must still be met. The task is to ensure that at the same time that overall operations are being improved, there is little variation from what is expected. Daily Management is a means both to control and to improve day-to-day operations.

A Daily Management process is essential when implementing Policy Management. It is essential for solving daily operational problems that all organizations experience. Part of senior management's role is to ensure that processes that are vital to meeting customer needs are in place. Managers and supervisors are the ones responsible for actually executing and checking this portion of the quality management system. In addition to ensuring that day-to-day operations are under control or daily improvement activities are underway, Daily Management is the means to maintain the gains realized from Policy Management activities.

Team Activity

With quality principles in place, policies adopted, training started, and problems identified, someone—namely, company employees—needs to *solve* the problems. This is where teams and teamwork come into play, and this is a great opportunity to begin tapping employee brainpower. Team activity is the means both to address Policy Management goals and objectives and to make improvements to daily operations. The characteristics of teams may differ depending on the type or nature of the problem to be solved. Typically, project teams are assigned problems by management, whereas natural teams or quality circles choose their own problems to solve. The average employee, unfortunately, will probably initially be somewhat skeptical about a company's turning over its problems to him or her to resolve. They may also be skeptical about using a disciplined problem-solving process or statistical techniques because they will have strong opinions about how things should be done without using such techniques.

Yet, for TQM to succeed, employees must know that they are one of the most important resources for making improvements in their company, and they must be taught the importance of using the right tools to solve problems. Once employees use the tools, they will quickly learn the importance of using *facts* over opinions. They will learn that opinions are easy to give, but fact-finding takes work and can often be frustrating. They will learn that when they use facts to support their ideas, their solutions are more readily approved by management.

Initially, employees sometimes doubt that anyone will listen to them if they do solve a problem, or if they are listened to, they wonder if management will take heed and implement their solution. To be successful with team activity, a work atmosphere must be developed where managers and workers listen to and respect each other's ideas. Building this type of environment is difficult, but a team activity approach is a very good means to begin building trust and respect.

Vendor Quality

A quality system to deal with vendors must also be developed. A vendor quality program is a natural extension of a total quality program. It is necessary for several reasons, but primarily because total quality cannot be achieved in a vacuum. Many companies spend nearly two-thirds of their revenues on products and services that come from outside the company. Such companies need assistance from their vendors to achieve total quality. A good vendor quality process can help ensure quality products and services.

It is not necessary to insist that the particular quality approach used by the company is also used by its vendors, but there should be systematic quality processes in place that can be checked to ensure that the company standards are met. This is not a matter of inspecting vendors' products, but actually inspecting their quality control processes. Vendors should clearly know what is expected of them in this regard.

ADDITIONAL STRUCTURAL SUPPORT FOR TQM

Dr. Kano's third pillar to support TQM is the techniques employed. Japanese methods teach us that over 90 percent of all problems can be solved using the seven basic statistical tools. Only very complicated problems require sophisticated analytical tools. Too often, we seem to be more impressed with the sophistication of the tools than the results achieved—we like to use calculus when addition would do. (Chapter 8 discusses some of the problem-solving techniques used.) Dr. Kano's model for a TQM management system is covered by a "roof of quality assurance" (i.e., a system that forces the prevention of problems and one that drives continuous improvement).

DEVELOPING A MANAGEMENT SYSTEM

TQM is a total management system that sets the direction of the company, tunes its engines, and helps realize the company's vision. TQM allows a company or organization to identify and develop an interaction among corporate problems and solutions, local problems and solutions, Policy Management efforts, Daily Management efforts, Team Activity, Vendor Quality, and the role of education and training. The management system that evolves is a focused approach to increasing customer satisfaction and achieving business objectives. In addition, artificial organizational structures can be avoided or used sparingly to accomplish the implementation. It is preferable to use the natural organizational structure whenever possible to promote and implement a quality plan.

TRAPS AND HURDLES

Various barriers will impede successful implementation of a total quality program. These cover two general areas: barriers that are organizational or structural in nature, and barriers that are "attitudinal" or behavioral in nature. A good deal of overlap exists between the two.

One key barrier is *senior management*. Without the total commitment of senior management, total quality will never happen. Commitment does not mean simply endorsing the undertaking, coming up with catchy phrases, and giving a few speeches. It means *total* involvement.

Senior management needs to be educated: they will need to attend courses in everything from promoting team activity to statistical process control (SPC). In some companies, senior management meets during evening hours and on weekends to expand their education on quality and to help define and refine the management system.

A second barrier is *middle management*. Middle managers are in some ways the "prima donnas" of the corporate world. They can represent a significant barrier in implementing change in an organization because they will often tell others what to do rather than try to do it themselves. To implement a quality program, middle management, like senior management, must become involved. That means education and participation.

A third barrier, not surprisingly, is *first-line supervision*. This is principally because of how first-line supervisors are selected. Traditionally, they have been selected because of their technical abilities. They are told, "You have done a good job and now we want you to tell others how best to do the job." This type of management does not necessarily contribute to a successful quality program. First-line supervisors must first learn to act as coaches and cheerleaders. Their job is to foster an atmosphere that allows employees to use not only their manual skills but their brains. Supervisors must avoid viewing employee teams as hindrances to accomplishing the job. The first-line supervisor must be thoroughly educated in the techniques of problem solving and must know how to coach employees effectively.

Another barrier is *staff*. In my career, I have come to learn a good deal about where power lies in an organization. Staff members often seem to behave as though the line organization works for them. Staff personnel are, after all, the caretakers of the corporate rule books, standards, and policies, so over the years they come to feel they know everything and that people in the line organization are somehow less cognizant of things than they. This has to do, in part, with the selection of staff.

Staff members are generally understood to be the local experts and, as a result, they are sometimes adverse to taking suggestions from others. For instance, engineering departments have individuals with highly specialized areas of expertise. When they receive an improvement solution from the line organization, particularly a first-line employee, they may sometimes dismiss it. They wonder how a first-line employee could possibly know more about the subject than they do? But for TQM to succeed, staff members must identify their internal customers' needs and, most importantly, know and appreciate that they work for the line organization.

First-line employees are not usually serious barriers. Employees, in general, want to do a good job and they have good ideas about how their jobs can be done. It is management's role to provide employees with the proper implements (e.g., statistical tools and a problem-solving process).

Another set of barriers includes time and attitude, amount of training needed, management styles, level of success, and artificial organizational structures. Time and attitude are significant because the CEO cannot simply will TQM to happen. It takes time, and senior management must be patient. TQM is a long-term investment—it is not a 90-day quick fix. It requires a company to "get back to the basics" and to concentrate on *improving* them.

The amount of training needed matters because it may seem that training will never end. The reality is that training will continue for an extended period. Quality begins and ends with education. All companies invest in training, some more than others. The allocation of the training budget will need to be changed to focus on training in the tools of quality. But, as noted, this does not necessarily mean that a company will have to spend more money.

Management styles are a barrier because certain styles are not complementary to a TQM approach. A highly autocratic management style, for example, does not fit. TQM is a consensus-building style of management that requires teamwork at all levels in an organization. It requires a great deal of respect for people, their ideas, and their abilities.

Success is a barrier because if any company is satisfied with its existing management approach, why would it consider changing? Successful organizations tend to have a difficult time justifying the necessity for basic change, but there are good business reasons for considering change, even if a company has been successful historically.

Finally, artificial organizational structures can and should be avoided or used sparingly to accomplish the implementation, because it is preferable to use the natural organizational structure whenever possible to accomplish the implementation and to promote a quality plan. Too many companies create unnecessary parallel organizations to implement TQM. They believe it is a way to avoid the resistance that occurs when change is introduced. Resistance to change is a natural occurrence—it must be faced and solved. Creating parallel organizations only postpones dealing with the issue.

CONCLUSION

There are various views about what TQM can offer a business. My own view is that a company should first have sound business reasons for adopting TQM. TQM should not be adopted simply because it seems like the latest management fad. TQM is a systematic approach for delivering customer satisfaction. It is a way of doing business that focuses the entire company on doing the things to achieve this end. If your company can satisfy its customers, its chances of achieving success will be enhanced.

Dr. Tetsuichi Asaka, one of the world's leading teachers in the field of quality, says that total quality control is "the systematic application of common sense." Yet no one ever said that "applying" common sense should be easy. Hence, the necessity for learning and for careful application of management concepts.

Dr. Noriaki Kano, another great teacher of quality, is somewhat more pragmatic about the idea of quality. He says that the best way for a corporation to expand sales and make a profit is to provide its customers with satisfaction through its products and services. Corporate executives who are making short-term decisions to improve this year's earnings without regard to what tomorrow may bring are jeopardizing the futures of their companies.

In this increasingly competitive world, businesses must adopt a management approach that listens and reacts to their customers. If your business does not, someone else's will. Being the best you can might not be good enough any more.

It is only through your customers that you can make a profit; it is only through your customers that you stay in business. A total quality management process can greatly enhance a company's ability to be competitive and satisfy its customers.

2

Quality and the Role of Management

INTRODUCTION

When I first started studying total quality, I heard Dr. Deming say that 90 percent of all business problems are caused by management. I thought this was a ridiculous statement. He was talking about someone *else's* company; that certainly was not true of *my* company.

As we at FPL began to analyze the root causes of some of our business problems, however, the vast majority of them pointed at *management*. They did not point directly at management; rather, they pointed at our written and unwritten policies. They pointed at construction standards. They pointed at our operation and maintenance policies and standards. They pointed at the organizational structure itself. These were the culprits and, unfortunately, it was management that was ultimately responsible for each and every one of them.

I thought I would never be able to admit it, but management truly does create the majority of problems. If you start with an open mind and begin to look deeply into a problem and its genesis, I would wager that you will find that someone in management has created it. Most managers remain unaware that they are creating problems, and other people in the organization are often too afraid to tell them. Yet ultimately the truth must be known!

SENIOR MANAGEMENT

Quality begins with senior management, but where does the actual quality *journey* begin? Senior management typically needs a somewhat definitive approach. Managers will want a foundational idea—a tentative road map—to know exactly where they should start.

If someone were to ask the CEO of a company to describe the company's management system, he or she would perhaps send the person to the vice president of information services or maybe to the human resources department. There, a discussion would probably take place about purchasing, payroll, production scheduling, human resources, and other such activities. These are all part of the general management system, and yet they are not the parts that really drive the company.

One reason the Japanese have made so many advances in the marketplace is that they have paid meticulous attention to studying their management systems. They typically examine not only their design and production processes, but also their management processes—those systems by which decisions are made, policies are established, and improvements are made. It is this rigorous examination and fine tuning of the management process that drives continuous improvement in Japanese companies.

Have you ever taken time to draw a picture of your own management system? If you have not, the following exercise may give you insight into how complex and how important your management system is for your business. Ask three senior-level vice presidents to draw a one-page picture of the company's management system. Tell each one that you have talked to the others and that none of them should collaborate on this assignment. Explain that the purpose of the task is to see how they view the company's business strategy, how strategy is established, how the company determines plans and priorities, and how improvements are made and maintained. Fundamentally, you want to get at the executives' views of how the company operates.

The managers might think you are a little crazy for making such a strange request. My guess is that, in the end, you will receive sketches that do not even remotely resemble one another. The lesson of the exercise is that, if senior managers cannot agree among themselves on the business system under which they operate, how can anyone expect to make improvements on it? And if the senior managers cannot agree on the business system, a great deal of confusion is bound to exist at lower levels in the organization. Key managers may be playing with different game plans, each one thinking that his or her view is correct. Despite this problem, however, senior managers continue to make changes to their management systems—only they do not think of this as changing the management system. Instead, they think they are addressing an isolated set of problems.

Before your company begins the arduous TQM journey, senior management must understand the fundamental business system under which it currently operates. The company's management system will strongly influence the way that changes to the corporate culture are made and the effect that such changes will have.

Figure 2.1 is a simplified overview of a management system. It shows how policy is established, how problems are identified, and how improvements are made and maintained. It describes how a business operates. How did your own company's senior executives' pictures compare with this one? Figure 2.2 shows the interaction between Policy Management, Daily Management, team activity, problem solving, and continuous improvement (all of which are described more fully later).

To start with, one thing I recommend is that senior managers reserve several days from their busy schedules to attend an executive conference on TQM. These conferences are important for three reasons. The first is that they allow those who are ultimately responsible for quality to get away from the office where they can more clearly think about what they and their company need to accomplish. The second reason is that, in such an environment, managers meet others who may share similar concerns

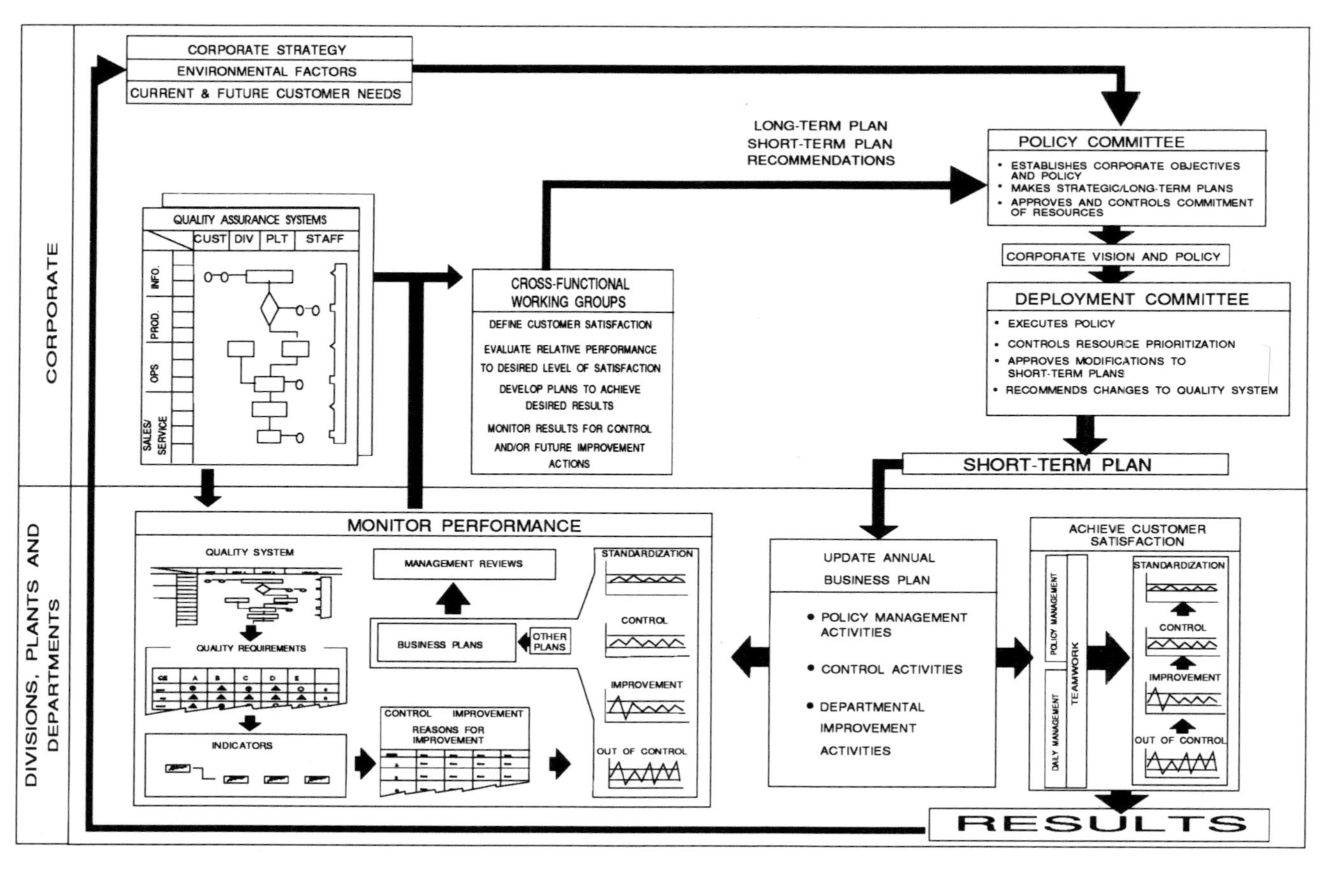

FIGURE 2.1. Simplified Overview of a Management System

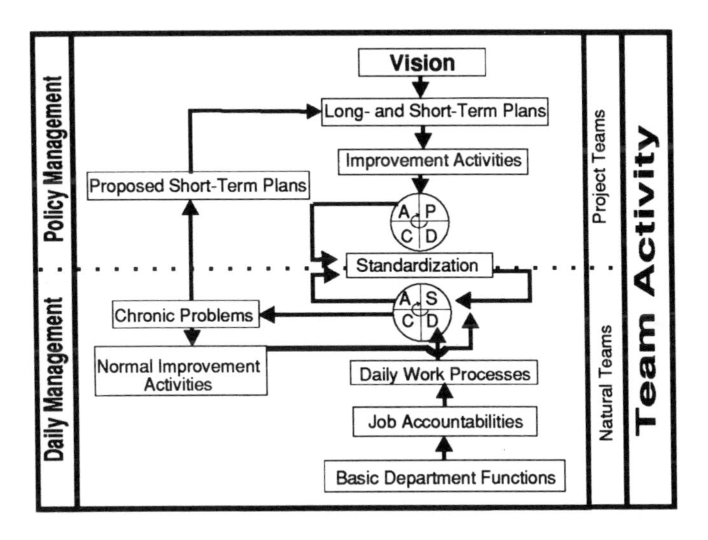

FIGURE 2.2. Management System Interactions

and anxieties. Finally, the conferences are a forum where managers hear valuable stories about others' efforts, accomplishments, and even failures.

If you develop a sincere interest in adopting a TQM approach, look within your organization for an assistant who is both tenacious and good at dealing with people. Assign this person, on a full-time basis, to the senior manager in charge of the quality effort. The assistant's task is to aid senior management in preparing a plan for developing and implementing total quality.

CREATING A SENIOR MANAGEMENT TEAM

Many companies already have an executive or policy committee. I highly recommend that existing management committees be used to direct the planning and design of their TQM system rather than creating new structures. Some companies have chosen their executive or senior management committee as the body to give life to their TQM effort. Others have created new management committees, called either a steering committee or a quality council. In general, your management lead team or committee should consist of members who are directly responsible for the overall operation of the company and who will be executing the quality plan and shaping its direction. (See also Chapter 5.)

Make sure that the executive committee, management committee, steering committee, or quality council has a clear picture of the major components, stages, and steps necessary to create a comprehensive approach. The quality plan will be your road map to success. Full ownership and commitment are required to make the plan work. There is no sense in trying to change the way a company does business unless there is unity of purpose within the top management ranks. Others can help the senior management team think the details through, but, in the end, senior management must make it work.

Quality begins not only with senior management, but also with education. In the early stages of developing a quality management plan, hold a series of seminars and training classes for the management team. Team members must be familiar with the terminology, strategies, problem-solving techniques, and statistical tools of quality improvement. They will need to know the planning and implementation process that will be employed and the various approaches one can take. They will also need to understand their own and their colleagues' expectations and what can realistically be achieved.

The senior management team is the essential source for creating and developing the policies of the company, for promoting other team activity, for applying cross-functional management, and for creating a work atmosphere in which TQM can grow and flourish. The team must demonstrate what "respect for people" really means. They must break down any corporate barriers to improvement. The senior management team must be on the forefront of providing help and of promoting cooperation.

DIAGNOSING A CRISIS

Dr. Noriaki Kano has devoted time to studying companies that have been successful in implementing a quality management system. His studies indicate that there were basically two types of successful companies: those whose success came by way of a crisis, and those that detected the beginnings of a crisis, or a perceived crisis, early on and took steps to prevent it.[1]

The first type of company will have faced loss of market share, a drop in earnings, and a loss of public confidence before taking corrective action. The second type of company will have been doing well, possessed good market share and earnings, and had good customer loyalty. Yet it perceives potentially troublesome events that, if not properly responded to, can put the company in a real crisis. Companies of the latter type watch new entrants into the market, perceive product obsolescence, and detect other external or internal events that stand to change the course of their company. Although it is better to be a company of the second type, for companies of the first type there are also ways to improve the situation and turn things around.

In preparing an initial draft plan for quality improvement, senior management must clearly decide *why* the organization should change and how best it should achieve this goal. In many ways this will be an easier task if the company is currently experiencing problems of crisis proportions, serving to highlight any clear and present dangers. If, however, the company is not experiencing a crisis, the task will require more careful consideration and evaluation. The senior management team will need to become convinced that a real potential for crisis exists and that they will need everyone's help in confronting it.

If senior management is unclear about whether a real or potential crisis exists, they should look for answers within the organization. One way to accomplish this is through the presidential or chief-executive diagnosis. This is the typical approach used by Japanese companies to diagnose the problems of the company. It does not mean that the president performs the diagnosis alone. I would encourage all senior managers to participate. The diagnosis is helpful in several respects:

[1]Source: Dr. Noriaki Kano

- Senior management will learn things from the organization that otherwise would have been filtered several times before senior executives became aware of them.
- The organization wants to know its senior management and wants to know that senior management cares about people and their problems.
- Senior management has an opportunity to tell the organization what it is thinking and to evaluate first-hand the health of the company.

The diagnosis is a good time for senior management to begin practicing and implementing one of the key principles of total quality—management by fact. Two questions must be answered: What are your problems? And, how do you or your people know? I am often amazed at how difficult it is for managers and employees to answer these two questions. I have participated in sessions with senior managers who have many excellent solutions to some yet unknown problems. This is because managers have been trained to think about solutions without really knowing about the problem. Even among those who can properly state a problem, few are able to substantiate their statement with facts. Most tend to use their "feeling" about it instead.

The two questions—what and how—may have to be asked several times before satisfactory answers are received. The executive diagnosis, however, is intended to be a fact-finding mission and not a witch hunt. If good answers to these two questions are received, these will help in the formulation and strengthening of strategy. A method such as Policy Management may then be used to boil down the issues to the most important ones—the ones that senior management is overwhelmingly convinced must be solved. Each problem must ultimately be tested against one simple criterion: if it is solved, will the viability and growth of the business be improved?

Another critical source of information for identifying problems and diagnosing crises is your customers. Ultimately, the goal of a quality management system is customer satisfaction. Customers are why the company is in business. If the company has not conducted a customer survey, do so or better yet use the information you already have available. Check complaint records, warranty-performance records, or even legal suits. These are all great sources of information for identifying problems. You will undoubtedly find some quality tools (e.g., quality function deployment) or even a simple checklist helpful in organizing customer requirements and matching them against company performance (see Chapters 3 and 4). Such an approach is invaluable for defining and breaking down business problems into actionable steps that, when set in place, can be measured and checked. Performing a management diagnosis and analyzing customer records can help clearly identify a crisis in your organization—if one exists—that virtually everyone in the organization can rally around.

If a crisis has not been identified within the company using any of these sources, check outside the company. The competition, government, or a variety of other sources are all useful. Benchmarking techniques, where performance is gauged against other companies, can help spot a crisis of major proportions. I say crisis because there needs to be some sense of urgency if a company wants to fundamentally change its approach and adopt TQM. Identifying a crisis is one of the best ways to create this sense of urgency.

ESTABLISHING A VISION

> "A vision without a task is but a dream. A task without a vision is drudgery, but, a vision and a task are the hope of the world."
>
> (Church in Sussex, England, 1730)

Typically, during the preliminary stages of TQM, an organization's senior management establishes the corporate vision, or if one already exists, it is reexamined. A company must have a clear vision and strategic plan before it can implement critical components of a total quality system. Several things must be kept in mind in creating a vision, the overall idea being to produce a simple statement that epitomizes the corporate direction.

First, a vision must be *exciting* for the organization. There is a need to "turn on" the organization (i.e., make it stimulating for people). Second, a vision should be *short and repeatable.* Corporate visions should not take up a full typed page. How could anyone possibly remember it? Everyone in the organization should be able to understand what it means and repeat it. Finally, the vision should be *directional.* The vision sets the compass of the ship. Everyone, including the customers, shareholders, and employees, needs to know where the vision will lead the company.

Several factors should be considered in the development of a vision. An evaluation of the company's strengths and convictions will help to lay out its core competencies. An appraisal of its weaknesses will help to identify gaps in performance. An assessment of the competition and a review of the external environment will produce a better understanding of the business arena and help to formulate a direction for the company. The vision should consider leveraging company strengths and overcoming its weaknesses to close the gap. The "seven new tools" of quality are often useful to help formulate a vision for the company (see Chapter 8).

ESTABLISHING CORPORATE POLICIES

Senior management has full responsibility for establishing the overall corporate agenda or set of business policies. After establishing or revising the corporate vision (or strategic plan), the senior management team needs to create a clear and understandable corporate agenda or prioritized set of policies.

To some, this may sound like management by objectives (MBO). MBO is, or has been, practiced by many companies; but I have seen few examples where this approach is put to good use. The failure of this method is not in its intent, but in its execution. Policy Management is a much more disciplined process than the MBO concept.

Often the failure of businesses in successfully implementing MBO lies in management's overestimating the organization's capabilities and in including too many items to be improved. This really is a "management by wish." It is a case of the superman syndrome. Even senior managers often forget that they have limited resources. The company will want to devote its resources to those problems or crises that, when resolved, bring it closer to its vision.

In creating corporate policies, take care in their wording. If not properly focused, the organization will be sent in too many directions. For instance, I once saw a corporate policy that stated: "Improve operations." This type of objective is so broad that the organization can do virtually anything it wants and claim in the end that the objective was reached. A policy that states, "Improve operations by reducing the defect rate 90 percent in three years," on the other hand, will drive the organization to focus its efforts on areas critical to the company's success. In addition, results will be more measurable and the persons contributing will be more readily identifiable. As a rule of thumb, if you cannot measure it, do not include it as part of the corporate policies.

Another important consideration for the senior management team is time. The time allowed for achieving the vision must be more than one business cycle. TQM is a long-term approach. In establishing the corporate agenda, a long-term plan must be used. The long-term plan is used when the company expects a particular issue or problem to take three to five years to resolve.

PROMOTING AND DEPLOYING POLICIES

Still another critical assignment for senior management is promotion. I am not in favor of slogans unless they help get you where you want to go. An example of a useful slogan is a corporate vision, which no company should be without.

There are two areas where senior management can really help: promoting team activity and employee suggestions. Senior management interest in these areas will help lower-level management understand what they must do. Attend award ceremonies, visit teams, and write personal notes to those who have contributed to the betterment of the company. The CEO is the chief public relations person for the company—so promote what needs to be accomplished.

Use every opportunity to promote quality activities. Pass on and promote success stories. Senior management should demonstrate that it appreciates the efforts being made. Promotional activities that demonstrate respect for people, cross-functional management, management by fact, and other quality principles should be conducted regularly.

Senior management is the key to success, for without its full involvement, TQM cannot and will not flourish. Do not start if you and your senior managers are not willing to spend the time and effort or if the senior management team does not have a similar view that such activities are essential for the continued growth of the organization.

EXECUTIVE VISITS AND PDCA

Another critical responsibility for senior management is to monitor progress. Here, another key principle of quality, the Plan-Do-Check-Act (PDCA) cycle, should be implemented. The "C" or check part of PDCA is one of the most important activities for senior management. Many companies are very good at planning and doing, but few are very good at checking their results (except for checking on financial results, which most companies seem to know how to do).

Generally, senior management will conduct a formal business review monthly. During that review, a more detailed review of one particular policy may be held. For instance, if there are six corporate agenda items or policies, each policy should be reviewed in depth at least twice a year.

Through these reviews, additional problems may be discovered. Senior management should give homework, if necessary, to those making reports, and the action taken in the interim should be reported at the next review, or sooner if it is a critical problem. Have the management team review at a set time and place. Keep the sessions open for others to attend unless there are business matters being reviewed that must be kept confidential. For instance, attendance may be restricted if a corporate policy to improve public safety is being reviewed and there is a risk that during the review session someone might reveal information that could jeopardize pending litigation or cause an action to be taken against the company. Other than these unique instances, reviews are educational and should be open to a wide audience within the company.

Reviews are important from a senior management point of view for several reasons. They pass on a message to the organization on what is important. The reviews help educate management on the root causes of problems and their potential solutions. The sessions are also useful to obtain information that can be used to promote quality efforts throughout the organization.

Critique each review—this is nothing more than practicing PDCA. Use what is learned and make the necessary changes for the next review. Practice what you are asking the rest of your organization to do. Manage by example. Policy Management is the responsibility of senior management. This is the one area that senior management must pay the most attention to in implementing a quality system.

In addition, after each business cycle, review the systems that have been put in place. No business system is perfect, and the system will need constant improvements as problems are analyzed. The company will also need to examine and standardize those things that went right to benefit from them in future business cycles.

As part of the checking process, consider institutionalizing an executive visit process. Several companies have found that they can get their executives out of the office and into the field by establishing a formal executive visit schedule and process. The visits are not intended to interfere with local management's responsibilities or prerogatives. The visits must be diagnostic and promotional. The purpose of the visits are:

- To promote the corporate policies and objectives.
- To promote quality activities as a way of doing business.
- To check on how improvements are taking place.
- To see if there are any business problems that have gone undetected.

A typical schedule might look like this:

8:00–9:00	Give a talk to employees, including a question-and-answer period.
9:00–10:00	Meet with the local lead team (see Chapter 5) to review their business and promotion plans.
10:00–10:30	Review one of the functional or task teams.
10:30–11:30	Walk through the workplace, interacting with employees.
11:30–12:00	Critique with local lead team.

The half-day spent will be personally rewarding not only to senior management, but also for the managers, supervisors, and employees who are reviewed. They will be excited because the visit will demonstrate that senior managers are practicing what they preach. It will show that senior managers care enough about them to have taken the time out of their business schedules to come and visit.

As a word of caution, the visits may sometimes have an emotional effect on local management personnel, particularly if local management is unaccustomed to seeing someone from senior management. If this symptom arises, it may be an indication that a sense of fear exists in the organization that must be driven out.

Remember that some people in the organization, including some key managers, may have never interacted with or even met someone from senior management. In addition to breaking down this barrier, there is an interesting side effect to executive visits. They are often an excellent means to improve the general appearance of offices, factories, and equipment. Managers and supervisors generally do not want to be embarrassed about the appearance of their facilities. In many cases, this side effect will help to improve the overall quality of work life.

Executive visits must be brought to some closure. Develop a simple and non-bureaucratic method to transfer knowledge. Executives need to share their experiences and findings among their peers. Sharing experiences will help senior management identify corporatewide problems and opportunities and will also help the senior management team improve the management system. Executive visits can be one of the most rewarding parts of the job. At FPL, I set time aside to discover how employees were feeling and to learn about their concerns, often encountering remarkable people doing remarkable things. Making the time to do this is well worth the effort.

Prevention and Standardization

Still another task of senior management is to ensure that gains made are retained. Sometimes senior management is so pleased that a particular problem is solved that all they want to do is celebrate. It is natural to be happy when a major problem is solved. But then what next? After successfully solving the problem, senior management should ask "And now what do we do?" The first stage in problem solving is to remedy the problem. After that has been accomplished, you must prevent it from recurring.

Standardization of the solution and countermeasures are the most common methods employed to prevent problem recurrence. If a problem is solved without standardization, the opportunity for the problem to recur remains. In the early stages of a quality program, people are so happy to solve a problem that they forget the importance of this step.

As a quality program matures and as analytical abilities improve, the organization will need to move to the next stage of problem solving. The organization must not only prevent the recurrence of problems, but also become skilled at predicting problems. This is commonly referred to as prevention by prediction. This level of sophistication will be particularly important for those involved in manufacturing, but the techniques can also be applied to the service sector. Prevention by prediction techniques requires a great deal of understanding about the cause and effect relationships of processes. It requires an understanding of life cycles and failure modes. For those who master these techniques, the rewards are great.

CROSS-FUNCTIONAL MANAGEMENT

The most significant change in senior management practice at FPL was the use of cross-functional committees. They produced significant changes in how people acted. They developed cooperation among managers, they resulted in the efficient reallocation of resources, and they broke down traditional corporate barriers.

Some senior executives tend to oppose such practices. They believe that someone should be given responsibility for an area and then be held accountable for it and nothing more. However, senior management must realize that one functional area cannot achieve results without the cooperation of others. Customers rarely receive a product or service from one functional area in a company. The customer receives the product or service across the organization and only through the cooperation of others.

While attending an in-house quality conference for a major electronics manufacturer, I heard a guest speaker talk about how the difficult part of management was not managing a functional area but managing the "white" spaces on the organizational chart. How can manufacturing be successful without the cooperation of engineering, design, or purchasing? How will the sales people be successful without the cooperation of nearly everyone else in the company?

When cross-functional committees were formed at FPL, I felt that they were going to be a waste of time—more meetings to attend. But the committees, which had been carefully assembled, nevertheless soon began to achieve solid results, to gain consensus, and to earn support throughout the organization over which the chairman took no direct control or responsibility.

For example, one problem area was formal customer complaints. One component of the corporate policy was to make a major reduction in the number of formal complaints to achieve greater customer satisfaction. A sales and service cross-functional committee was formed. A major complaint area identified was inaccurate bills. A detailed analysis of the problem revealed that several specific sub-areas needed to be addressed to eliminate billing as a category of complaint. The meter reading department sometimes caused billing complaints because they occasionally read a meter incorrectly. The meter maintenance department caused billing complaints because occasionally they installed defective or incorrect meters.

The computer operations department caused billing complaints because they occasionally ran the billing programs with the wrong parameters. The information systems department occasionally made incorrect modifications to billing programs. The accounting department caused complaints because they occasionally sent the computer operations department incorrect billing and tax information.

The customer service department caused billing complaints because they occasionally entered the wrong information in the customer record. The marketing department, the purchasing department, the collection department, and the payment processing department all occasionally made errors. Each department may have made only a few errors, but the cumulative effect was significant. No one department's individual record looked unsatisfactory, yet customers were complaining. To overcome these types of service problems, a committee was established representing major departments that had a direct affect on meeting customers' quality requirements. A sales and service cross-functional committee was established. The members of the committee were committed to solving the billing-related customer complaint problem, as well as several other service-related problems. They did this by establishing communications, internal requirements, and practicing cooperation between their respective departments.

Managers who believe that single-function responsibility and accountability is the only way to run an organization have something to learn from this. I doubt that these managers would have been able to identify this type of billing problem in the first place. Typically, a highly functional organization tends to look to others to blame when things go wrong. My experience is that functional organizations with no cross-management direction tend to live in their own world with little care about other organizations' problems. This type of structure produces people who are uncooperative. Under a strong functional structure, this type of problem often remains hidden.

I have worked under several different management approaches, and I hope that I never again will be subjected to a highly centralized style of management. It breeds distrust, misinformation, fiefdoms, autocrats, and other problems. Managing the "white" spaces, on the other hand, is tricky business, but has proven very successful for the Japanese and many U.S. companies. Cross-functional management expands the organization's knowledge of the business and helps develop a sense of teamwork and cooperation.

CONCLUSION

As with most important outcomes in business, management must provide leadership. It is no different with quality. Without management's personal attention and direction, programmatic attempts to institutionalize quality will fail. Quality leadership is executed not only by supporting and promoting the underlying concepts and structures of this management practice, but also by doing. Management must lead the way by example, by designing and communicating its quality plan, by participating in quality practices, by providing a clear business strategy and vision, and by setting the business objectives to be achieved.

3

Policy Management

INTRODUCTION

Without question, the most important TQM process component to establish when launching a quality effort is Policy Management. Policy Management is a systematic business planning process that requires management to direct corporate attention and resources to a few selected high-priority areas that, when addressed, can help a company achieve its business strategy and vision. When executed correctly, Policy Management can generate major improvements for any organization. Policy Management is a method to establish and execute long-term and short-term business strategies. A Policy Management process focuses company resources on the "vital few" important problems a company has.

Policy Management is a method to "align the vectors" in a company (see Figure 3.1). In the best of companies, one finds an enormous amount of good intention among department managers and division heads. All want to do a good job—or at least what they feel is a good job. But most companies lack a method or system to align the department heads and divisions to work toward a common goal or purpose. Policy Management provides such a system.

Most companies also have an annual process to establish their priority areas or corporate agenda for the following year. Some companies even have a process that sets up the corporate agenda for a longer period (i.e., a long-range plan). Many companies have followed the practice of management by objective (MBO) to establish their annual plans. There is nothing intrinsically wrong with the theory of MBO; in fact, the principles form the basic foundation for Policy Management. But even Peter Drucker would probably be disappointed at the application of MBO as practiced by many companies.

Some companies using MBO may list more than 20 items to be accomplished for the next year. Yet no company is so rich that it can allocate resources to make major improvements in so many areas of concentration. I recently received an annual plan from a large, very well-known company and was shocked to find that it had included 65 major items to be accomplished in the next fiscal year. This was obviously nothing more than a management "wish list". It appeared that the plan was a result of the executives waking up one morning and saying, "If we could magically cure all of our problems this is what we would like to do."

What is needed is a systematic method to narrow the focus of attention — a method to concentrate resources on the most important areas and gain commitment from all organizational levels able to make a contribution toward meeting the objectives. All key business factors need to be included as input in a process that will provide meaningful output (see Figure 3.2).

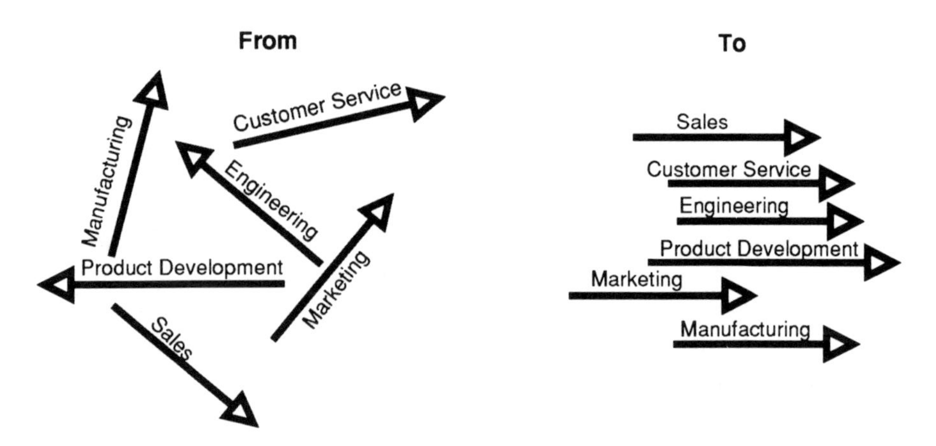

FIGURE 3.1. Align the Vectors

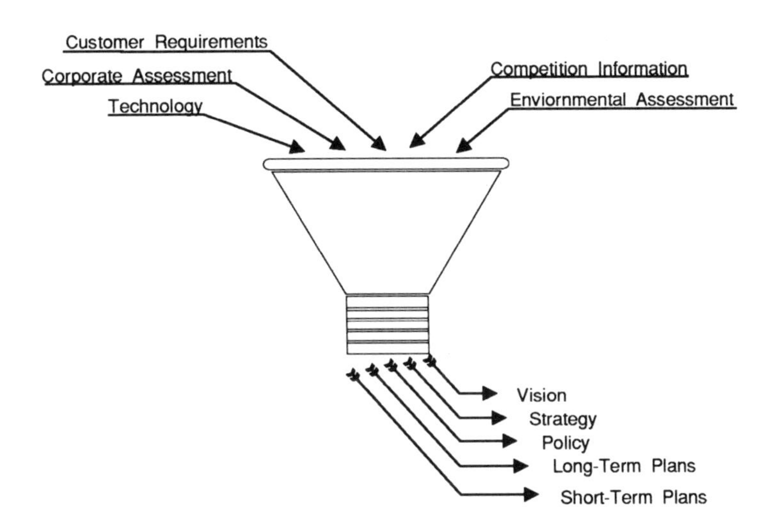

FIGURE 3.2. The Role of Top Management

If your company does not practice MBO, the general management process itself will undoubtedly have some means or system to absorb the incredible amount of information received from different sources, to organize it in some fashion, and to develop and issue plans. But sometimes the process seems closer to magic than management. Policy Management adds value to these more unstructured, often creative practices and adds discipline to the application of MBO in several respects:

- It is a systematic process that provides the means of identifying and achieving objectives.
- Objectives and targets are supported by analysis.
- Contributions necessary to meeting the objectives are identified within the organization.
- There is a structured checking process rather than the traditional year-end review.

Another failure of many companies' annual plans is that they are written only from the *company's* point of view and give little, if any, consideration to the *customer's* point of view. From 1972 to 1984, my former company followed the practice of establishing the next year's agenda using a traditional MBO approach (i.e., including too many things to be accomplished without really thinking about the resources needed to accomplish them, or wording the objectives so vaguely that any action taken could be claimed as making a contribution to the objectives). The most unfortunate part, I thought, was the agenda's heavy concentration on financial matters—setting objectives from the company's fiscal point of view with little, if any, consideration for quality as defined by our customers.

Each year the objectives were similar. For instance: "Improve earnings by limiting operating and maintenance costs," or "Improve earnings by limiting growth in the work force." Unfortunately, the corporate agenda was met only two times during the period from 1972 to 1984.

In 1985, we began to focus on the requirements of the customer and develop a corporate agenda based on the *customer's* viewpoint. We began looking at things we identified as the most important to customers and concentrated on improving the quality of the service we provided our customers. We also limited the corporate agenda to fewer high-priority areas. We concentrated our efforts by allocating resources to support key areas identified for improvement.

Regulated companies, like my former company, have limitations on their earnings—caps, if you will. During the period from 1985 to 1990, when we practiced Policy Management, we not only made major improvements in areas that were important to our customers, but the company earned at or near the its maximum allowed earnings. To the best of my knowledge this had never happened before in the history of the company. There were several factors that caused this to happen, but I believe that the change in philosophy and practice of Policy Management had the most to do with the result.

There is a theory about why corporate agendas written from a company viewpoint often fail, particularly agendas containing cost cutting or cost containment as their main objectives. When employees and middle managers read this type of corporate agenda, they tend to be put off or become scared. Each reads the agenda as though it affects them personally. Somehow they think, "They (senior management) are talking about my job." When this type of thinking develops, the best commitment that can be expected is passive compliance.

On the other hand, when corporate agendas are established from a customer's viewpoint and with an emphasis on quality, the picture changes in middle management's and employees' minds. Employees and managers can read the corporate agenda and say, "Here is something I can contribute to—for instance, improving customer service." People no longer feel threatened. They know that their actions can improve the quality of the product or service that the customer receives and, in most instances, can help reduce costs and increase company profits.

THE POLICY MANAGEMENT PROCESS

The Policy Management process involves three distinct steps: establishing policy, deploying policy, and implementing policy.

Establishing Policy

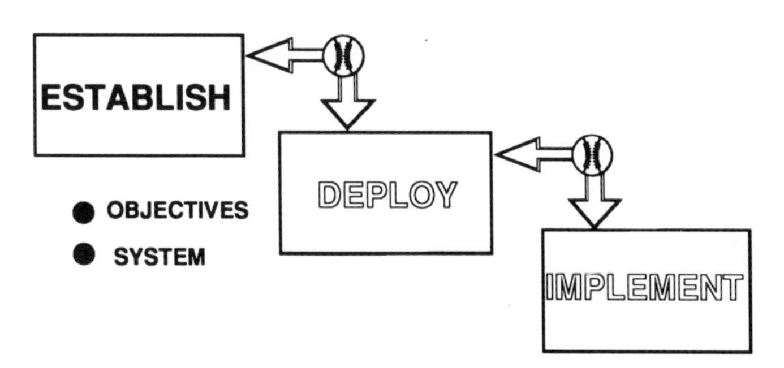

FIGURE 3.3. Establish Policy

Establishing the vision, strategy, policy, direction, goals, and objectives are the responsibilities of senior management (Figure 3.3). Senior management must map out the future course for the company. Although this responsibility is the same for both Western and Japanese companies, few Western managers seem to grasp or appreciate the methods that Japanese companies use to achieve their very considerable results. Establishing policy through the use of a Policy Management system is a role senior management plays in Japan in charting the future success of companies there. Although establishing policy will not in itself ensure success for any company, it can help significantly in achieving market success.

Many sources of information can be used to develop and establish policy. One should use all sources that make sense for one's business to develop the best picture of current business problems. Defining or establishing customer requirements is a must, and Policy Management can assist here. An assessment of the external environment and of internal company operations and organization, a review of competitive information, and an assessment of changes in technology are just a few of the sources that should be drawn upon. A systematic evaluation of this information through Policy Management will help to refine business strategy and long- and short-term plans and to focus on meeting overall corporate vision.

In Chapter 1, I mentioned that there are three broad source areas to consider in developing and establishing policy:

1. Customer requirements compared to company performance.
2. Internal business problems.
3. The external business environment, including competition and new technology.

These areas may be considered in terms of two main categories: "the voice of the customer" and the "voice of the business" (see below). A consultant friend of mine would also add "the noise of the competition" as an important ingredient in defining policy. I tend to view competitive issues as well as technological issues as integral ingredients to the two main categories.

"Voice of the Customer": Establishing External Customer Requirements

What Japanese companies seem to do so well is to focus their attention and resources on the most important problems or issues facing them. It is this ability that I believe makes the critical difference. In these quality-oriented companies, the basic starting point is ascertaining the customer's requirements and comparing them to the company's performance in delivering them. The task here is to identify the "gap" between what is expected and what is delivered—or rather perceived by the customer to be delivered.

Most companies already have a gold mine of information about their customers, but do not structure the information so that it is useful. Some of the most common information available in a company that is beneficial when ascertaining customer's requirements includes:

- Warranty claims and customer complaint records.
- Marketing information.
- Customer surveys.
- Customer focus groups.
- Benchmarking data.

All these categories of information are excellent if the information is properly interpreted and organized. You should use what is available; do not necessarily wait until you have a statistically valid survey, as some might advise. Do something with what you already know, then you can more carefully plan a customer requirements survey. Use whatever survey information you already have available. Look at existing customer complaint and warranty claims records. These records can provide a wealth of information about what customers require. Use the knowledge of those who work directly with the customer—the sales people and the customer service people. They have valuable information that can greatly improve the ability of a company to satisfy customers' needs and requirements.

Conduct customer requirement surveys only after the information you already have is exhausted. Remember, customer surveys can be very expensive, so if you undertake one, much care should be taken ahead of time to determine what it is you wish to learn. There are experienced consultants and, often, very good in-house experts who can facilitate these types of surveys. Policy Management relies not on customer *attitude* surveys, which also generate important information, but on customer *requirement* surveys and company performance surveys.

By carefully gathering together the vast amount of data and using such summarizing techniques as an affinity process (see Chapter 8), you can produce a concise listing of what customers require. The basic format, organized into a table, is known as a customer needs table (see Figure 3.4). Customer requirements can be broken down and grouped into several categories or levels. These may be termed customer requirements (i.e., what customers want), primary-level requirements, and secondary-level requirements. Often a company delivers its products or services to several different market segments. If this condition exists, group these requirements by customer segments. It is the secondary customer requirements that will be evaluated to determine the "gaps" in company performance. These will also be the items used to develop and establish policy.

Customers may not always be able to state clearly what exactly they want. It is the company's responsibility to listen carefully to customers and interpret what they are saying. For example: customers may say, "We want you to improve your documentation." Customers often give *solutions* for problems rather than definitions of requirements—they try to help you out. In this example, the customer may be asking to receive more, or better, information. Improving documentation may be one method, but there may be others to consider. The company must be the creative catalyst in satisfying the customer. Requirements may be lengthy and will have to be broken down and classified. One company I visited learned of a customer's requirement by observing the customer in the customer's work place over time. Through observation, the company was able to identify some requirements of which the customer was unaware.

To provide clarity to company personnel about customer requirements, primary and secondary customer requirements should be organized in terms of essential quality characteristics: quality, cost, delivery, and safety. The requirements must then be quantified or weighted to gain an understanding of their rela-

Customer Requirements

- Product & Delivery Quality
  - Give me dependable products
    - Provide products that I need when I want them
    - Anticipate my changing needs and act on them
    - Provide products that work all the time
    - Provide products that are easy to use
    - If it breaks, provide me with a convienient place for repairs
- Service Quality
  - Meet your commitments
    - Keep the commitments that you make with me
    - Keep appointments
    - If you can't meet your commitments, tell me in time to cause me the least hassle
  - Give me confidence that you can do the job
    - Don't make mistakes
    - If you make mistakes own it, apologize, & make it right
    - Be my expert, help me
  - Provide courteous customer service
    - Treat me with respect
    - Be friendly
    - Be flexible, understand & respond to my individual needs
    - Don't pass me around, take on my problem & fix it
    - Treat me fairly
    - Give me fast easy access to someone who can help me
  - Communicate with me in a clear manner
    - Share useful information that is specific to my needs when I need it
    - Speak to me in my language, not yours
    - Keep me updated on your products & services
- Cost
  - I want my money's worth
    - Charge prices that are fair to me
    - Give me ways to save money & make more money
    - Give me a break for doing a lot of business with you
    - Don't nickel & dime me
  - Send me a bill I can use
    - Bill me accurately
    - Make my bill easy to understand
    - Bill me according to how I run my business

FIGURE 3.4. Customer Requirements

tive importance to the customer. This information can be gathered from survey information, by company personnel dealing with customers, and from customer complaint and claims records. A ranking of one to five is used, five being a very important requirement (see Figure 3.5). A great deal of care must be taken in these early stages. The results of the weighting will most likely cause action to be taken by the organization. The desired effect is to have the organization sent in the right direction the first time.

Next, evaluate the company's performance in meeting the requirement. Rank this information using the same scale that was used to rank customer requirements (see "Current Position," Figure 3.5). One way to evaluate performance is simply to ask the customer, "How are we doing in meeting (the specific requirement)?" If you have survey information, use it. You can also conduct focus groups using your customers—a relatively inexpensive means. Another method is to survey company personnel who deal directly with the customer.

In using company data from company records, care must be taken because company data tends to measure things from a company point of view. Establish objective criteria that measure performance from a customers' point-of-view. For example, when FPL surveyed its customers we discovered that customers were not very pleased with our performance in keeping the lights on. We were mystified by the survey results because we thought our performance had greatly improved. We always kept in-house measurements of our performance because we knew it was an important characteristic of the business—something we knew we needed to do a good job on. It was the heart of the business. We called it service availability; the records had been kept for many years.

When we examined our information, we wondered why customers seemed concerned. The examination revealed that over the past few years, several new maintenance programs designed to improve service availability had begun and the programs seemed to be working successfully. Improvements had been made every year for the past three years. The data showed that the service availability index stood at 99.9876; the lights were on an

Customer Requirements	Total Weight	Importance (1-5)	Current Position (1-5)	Plan (1-5)	Market Accent (1.2, 1.5)	Competitive Position
	Weights					
Product & Delivery Quality						
Give me dependable products						
Provide products that I need when I want them	0.0	4	3	5		5
Anticipate my changing needs and act on them	0.0	3	3	4		4
Provide products that work all the time	0.0	5	4	5		5
Provide products that are easy to use	0.0	3	3	4		3
If it breaks, provide me with a convienient place for repairs	0.0	5	4	5		4
Service Quality						
Meet your commitments						
Keep the commitments that you make with me	0.0	5	2	5		5
Keep appointments	0.0	5	3	5		4
If you can't meet your commitments, tell me in time to cause me the least hassle	0.0	4	2	4		3
Give me confidence that you can do the job						
Don't make mistakes	0.0	4	2	4		2
If you make mistakes own it, apologize, & make it right	0.0	4	2	5		1
Be my expert, help me	0.0	4	3	4		2
Provide courteous customer service						
Treat me with respect	0.0	5	4	5		3
Be friendly	0.0	1	3	4		3
Be flexible, understand & respond to my individual needs	0.0	5	2	5		5
Don't pass me around, take on my problem & fix it	0.0	4	3	5		5
Treat me fairly	0.0	4	3	5		5
Give me fast easy access to someone who can help me	0.0	4	3	4		2

FIGURE 3.5. Ranking Customer Requirements

average of 99.9876% of the time. How could anyone do better? This was near perfection. How could this be a great concern for our customers? How much more reliable could one be?

One day, however, one of our managers recalculated the index to look at the same information as a customer might view it. What developed was a service *un*availability index that measured the average time the lights were *not* on. The data revealed that the customers were experiencing an interruption, on average, of 100 minutes a year.

We began to appreciate what our customers were saying. Customers expect the lights to be on *all* of the time. Although they may not spend time and effort measuring how well we are doing, they do notice whenever the lights are out or even when there is a momentary service interruption.

This is particularly true in the era of the digital clock. All electrical systems are designed to clear faults. Clearing a fault is a safety feature. But our survey data revealed that momentary interruptions designed into the system to clear faults were no longer acceptable to customers. In the past no one noticed—that is, until the digital clock was introduced. Nowadays everybody has a blinking reminder of when the power company has interrupted service.

Even in our industrial market we found this to be an increasingly important requirement. Electronic process control is used in manufacturing. Interruptions of service cause companies headaches, loss of production, and increased costs. Likewise, in the commercial sector computer downtime acts as an important gauge for customers to measure our inability to keep the lights on all the time. When there is a momentary interruption, everyone knows.

We looked at other data and discovered that, although the service levels had improved, our customers' complaints in this area had risen dramatically. This was surprising. We did a little benchmarking to compare ourself to other companies. We discovered that several companies were doing much better than we were. Our customer's requirements were changing, and we were not responding to the changes quickly enough. By looking at the data from a customer's point of view we began to understand better what their requirements were and found ourselves in a better position to determine where room existed for improvement.

Benchmarking can and often is used in this step. I do not want to dwell on the techniques used in benchmarking, because there are books already available on the subject. There are also a number of consulting firms and organizations that have excellent data bases to assist a company in identifying the "best in class." But benchmarking can help you identify the "gap" between customer requirements and company performance. Although there is a great deal of discussion today about benchmarking (largely attributed to the fine work done by Xerox), the concept has actually been around for a long time—generally referred to as competitive analysis. Xerox changed the view of competitive analysis by looking beyond its direct competitors. Instead of doing classical competitive analysis, Xerox began to understand that the business was a series of processes and that what needed to be evaluated on a competitive basis was the process, not the end result. They looked for best in class *in process* no matter what industry a particular company might operate in. Benchmarking, then, is an extremely valuable tool to help evaluate your current level of performance.

After you have determined your current level of performance, next determine the required or needed level of performance (see "Plan," Figure 3.5). This may often be *higher* than the customers themselves require, either because the benchmarking data suggests that this should be so or because higher targets will allow the company to keep apace of its competitors' benchmarking advances. If, for instance, a particular customer requirement is ranked high—a 4—and the current performance of the company is relatively low—a 3—you may need to set the target at 5 to satisfy the customer *and* keep up with the competition.

Next, determine if there is some potential "market accent" or "sales point" that could be used by sales and advertising personnel to distinguish your product or service from the competition (Figure 3.6). Use a value of 1.2 if there is a good sales point, one that distinguishes the product or service, and 1.5 if the sales point is

Customer Requirements	Total Weight	Importance (1-5)	Current Position (1-5)	Plan (1-5)	Market Accent (1.2, 1.5)	Competitive Position
Product & Delivery Quality						
Give me dependable products						
Provide products that I need when I want them	8.0	4	3	5	1.2	5
Anticipate my changing needs and act on them	6.0	3	3	4	1.5	4
Provide products that work all the time	9.4	5	4	5	1.5	5
Provide products that are easy to use	4.0	3	3	4	1	3
If it breaks, provide me with a convienient place for repairs	6.3	5	4	5	1	4
Service Quality						
Meet your commitments						
Keep the commitments that you make with me	18.8	5	2	5	1.5	5
Keep appointments	10.0	5	3	5	1.2	4
If you can't meet your commitments, tell me in time to cause me the least hassle	8.0	4	2	4	1	3
Give me confidence that you can do the job						
Don't make mistakes	8.0	4	2	4	1	2
If you make mistakes own it, apologize, & make it right	10.0	4	2	5	1	1
Be my expert, help me	8.0	4	3	4	1.5	2
Provide courteous customer service						
Treat me with respect	6.3	5	4	5	1	3
Be friendly	1.3	1	3	4	1	3
Be flexible, understand & respond to my individual needs	15.0	5	2	5	1.2	5
Don't pass me around, take on my problem & fix it	8.0	4	3	5	1.2	5
Treat me fairly	6.7	4	3	5	1	5
Give me fast easy access to someone who can help me	5.3	4	3	4	1	2

FIGURE 3.6. Weighting Customer Requirements

clearly a competitive advantage. For example, if the product being sold has a reliability record far better than any competitor's, a 1.5 weight can be given. A weight should be assigned only if the company always meets or exceeds the customer's expectations for the requirement—something that the company can do better than its competitors—or when performance on the requirement, if dramatically improved, can give the company a significant competitive advantage. Special weight should be given to these requirements to help set your company apart from the competition.

Once customers' requirements and priorities have been established, current and planned company performance levels ranked, and any potential sales points noted, a final weighting of each customer's requirement may be calculated and normalized if desired (Figure 3.6).[1]

Any additional information should also be included. One source of such information is governmental regulatory bodies such as the Environmental Protection Agency (EPA). The EPA acts as a proxy for the public. It speaks for the public by establishing rules and regulations designed to protect the public's interest. Few customers can specify such requirements. These items are indirect customer requirements and should be listed on the table in the same manner as direct customer requirements, but labeled "additional customer requirements" to distinguish them from the others. These indirect requirements should also be weighted. Unlike the direct customer requirements that can be weighted based on survey data, however, the weighting of indirect requirements will take a little imagination. This is one of the few times that *experience* rather than *facts* can be used to make an initial cut.

At this point there will be a list of high- and low-priority areas or potential "candidates" for incorporation into company policy. The customer requirements with the highest weights should be considered first for inclusion in policy.

The customer needs table is useful not only to senior manage-

[1]The formula to use here is as follows: total weight = importance (plan ÷ current position) × market accent.

ment in helping to evaluate gaps in performance and in developing and establishing policy, but also has numerous other important uses throughout the organization. To make the customer needs table more meaningful and useful to the organization, a number of additional steps should be carried out. After establishing direct and indirect customer requirements, determine what the company must do to meet those requirements. What actions must be taken? What processes must be engaged? What specifications must be met? What are the business steps the organization needs to take to meet the customer's requirements?

Each key business process should be examined to determine the influence it has on meeting the customers' requirements. If there is a heavy influence, a weight of nine times (9×) the customer-weighted requirement is assigned to the block corresponding to the process and the requirement (see Figure 3.7). If there is a medium influence, a weight of six is used as the multiplier (6×). If the influence is low, a weight of three is used (3×); and if no influence is present, a weight of zero is used.

The table will form the basis for helping lower-level managers assess potential areas for improvement and for evaluating functional areas that have a great deal of influence on customer satisfaction as defined by the requirements. The table also provides senior management with a view of where best to direct (or "deploy") policy. The end product is a weighted quality-requirement matrix describing, in quantitative terms, all customer quality requirements. Use it as a tool to begin formulating corporate policy and the business' overall direction.

The lowest organizational levels in the company will be able to use the customer needs table to refine the customer quality requirements into progressively more "actionable" items. If, for instance, one requirement is defined as considerate customer service, to meet that requirement the company would have to treat the customer in a courteous, professional manner, and possibly show that people are caring and concerned about the customer's needs. To treat the customer in a courteous and professional manner, one requirement might be that you have a proper greeting. Once you have established a proper greeting you will have reached the actionable level (i.e., completed actions to meet the customer's expectations). This process should continue until all

Customer Requirements	Total Weight	Importance (1-5)	Current Position (1-5)	Plan (1-5)	Market Accent (1.2, 1.5)	Competitive Position	Market Research	Market Planning	Product Development	Product Management	Advertising & Promotion	Engineering Design	Construction	Installation
	Business Activities						Marketing					Construction		
	Weights													
Product & Delivery Quality														
Give me dependable products														
Provide products that I need when I want them	8.0	4	3	5	1.2	5	72	72	72	72	24	72	72	72
Anticipate my changing needs and act on them	6.0	3	3	4	1.5	4	54	54	54	36	18	54	54	54
Provide products that work all the time	9.4	5	4	5	1.5	5	28	56	84	84	28	84	84	84
Provide products that are easy to use	4.0	3	3	4	1	3	24	24	36	36	12	24		36
If it breaks, provide me with a convienient place for repairs	6.3	5	4	5	1	4		19	38	38		38	38	19
Service Quality														
Meet your commitments														
Keep the commitments that you make with me	18.8	5	2	5	1.5	5	56	113	56	113	56	169	169	169
Keep appointments	10.0	5	3	5	1.2	4		30	30	30		90	90	90
If you can't meet your commitments, tell me in time to cause me the least hassle	8.0	4	2	4	1	3						72	24	72
Give me confidence that you can do the job														
Don't make mistakes	8.0	4	2	4	1	2		24	48	48	24	72	72	72
If you make mistakes own it, apologize, & make it right	10.0	4	2	5	1	1				60	30	60	30	90
Be my expert, help me	8.0	4	3	4	1.5	2	48	48	24	48	48	72		72
Provide courteous customer service														
Treat me with respect	6.3	5	4	5	1	3	19	19		19	56	19	38	56
Be friendly	1.3	1	3	4	1	3				4	12	12	4	8
Be flexible, understand & respond to my individual needs	15.0	5	2	5	1.2	5	45	90	90	135	90	45	135	135
Don't pass me around, take on my problem & fix it	8.0	4	3	5	1.2	5			24	48	24	24		72
Treat me fairly	6.7	4	3	5	1	5	20	20			60	20	20	40
Give me fast easy access to someone who can help me	5.3	4	3	4	1	2	16	16		16	32	32		32

FIGURE 3.7. Customer Needs Analysis

quality requirements, and their specific characteristics, become actionable. At the actionable level one begins to use the TQM process component of Daily Management rather than Policy Management (see Chapter 4).

Your organization will find multiple uses for the table. It will be one of the best investments you make. Its most important feature is that it provides a permanent record of what is important to the customer. The desire to dig deeper to understand your customer's requirements is the most important part of establishing corporate policy.

"Voice of the Business": Internal Business Problems

The second crucial source of information in developing corporate policy comes from *within* the company—an evaluation of internal business problems. There are several techniques that can be employed here.

One technique is to establish a CEO or presidential diagnosis. This process can take a great deal of the CEO's time, but it will prove invaluable. A diagnosis requires that the CEO and the senior management team visit virtually every location or division in the organization. The purpose of the visits is to learn what employees and managers view as chronic problems. It is surprising what insights can be gained. Through these visits, senior management will discover problems at the local level. As more and more locations are visited, more problems common to company divisions will be discovered. These problems also must be evaluated for possible inclusion in corporate policies.

Local problems that are identified and that are limited to a particular management unit should be discussed between local and senior management during the executive visit. This type of problem must be left to local management to solve. These visits may uncover some disturbing things. But if harsh disciplinary action is taken against local managers because of what is discovered, during the next visit problems may not be expressed for fear of further retaliation. Executive visits should be fact-finding missions to identify corporate priority areas. Local management authority must not be disturbed.

A second approach used by many companies as part of their annual business-planning process is the "reason for improvement" worksheet, as developed by lower level managers for each responsibility area. This process drives the improvement opportunities from the customers' point of view and becomes the foundation for local management's execution of the annual business plan. Staff members compile the preliminary business plans from the various business units to look for common problems across the company. Staff members then recommend to senior management items that should be considered for inclusion in corporate objectives.

At this point you will have two lists of potential candidates for inclusion in policy statements—one list based on the voice of the customer, the other based on the voice of the business. Pare down the number of candidates on the lists to no more than a total of six or seven. Concentrate your attention on the most important issues. A matrix analysis is often useful to see the relationship between customer priorities and business problems (see Chapter 8). Often there is a close relationship. The use of a matrix analysis can assist senior management in the formulation of policy.

Establishing policy is both a subjective and objective process—subjective because there are relationships between business problems and customer problems that cannot easily be recognized through the use of data, and objective because such data can nevertheless be used to assess areas needing improvement and to establish the scope of the problem. The selection process is critical if you want to achieve success in using Policy Management as a tool to make major improvements. The items identified as the best candidates must be the most important areas—those that will help achieve the company vision, accomplish business strategy, and satisfy customers. Keep asking, "What is the problem? Are the items identified in line with the corporate vision? Have we identified the right things from the customer's point of view? Will improving these items give us a competitive advantage? What is the urgency? What are the consequences if we fail to take action and improve?" There are no hard scientific tools available to absolutely determine policy, though there are some that assist (see the seven "new tools" of quality covered in Chapter 8). Ultimately, the tool that must be used to establish policy is called management judgment.

The initial outcome is that the senior management team should develop a series of policy statements in draft form. These "draft" policies must be tested on the organization to see how they are interpreted. Policy statements must be clear and understandable to the entire organization. There should be no doubt as to what needs to be accomplished and who is responsible for accomplishing it. Keep refining the policy statements over and over until it is clear that the organization knows what is intended and how best to proceed.

Target setting is next, and this is a critical step. An initial target for improvement should be established for each policy statement. For example, your policy statement might be, "Achieve customer satisfaction by reducing the defect rate by 90 percent in three years." Another policy might be, "Reduce cycle time by 25% of the current level over the next three years." Targets should be very aggressive and set to reach "what is possible". Benchmarking data will again help you know what is possible. Remember, though, that the best in class are probably working continuously on improvements. If you want to be only as good as the best *today*, you may find yourself substantially behind by the time you actually *get* there! Another way to determine what is possible is to examine the company's historical records. Often there is evidence that the company did very well at one time and levels of performance deteriorated over the years. If it was achieved in the past, it probably can be achieved again. Targets should again be extremely aggressive and yet reflect convincing evidence that they are possible. They will send a clear message to the organization about what is expected.

One of the corporate policy items at FPL had initially been targeted for a 50 percent improvement in three years. There were some departments that spent their beginning efforts determining why the target was impossible to achieve. The department heads complained that the targets were too aggressive and impossible to achieve. They did not examine what could be done to contribute to the improvement. Management did not relent and reduce the target. Departments were asked to go back and examine the root cause of the problem. It was agreed that if the root cause could not be identified, or if corrective action was impossible, management would then consider changing the target. The departments never returned with a negative analysis. As a matter fact, the problem identified was improved by 75 percent in three years. It turned out that the initial target had not been aggressive enough!

Companies that have been truly successful in implementing TQM are aggressive: they set and achieve improvement targets that many feel might be impossible. Most organizations tend to underestimate their capabilities and do not challenge the resources they have to make dramatic changes.

Deploying Policy

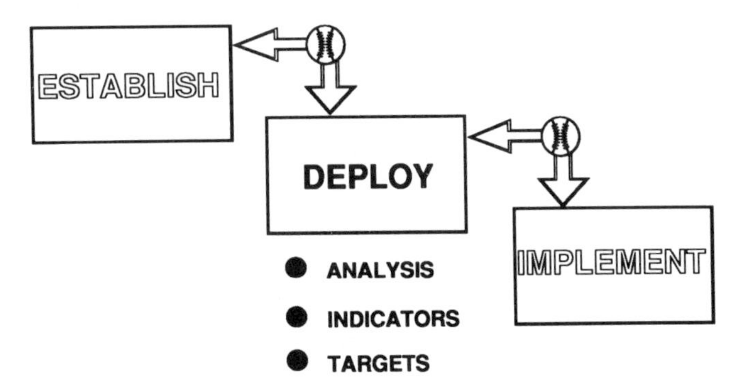

FIGURE 3.8. Deploy Policy

Deploying policy is the second major phase of the Policy Management process (see Figure 3.8). This is a method to launch initial policy statements and receive commitment from the rest of the company, or at least those departments that can make a contribution to the targeted improvements. Through this process, organizational commitments to meeting corporate policies are laid out and refined. Not every department can or should contribute to every item; the customer needs table will help identify who can make what contribution.

During the deployment phase, each department develops an analysis of the current situation as it applies to them, looking for ways to translate improvement targets into actionable steps. From that point, there is negotiation up and down the corporate chain to settle on what a given department can commit to and how it should go about it. The term "catch ball" is used by many Japanese companies to describe this negotiation phase of the process—a process of refinement and agreement on the final targets. Once the individual targets are negotiated and set, the final version of the corporate policy is issued.

Some people think that deploying policy is nothing more than deploying targets. But targets without methods are meaningless. During the deployment phase, each department develops its analysis *and methods* to establish countermeasures. This gives each department a fuller understanding of what it will have to do to make a contribution and what, if any, additional resources will be required. It places departments in a position either to plan a reallocation of resources or to prepare their business plans and arguments regarding what additional resources they may need. Generally, *additional* resources will not be needed—instead, resources should be reallocated among departments.

Once departmental analyses are complete for corporate level policies, each department begins to finalize its part in the business plan and issues a draft policy statement of its own. This policy statement includes not only what senior management has already negotiated with local management (through "catch ball"), but also any high-priority improvement opportunities limited to the local unit. The latter is sometimes referred to as the "will of the manager." From a corporate point of view, one now has a means of tracking and checking on improvements, allowing one to move to the third phase: policy implementation. Policy Management is part of the business planning process. As such, budgeting and resource allocation processes should also be incorporated into the management and deployment of policy.

A system of indicators must be established to track progress and commitment. There are several great tracking systems that have been developed. One of the best and most useful methods is called the "flag system," as developed by Japanese manufacturers. Flag systems give a fairly comprehensive view of the status of a particular policy in a very concise manner. At a glance, the progress or lack of progress can be seen. Flag systems can range from simple to complex; they can show not only the contributions and progress made by each management unit, but also the root causes of the problem.

Choosing the right indicator can be frustrating. If the indicator is not properly chosen it can be very misleading, masking the size of the problem or causing a bigger problem than the one you originally started with. Choosing an indicator that reflects the customer's point of view will help produce better results. Suppose, for instance, a critical customer quality requirement for a given product is reliability (rather than, from a company point of view, the mean time between failures). The specific requirement might be that the product be capable of performing 24 hours a day for one year without any downtime. The records show that the product meets the requirement 99.97% of the time. But customers do not see the 99.97% reliability rating; instead, they see 157.7 minutes a year that the product is *not* reliable. Caution must be exercised when using numbers that are the result of averaging several numbers. An average number, such as 157.7 minutes, often hides the seriousness of the problem. It does not tell you the variation. For instance, some customers may be experiencing 600 minutes of downtime. Indicators must be chosen to reflect expected quality outcomes as seen by the customer.

Avoid indicators that measure activity. Activity-based indicators show activity, but do not necessarily track quality. I once saw a proposal that suggested measuring the number of processes that were documented in the company's business system. This type of indicator can result in chaos. It tells employees that the company has more interest in the *appearance* of quality than in *real* quality.

Avoid financial quality indicators as well. Financial results should be the natural outcome of quality processes and not the sole purpose behind quality efforts. I once saw a senior manager of a company propose a reduction in costs as the prime indictor of effectiveness in delivering service. Often it is easier to reduce costs than to improve quality. I think this is why people revert to such indicators—to avoid the more difficult issue of controlling quality.

Finally, it would be useful to consider assigning a senior manager or executive—a policy "champion"—to coordinate company-wide activities for each corporate policy. This person's job is to minimize duplication of efforts and to provide resources or assistance to departments that request help. The coordinating executive or policy champion becomes the traffic cop who keeps order and maintains the master analysis for that particular policy. The coordinating manager or executive often becomes the chairman of a cross-functional committee that addresses a series of quality requirements. However, coordinating executives are not necessary in every case. The use of this role should be limited to where it is likely that a great deal of duplication of effort might occur and where resources need to be tightly controlled. Each company is different, and how policy is deployed must fit the organization's needs.

Implementing Policy

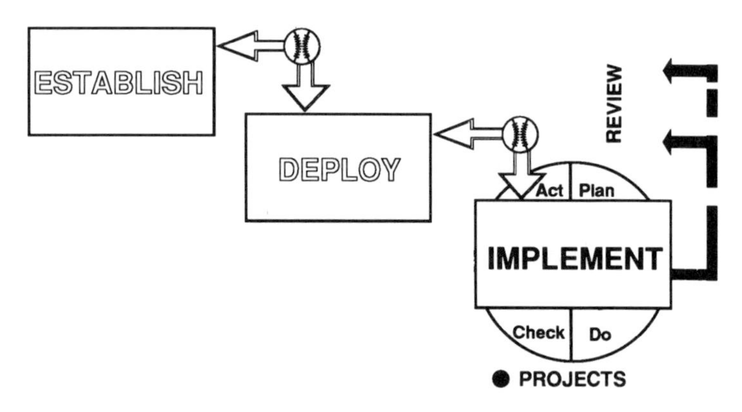

FIGURE 3.9. Implement Policy

The last major phase, implementation, is where the new policies and methods are actually put into effect (Figure 3.9). This is when things happen. Projects progress! Improvements are seen! Several successful methods can be employed in implementing policy. The methods largely depend on the natural organization—how it operates and how it is structured.

Companies that have done well in this phase have used several useful techniques. One purpose of the implementation stage is to produce a "multiplying" effect in the organization. In other words, if a successful policy or problem-solution is implemented in one unit of the company and can readily be adopted by other units, the effects are seen to multiply as success stimulates further success. A mechanism or system must be in place to achieve this effect. One technique here is, again, to pick a corporate champion for each policy adopted. The champion should be someone who is respected in the organization, who has knowledge about the subject, and who has good interpersonal skills. Typically the champion should be a member of senior management. By picking a member of senior management, a clear message is sent about the importance of policy to the organization.

The champion's job is promotion and coordination to remove barriers to achieving the results desired, and to keep track of and present the progress being made. The champion also has the responsibility of ensuring that company resources are being used effectively. Often, policies are deployed to good effect but are not deployed efficiently. Effectiveness may be judged by the number of business units making a contribution to targets. However, different units may end up working on the *same* problem (or same aspect of a larger problem) and develop conflicting solutions. This is, of course, a waste of resources and reduces efficiency. The policy champion can help bring the units together so that they may reduce the overall level of resources and come up with a common solution. The likelihood of different groups coming up with different or alternative solutions is lessened with this type of coordination. When different groups select alternative solutions, the chances of standardizing the improvement are diminished. The champion can help coordinate the various efforts and eliminate conflict. The champion operates in a cross-functional management mode, yet does not take over line responsibilities for the policy. The last role of the champion is to help ensure resources are properly allocated or reallocated to support the policy.

Other methods used to implement policy include assigning corporate teams full-time to work on the policy. This method limits the participation in improvement activities to a select few and may defeat the notion of soliciting improvement opportunities throughout the organization, but the method has merit because resources are devoted full time to the effort. Another method involves publishing the policy without any coordination efforts. This method is simple, but may cause an inefficient allocation of resources.

To make sure that progress is being made on each of the policies, a monthly check by senior management will be necessary. This will instill in the organization the importance of corporate policies to management. Each month senior staff will meet with the coordinating executive (champion) to review progress. Every policy should be reviewed. A 10- to 15-minute presentation for each policy is made. As part of the monthly review, one policy item should be reviewed in depth, inviting members of the various teams working directly on that policy to present their case.

This review must go beyond a "How's it coming?" explanation. The presentation should include review of the team's analysis of problems, the countermeasures employed, and the results obtained (see also Chapter 8). Often the coordinating executive will bring in several presenters who will go over the particular areas each is working on to make a contribution. If, for instance, you have six specific policies, you will be able to review each in depth at least twice a year.

This type of review also takes place at the local level, where local management reviews its own and the corporate policies monthly. A critique at the conclusion of each session should be included, together with homework for the participants (if warranted). Each year senior management should carefully examine the entire process used to develop, deploy, and implement policy and make appropriate changes to improve the process. The complete Policy Management cycle is shown in Figure 3.10.

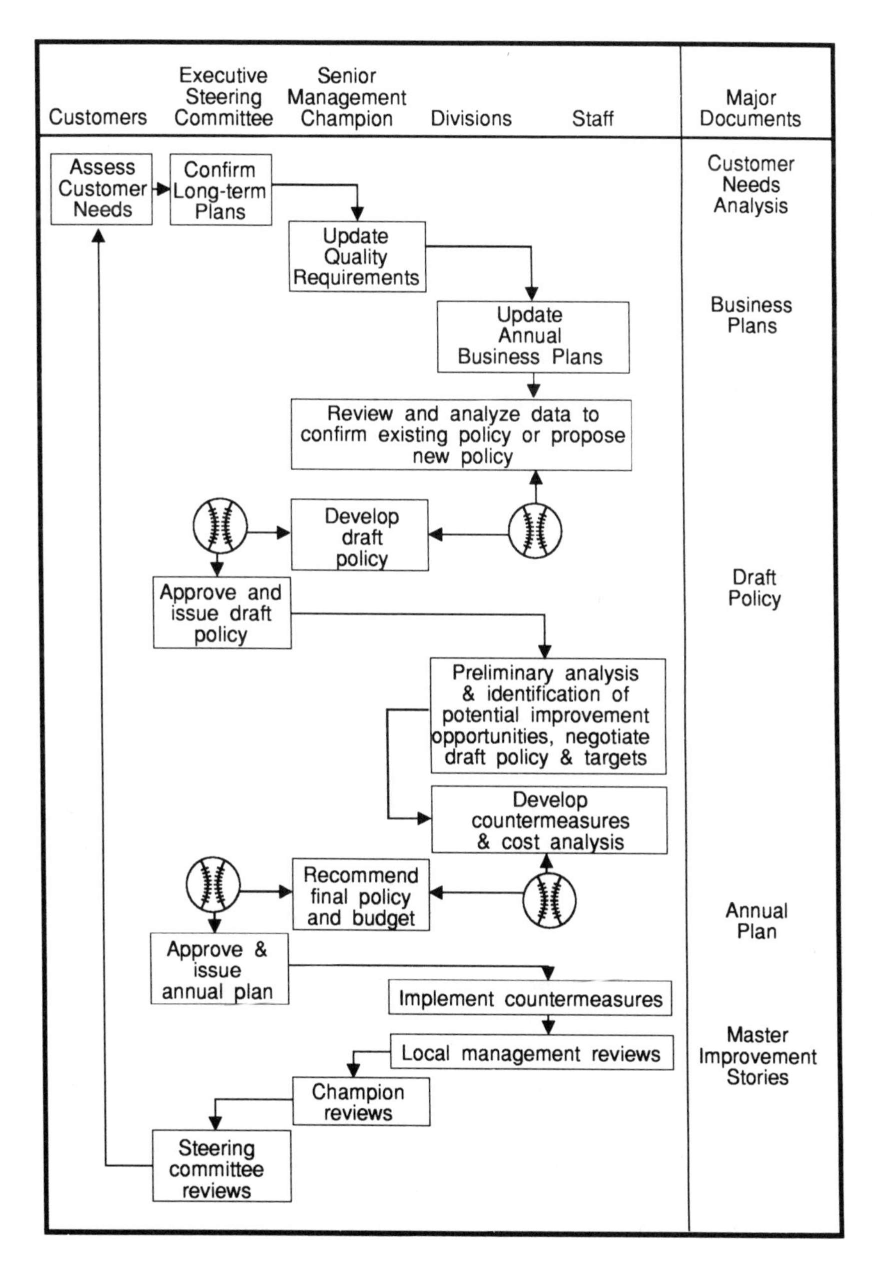

FIGURE 3.10. Policy Management Cycle

POLICY MANAGEMENT IN MULTI-DIVISIONAL COMPANIES

Companies often find it difficult to develop unity of business purpose when their company contains diverse business segments. When there are varying business interests, the business segments often act as though they are the most important or the only entity that counts. The business segments may not relate very well to the overall structure of the company. Business segments often compete with one another for resources and, in some cases, for market share. They may hide their "edge" from one another. Internal competition, though regrettable, abounds.

Such competitive spirit has no place within a company. It is destructive! It breeds mistrust. It wastes valuable resources. There are plenty of opportunities to compete outside and the competitive spirit needs to be directed to areas beyond the corporate boundaries. Policy Management can be an effective means to tie business together under one umbrella—to bring unity to the company.

Under normal circumstances, policy formation is difficult. It takes a great deal of thought and effort to boil down the issues to a critical few that have the most impact on the overall success of the company. In a diversified company, the task becomes even more complex. If the CEO establishes policy from the top without concurrence from the business units, there is little hope that the policies will be understood or implemented well. When different business segments exist, it is best to begin the work of policy formation at the individual business unit level. Policy Management is a business planning practice and most business planning starts at this level anyway.

Begin by developing the "Voice of the Customer" for each business unit (see Figure 3.11). If you were to try to do this at the corporate level first, the business segments might find the results unconvincing; there would never be full ownership. After each business segment properly identifies the voice of the customer, invite a representative from each business segment to a workshop to evaluate the customer needs tables.

More often than not, what is discovered is that there are

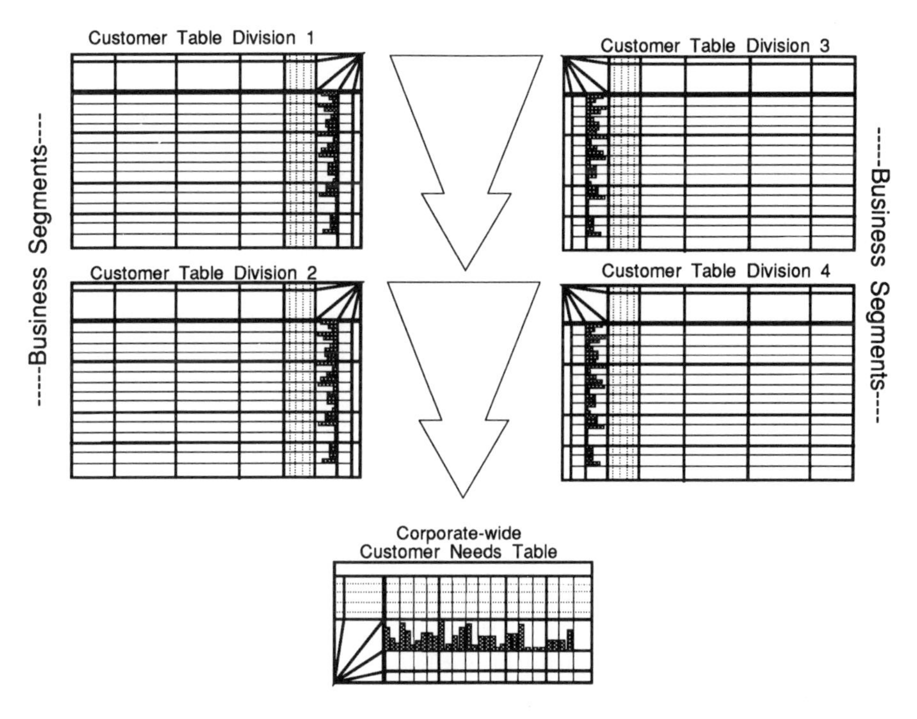

FIGURE 3.11. Customer Needs Analysis for a Multi-divisional Company

common customer requirements that appear regardless of the nature of the business. This makes good sense, but one cannot simply assume that it would be the case. Have the unit representative select the top 20 customer requirements from each of the business segment tables – the ones with the largest gaps in performance from a customer perspective. This is when you may find the requirements with the largest gaps to be common to each of the business segments, probably due to the overall corporate culture that permeates each business. Because each business segment may word the customer requirement in a slightly different manner, you will need a method to develop a common definition and understanding. One tool to help combine the requirements is the affinity diagram (see Chapter 8).

The second task for each business segment is to develop its "Voice of the Business." This activity has two purposes. The first is to develop a systematic method to identify each business segment's chronic business problems. The second is to provide the corporate hierarchy with a tool to look for common business problems among the different business segments. There are likely to be common business problems among the business segments, just as there were common high-priority customer requirements. Even if the analysis does not show that there are common problems, the exercise is useful because it provides each business segment with a list of improvement opportunities where Policy Management can be applied. The same techniques used for combining the "Voice of the Customer" can be used to develop a common list of business problems at the corporate level (see Figure 3.12).

Armed with the two tables, the company's strategic plan, and any other summarized analyses that look at future customer needs, environmental factors, competition, and business and technological forecasts, a corporate policy plan can be developed (Figure 3.12). Using this approach, the policy plan will make sense. It will be focused on the vital few issues that will improve the overall direction of the company. In addition, the policy plan can be supported by each of the business segments, because it was their analyses that provided the input for the development of the plan.

There are several quality tools that can assist the senior management team in evaluating the information before them. Data matrix analysis, QFD type analysis, affinity diagrams, and a whole host of basic graphical tools can be used (see Chapter 8). All information should be boiled down to graphical representations that give a visual picture of the relationships among the data at hand. I have worked with diversified companies that were able to take complex business problems, highlight the most important areas, and reduce the entire set of data to simple matrices that an entry-level employee could understand.

Once again, however, there is no absolute magic that will tell senior management what the best policy is. The tool that ultimately must be used is called management. Only management can decide the final policies to be adopted.

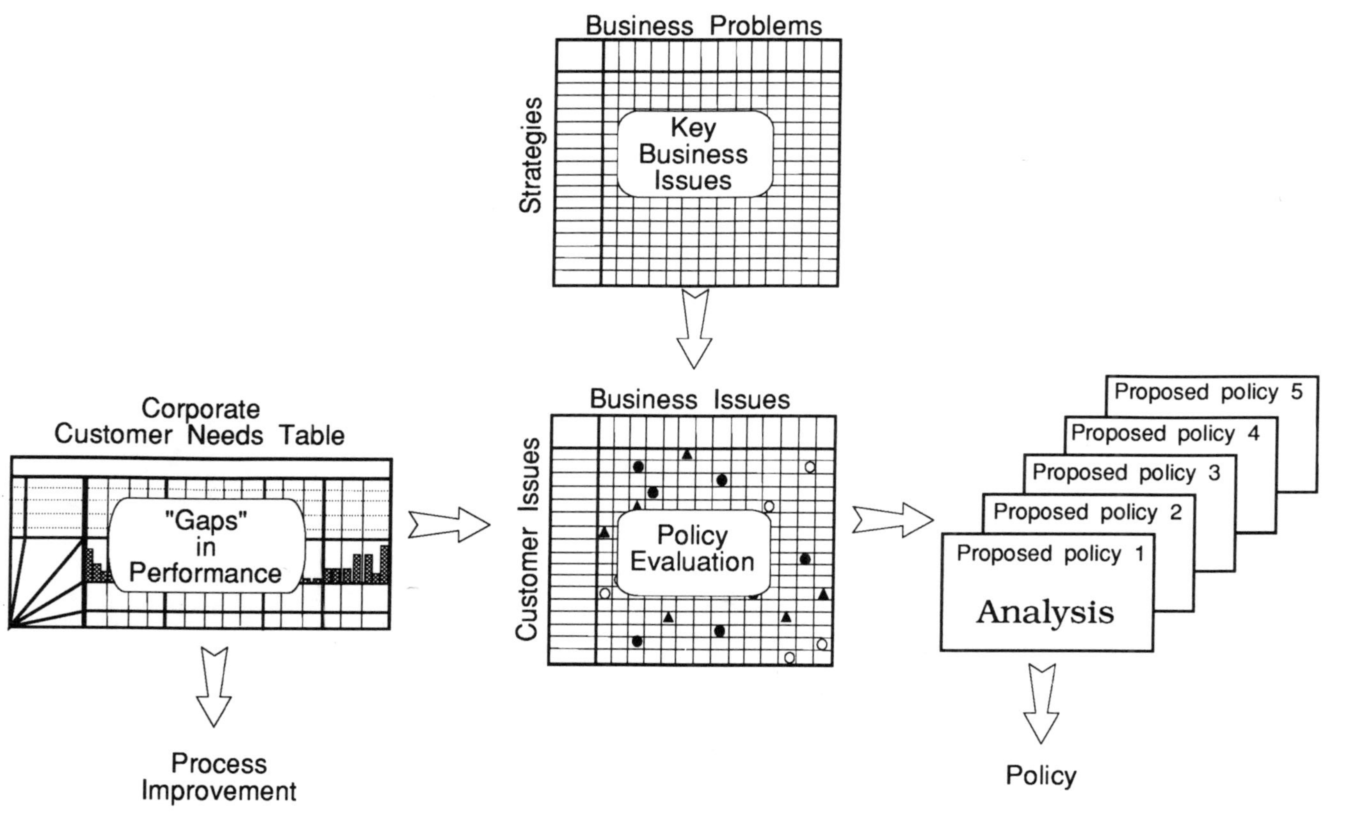

FIGURE 3.12. Policy Management in a Multi-divisional Company

Selecting Indicators

Selecting an indicator that will accurately track the progress made for each corporate wide policy is equally challenging. The measurement must be understood by each business segment and must be useful to them. There is a tendency for companies that have diverse business segments to develop measurements that are strictly financial in nature. This tendency is understandable because managers in corporate holding companies are trained very well in this type of measurement. It is the language of business and sometimes is the only system that can be uniformly communicated and understood. But no matter how common these monetary measures may be, it is tragic when they are used as the ultimate "score card" for tracking progress on a policy. Use of these indicators sends a clear message that senior management is interested only in financial results and that quality is simply a side issue. This is unwise from both an operations and marketing standpoint.

If one of the large gaps identified from the customer needs table is, for example, "timely action," the corporate measure for this could be either the number of times or the percentage of time that the business unit failed to fill the customer's request within the time frame desired. This type of measurement can readily be interpreted by the relevant business segments. They can look at their activities and determine what, exactly, "timely action" means for them and their customers and at the same time provide consistent tracking information at the corporate level.

There are numerous cases where selection of the wrong indicator resulted in wasted effort and, in some cases, unintended consequences or even malfeasance by the organization. You get what you measure! By measuring things from a customers' perspective, you are unlikely to generate activity that can result in embarrassment to the company. If you improve those things that are most important to the customer, the result can only be greater customer loyalty; and if you price things correctly, the result should be what financial managers find most important—an improved bottom line.

Coordination of Policy

In multi-divisional companies, the coordination of efforts becomes even more critical. The likelihood of duplication of effort or misinterpretation of policies is great. Again, a good way to avoid these situations is to select a senior executive or "champion" to coordinate efforts for a given policy. The task of the champion is to encourage the business segments to support the policy. In this role, his or her job is counselor, advisor, and persuader. The champion must be respected by the entire organization and have good human relations skills. The second role is one of tracking and reporting. This role is for increased efficiency. By having one person summarize the activities of each business segment, the CEO and senior staff can get a quick update on the status of each policy every month. If classic reporting techniques are used, the policy will take too long to be reviewed. This will probably happen only once before reverting to MBO-type activities where the policy does not get reviewed at all or, at best, once a year.

To support the company champion, each business segment selects its own coordinator or "co-champion." The company champion and the business-segment or co-champions become, in effect, the steering force for the policy they coordinate. Co-champions should have the same characteristics as the champion (i.e., be respected by the organization and have good human relations skills). In addition, co-champions should have skills related to the policy being supported and be high enough in the business segment to have influence.

Although Policy Management is more difficult in multi-divisional companies, it is not impossible. One need only give greater consideration to organizational aspects as well as to the system of implementation. A complete system is shown in Figure 3.13.

CONCLUSION

The process of Policy Management is a corporate system. Its primary purpose is to create a systematic means to establish overall

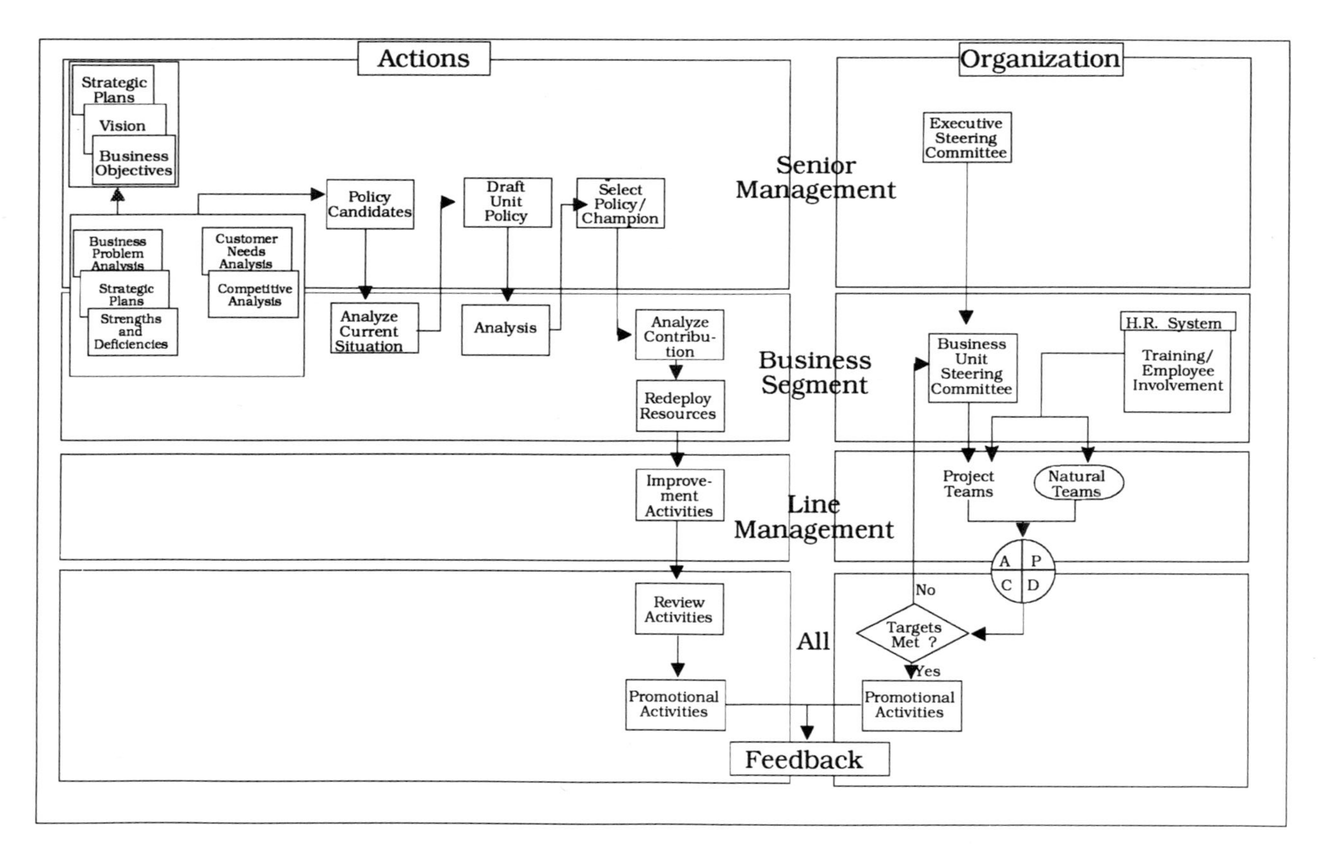

FIGURE 3.13. Policy Management System in a Multi-divisional Company

corporate priorities, implement strategies, and achieve a corporate vision. The same system is repeated at all levels of the organization. The method is used by divisions and departments to determine not only how they will contribute to meeting corporate objectives, but how they will develop and meet their own local-level objectives for high-priority problems.

Policy Management is an integral part of the overall business planning cycle. It must be integrated fully with the financial planning processes to ensure that reallocation of resources occurs as necessary. The system cannot be viewed separately from normal planning activities—it must be incorporated as part of the overall management process.

The Policy Management process is far superior to a typical MBO program that generally reviews results at the end of a year. Policy Management is a proven, disciplined process that drives major improvements in an organization. It enables a company to become quality-driven and customer-driven.

4

Daily Management

INTRODUCTION

Although Policy Management may be the most important TQM process component to institutionalize in developing a total quality company, Daily Management is also critical for achieving overall success. This process component, sometimes referred to as "quality in daily work" or "quality in repetitive work," is a means for identifying, controlling, and improving critical day-to-day operations. Daily Management attacks the many "trivial" problems that every organization faces. It provides a means for making hundreds, if not thousands, of minor improvements that, in accumulation, can produce very significant results. These improvements, moreover, are the kind that are often quickly noticed by customers.

Whereas Policy Management falls more on senior management, Daily Management is more dispersed. Senior management's responsibility is to ensure that the concepts of Daily Management are taught and understood, and that the means are put in place to make sure that they are practiced by the organization. Daily Management must be led by those who run the day-to-day operation of the company—middle managers, supervisors, and first line employees.

As an organization implements Policy Management, management may find that the participation by the employee population is limited. Daily Management steps in to provide a programmed approach to extend the application of quality concepts and practices to the entire organization. The application of Daily Management concepts can and should be practiced by every department, section, and work group within the organization.

It is virtually impossible (and not advisable) for an organization to put in place a system that controls or improves every process all the time. Formal control systems based in additional technology and administrative layers can, if misapplied, become counterproductive. Few companies can afford these more elaborate schemes and fewer still require this level of precision and control. Daily Management is a system of process control that, together with the other TQM process components, provides a comprehensive approach to solving problems and improving the organization.

There is no one magical way to implement Daily Management. It depends on the nature of the activities to which it is applied. Careful thought must be given to the specific methods chosen. Companies may employ a variety of methods—matching the proper ones to the processes at hand. Senior management should be familiar with alternative ways that this process component can be implemented and with how the overall process complements Policy Management and enhances the quality levels of the company.

USING THE CUSTOMER NEEDS TABLE

One way to narrow the field of possibilities for applying Daily Management is to use the customer needs table that was developed to identify candidates for inclusion in corporate policy. Recall that the customer needs table compares weighted customer requirements against the process that delivers a product or service. Because the table was developed by looking at how each key process relates to the customers' requirements, a ready-made prioritization scheme for managers and supervisors is available. The highest-weighted processes, as identified by the tallies at the bottom of the table (see Figure 4.1), are the processes that show the greatest need for control and improvement. In this way Daily

Construction			Customer Sales & Service							
Engineering Design	Construction	Installation	Sales	Order Entry	Bill Rendering	Payment Processing	Collections	Training & Support	Customer Systems	Quality Assurance
72 ●	72 ●	72 ●	24 ▲	48 ■	48 ■		24 ▲	48 ■		24 ▲
54 ●	54 ●	54 ●	18 ▲	36 ■				18 ▲		
84 ●	84 ●	84 ●	28 ▲	56 ■						28 ▲
24 ■		36 ●	12 ▲	12 ▲				24 ■	24 ■	12 ▲
38 ■	38 ■	19 ▲		19 ▲				19 ▲	19 ▲	
169 ●	169 ●	169 ●	169 ●	169 ●			169 ●	113 ■	113 ■	
90 ●	90 ●	90 ●	60 ■	90 ●	30 ▲	90 ●	90 ●	90 ●	60 ■	30 ▲
72 ●	24 ▲	72 ●	24 ▲	72 ●	24 ▲	72 ●	72 ●	72 ●	24 ▲	24 ▲
72 ●	72 ●	72 ●	72 ●	72 ●	72 ●	72 ●	72 ●	72 ●	72 ●	72 ●
60 ■	30 ▲	90 ●	90 ●	90 ●	60 ■	60 ■	90 ●	90 ●	30 ▲	60 ■
72 ●		72 ●	72 ●	72 ●		24 ▲	72 ●	72 ●	72 ●	72 ●
19 ▲	38 ■	56 ●	56 ●	56 ●			56 ●	56 ●	38 ■	19 ▲
12 ●	4 ▲	8 ■	8 ■	4 ▲			8 ■			4 ▲
45 ▲	135 ●	135 ●	135 ●	135 ●	45 ▲	45 ▲	135 ●	90 ■	45 ▲	45 ▲
24 ▲		72 ●	48 ■	72 ●		48 ■	48 ■	72 ●	48 ■	24 ▲
20 ▲	20 ▲	40 ■	60 ●	60 ●			60 ●	60 ●	40 ■	20 ▲
32 ■		32 ■	48 ●	48 ●	32 ■	16 ▲	48 ●	48 ●	32 ■	48 ●
18 ▲	18 ▲	36 ■	54 ●	54 ●	54 ●	18 ▲	54 ●	54 ●	36 ■	18 ▲
22 ▲		65 ●	65 ●	65 ●	65 ●		65 ●	65 ●	65 ●	22 ▲
18 ▲		18 ▲	54 ●	54 ●	18 ▲		18 ▲	36 ■	54 ●	18 ▲
28 ▲		28 ▲	56 ■	28 ▲	56 ■			56 ■	56 ■	
		19 ▲	58 ●	58 ●			19 ▲	38 ■	38 ■	19 ▲
				9 ▲			18 ■		9 ▲	9 ▲
6 ▲		6 ▲	6 ▲	12 ■	6 ▲				6 ▲	6 ▲
15 ▲		30 ■	15 ▲	45 ●	45 ●	45 ●	30 ■		30 ■	15 ▲
		24 ▲		24 ▲	72 ●					
			6 ▲	6 ▲	18 ●		6 ▲		6 ▲	6 ▲
1065	847	1399	1238	1466	645	490	1154	1193	916	595

FIGURE 4.1. Top Priority Processes

Management is approached from an external customers' point of view and complements Policy Management.

Daily Management is an inexpensive way to identify and focus the organization on the most important process-improvement areas. It is a method that helps managers and supervisors allocate or reallocate their limited resources to necessary improvement activities. The higher the weight for the process, the greater the likelihood that the process is significant from a customer point of view and the greater the opportunity for improvement. The following sections describe four ways to use the table for Daily Management.

Organizational Design Approach

The customer needs table is basically a quality function deployment (QFD) method as developed in Japan. QFD is used primarily for product design and manufacturing. By using QFD for Daily Management, the tool provides a method to design or redesign the organization's approach to meeting customer requirements. By using this "organizational design approach" to satisfy customer needs, the processes that have the greatest effect in terms of customers' requirements, as well as those that show the greatest "gap" in company performance, can be targeted for improvement (Figure 4.1). This is the best place to start in introducing Daily Management. The top-priority processes in need of improvement and control in Figure 4.1 are installation, sales, and order entry.

Next, supervisors or project teams flowchart the process that has been targeted to show graphically how things are currently accomplished. There must be a clear picture of the activities that take place. The processes selected for improvement or control must be carefully examined to locate any points in the process where breakdowns occur—points where the company fails to meet customers' expectations. Data must then be gathered to specify the extent of the failures, and indicators need to be established to track progress.

When the customer needs table is used in this manner to introduce Daily Management, project-team activities rather than quality circles or natural teams are normally employed (see Chapter 5). Project teams differ from quality circles in that team members are selected by management based on problem-solving ability rather than having team members volunteer. They are also assigned to a problem by management (rather than choosing a problem of their own) and are disbanded once the problem is solved (rather than remaining as an ongoing resource). The reason for using project teams is that the organizational design approach usually requires a higher level of skill, particularly if the improvement process involves a series of subprocesses. The end results can also substantially influence policy-related matters, because the processes targeted for improvement are identified from a customers' viewpoint.

Process-Streamlining Approach

A second way to use the customer needs table is to look *across* the table to see if there are any highly weighted customer requirements that have several different processes or business steps that impact the requirement (see Figure 4.2). If this condition exists, it could indicate that too many organizations and processes are given split responsibility for meeting customers' requirements. It forces the old adage: if everyone is responsible, probably no one is responsible. When there are multiple processes, each with its own type of variation, the chances of achieving a high level of customer satisfaction are more remote—unless each process is kept under tight control.

One good solution is to "reengineer" the stream of interrelated processes to minimize any variation and to enable better assignment of accountability and responsibility for the outcome desired. One hesitates to use the term "reengineering" here because it has become somewhat faddish. But both the concept and the practice are actually old industrial-engineering standbys that mean, simply, streamlining the process.

If you choose the process-streamlining approach for implementing Daily Management, you will again need to employ project teams made up of people from different departments or disciplines. Team members should have both the technical skills

Customer Requirements	Total Weight	Importance (1-5)	Current Position (1-5)	Plan (1-5)	Market Accent (1.2, 1.5)	Competitive Position	Market Research	Market Planning	Product Development	Product Management	Advertising & Promotion	Engineering Design	Construction	Installation	Sales
	Business Activities						Marketing					Construction			
	Weights														
Product & Delivery Quality															
Give me dependable products															
Provide products that I need when I want them	8.0	4	3	5	1.2	5	72 ●	72 ●	72 ●	72 ●	24 ▲	72 ●	72 ●	72 ●	24 ▲
Anticipate my changing needs and act on them	6.0	3	3	4	1.5	4	54 ●	54 ●	54 ●	36 ■	18 ▲	54 ●	54 ●	54 ●	18 ▲
Provide products that work all the time	9.4	5	4	5	1.5	5	28 ▲	56 ■	84 ●	84 ●	28 ▲	84 ●	84 ●	84 ●	28 ▲
Provide products that are easy to use	4.0	3	3	4	1	3	24 ▲	24 ■	36 ●	36 ●	12 ▲	24 ■		36 ●	12 ▲
If it breaks, provide me with a convienient place for repairs	6.3	5	4	5	1	4		19 ▲	38 ■	38 ●		38 ■	38 ■	19 ▲	

FIGURE 4.2. Priority Areas for Process Improvement

and the business acumen to make the necessary changes. The changes to be implemented could present difficulty in that they may affect several organizations; such improvements most likely will require organizational changes or changes in responsibility assignments. Typically, one can expect some organizational resistance because the changes can be profound.

Implementing Daily Management activities using the first two approaches can have a great impact on the overall effectiveness of an organization. The two approaches can result in significant cost reductions and produce improvements noticed by the customer. Using these methods requires a complete examination of how work is accomplished in the business unit and the delivery of quality characteristics. If improvement activities are centered around these two approaches, senior management may need to be involved to eliminate any resistance to recommended changes.

Examination-By-Function Approach

The customer needs table can be used in a third way to implement Daily Management on a broader scale. This approach may be used when there is a desire for widespread implementation of improvement activities and when resources are not constrained. Because each major business process is represented on the table, each separate business function can identify how it contributes to meeting customer requirements (see Figure 4.3). The employees and their managers can examine which processes are critical to meeting the requirements and determine whether the processes are in need of improvement or should simply be kept under tight control. Begin by first examining the highest-weighted individual blocks under each major business process column. Determine the sub-processes that affect the customer requirement associated with the process. Flowchart the sub-processes to gain an understanding of them and the larger process, where they need to be controlled, and where they need to be improved.

QFD-Type Approach

A fourth way to use the customer needs table arises when primary quality requirements and characteristics are influenced by a *limited* number of organizational units. This approach uses quality

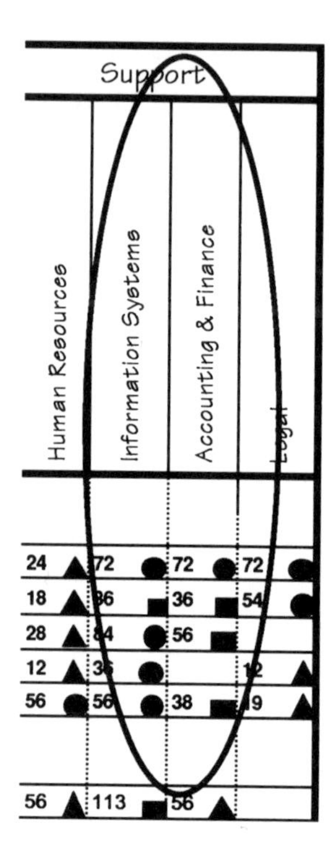

FIGURE 4.3. Department Areas for Improvement

function deployment techniques to rethink or redesign the methods used to deliver a given quality requirement. This approach is effective for both manufacturing and service companies.

First, a particular quality requirement is established and its primary and secondary characteristics are defined to a level where they become actionable. Each quality requirement typically entails a number of different actions. There will neither be the resources nor the will to control each and every actionable step—only the most critical ones. After the most critical actions are identified, processes are put in place to control and improve the results desired.

Assume, for example, that one of the customer quality requirements is considerate customer service. How do you go about defining what considerate customer service is and how do you ensure that it is delivered to your customers?

TABLE 4.1. Customer Quality Requirement

Quality Requirement	*Primary Requirements*
Considerate Customer Service	• Treat me in a courteous manner • Be caring and concerned about me

An easy way to find out is to ask them. You will, however, need to facilitate this process because customers often have a difficult time expressing their specific needs and requirements in terms meaningful to the producer. They often try to help by providing perceived *solutions*. Focus groups can help when properly facilitated. Complaint records can also be a source of information to help define considerate customer service. Basically, this vague concept needs to be made understandable and actionable.

Start by defining the primary characteristics that make up the quality requirement; then define the secondary characteristics and the tertiary characteristics. Actionable steps should emerge when tertiary characteristics are defined (see Tables 4.1–4.3).

At this point you have defined a comprehensive, actionable process derived from quality requirements established from a customer's point of view. To ensure that you deliver what the customer requires, a control and checking process must also be established. Use the most critical tertiary characteristics as checking and measurement points. One cannot measure every

TABLE 4.2. Primary and Secondary Requirements

Primary Requirements	*Secondary Requirements*
Treat me in a courteous manner	• Greet me properly • Speak clearly—use good grammar • Have a pleasant voice • Be courteous in your responses to me
Be caring and concerned about me	• Offer assistance • Listen to me and do not interrupt • Be attentive to me

TABLE 4.3. Secondary and Tertiary Requirements

Secondary Requirements	*Tertiary Requirements*
• Greet me properly	• Identify the company • Givc your name • Ask "May I help you?"
• Speak clearly—use good grammar	• Use proper grammar— avoid slang • Speak in complete sentences • Speak clearly
• Have a pleasant voice	• Use voice inflection to show interest—avoid monotone
• Be courteous in your responses to me	• Be polite and patient • Use "yes" and "no"—avoid "yeah" and "huh"
• Offer assistance	• Ask the customer if you can provide further assistance
• Listen to me and do not interrupt	• Be patient at all times
• Be attentive to me	• Acknowledge the customer's comments • Avoid expressions of annoyance or frustration

little thing—look for items that are most meaningful to the customer, and keep these under control.

* * *

The customer needs table can be used in at least four different ways to introduce the concepts and practice of Daily Management. These include: (1) driving improvements based on identifying the biggest gaps between your performance and your customers' requirements (organizational design approach); (2) looking for quality characteristics that appear to require too many processes to achieve (process-streamlining approach);

(3) examining the quality elements for each business function (examination-by-function approach); and (4) concentrating on a particular quality requirement. Still another method is to approach Daily Management recognizing that each and every department, division, section, and group exists ultimately to serve the customer and efforts must be focused on job accountabilities and responsibilities.

JOB ACCOUNTABILITIES AND DAILY MANAGEMENT

Identify Department Basic Functions and Job Accountabilities

A more traditional approach to introducing Daily Management, and one that can have widespread application in any organization, is to begin with fundamentals—department basic functions. This approach can be effectively implemented in every department.

All departments or units within an organization exist for some reason; they have a charter or reason for being. These are the "department basic functions." Begin by dusting off the mission statement, charter, or whatever is used to describe the core responsibilities of the department or section. If a department does not have a clear understanding of its basic functions, department heads should create a mission statement. If one exists but it is not current, update it.

Every employee in a department should know clearly why their department exists and what is expected of them. If there is a clear definition about the department basic functions, then there are a number of tasks or jobs that must be performed. Each job or task should accomplish a result. The expected results can be called "job accountabilities." Establish or confirm the set of basic job accountabilities. When job accountabilities are related to customer requirements, employees have a better understanding of how the customer is affected by their actions. Every job accountability usually entails one or more daily work processes. The place of department basic functions, job accountabilities,

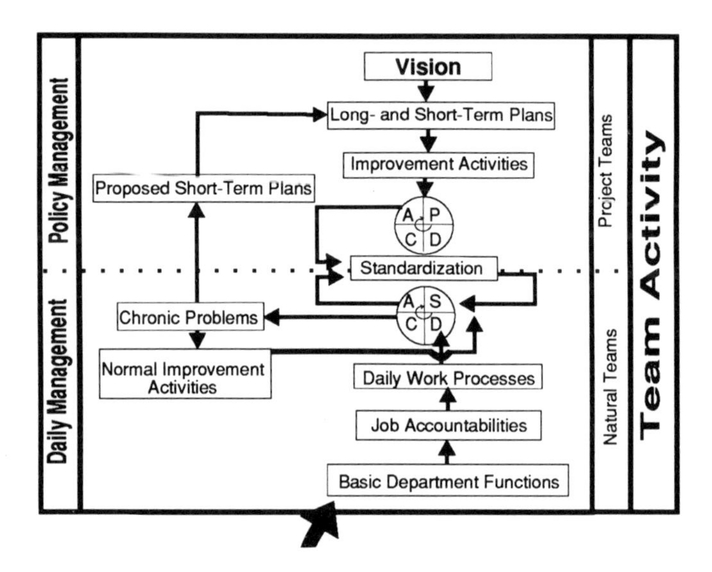

FIGURE 4.4. Daily Management Work Processes Within a TQM System

and daily work processes within a complete TQM system is illustrated in Figure 4.4.

The set of job accountabilities provides a means to begin examining what areas are in need of improvement and continued control. Although this approach is fairly straightforward, it may reveal some organizational difficulties—particularly when there is more than one unit with the same department basic function. This is not an uncommon condition: many organizations have geographically-separated offices or plants whose basic function is the same.

For example, given the nature of the public-utility business, at FPL we had more than one unit carrying the same functional responsibility: we had several different district offices, several service centers, and several engineering offices. The managers of these departments were asked to identify their "top priority jobs" (i.e., to list their job accountabilities and to identify those activities showing the greatest "gaps" in performance). When we examined the responses, we noticed that departments with the same basic functions had identified very different sets of job accountabilities. We wondered if the managers were working for the same company!

I began to realize that we had an organization that was potentially out of control. Everyone was apparently doing their own thing; there was not agreement on the fundamentals of the task (i.e., neither unit basic functions nor individual job accountabilities). No wonder we were having difficulty meeting customer requirements and no wonder we received so many customer complaints. We had discovered variation at its worst.

As a word of caution so that you do not interpret this to mean that all geographically separated units must always do exactly the same thing—they should not. Every organization or unit must adapt to local conditions and local customer requirements, but the basic task or function should be the same. Variation from this should be allowed only when there is a specific local need involving customer requirements that must be met.

Identify Products and Services

Another way to begin, which may be better for organizations that have well-developed departmental mission statements, is to develop a list of the products or services produced (see Table 4.4). This is a simple task, one that will not take a great deal of

TABLE 4.4. Department Product and Service List

Products and Services
Sale of exercise equipment
Marketing data
Sales data
Report on equipment sales
List of sales personnel who have been trained
Report on vacant sales personnel positions
Report on budget variances
Budget estimate for the rest of the year

resources. If the organization cannot identify any outputs, it should be disbanded; it has no purpose for being!

Identify the Process and the Customer

Identify the process or processes that produce each product or service. This will provide a list of what takes place to create the output of the process (see Table 4.5). A flowchart of the process can be helpful to identify customers of the process and points of interaction with other parts of the organization. Identify the customers of the product or service and add them to the list. The customer for most products or services is probably an internal customer but can also be an external customer. The best approach here is to think of the customer as the "next process." Often we think of customers only in terms of those who pay directly for products or services we offer (i.e., external customers). Keep in mind that the idea of the customer as the "next process" expands the classical understanding of "customer" to include not only those whom we traditionally consider customers, but also the myriad internal customers who may never see the ultimate customer. The concept of the internal customer helps strengthen cooperation within the organization and becomes an integral part of satisfying the ultimate customer's requirements.

Identify the Valid Requirements

For those processes whose customers are internal, identify their valid requirements (see Table 4.6). The concept of *valid requirements* is sometimes difficult to appreciate. If, for instance, you were to ask an internal customer what he or she required of a department for a particular report it produces for them, they might respond by saying that the report should be given to them before the end of the month. When, however, you examine the information needed for the report and realize that the data necessary to produce the report are not available before the tenth of the following month, obviously, this creates an impossible situation. The requirement is not valid.

TABLE 4.5. Processes and Customers Who Support Department Products and Services

Products and Services	*Processes*	*Customer*
Sale of exercise equipment	Take orders and answer customer requests	Sales VP
Marketing data	Collect, analyze, and report market data	Planning Department
Sales data	Prepare sales report	Planning Department
Report on equipment sales	Prepare report on sales by type	Purchasing Department
List of sales personnel who have been trained	Report on sales personnel who have been trained	Human Resources Department
Report on vacant sales personnel positions	Report on open sales personnel positions	Human Resources Department
Report on budget variances	Evaluate cost of operation vs. budget – prepare report	Budget Department
Budget estimate for the rest of the year	Analyze and forecast budget needs for year end	Budget Department

TABLE 4.6. Customer Valid Requirements

Products and Services	*Processes*	*Customer*	*Valid Requirements*
Sale of exercise equipment	Take orders and answer customer requests	Sales VP	• Achieve sales quota • Provide accurate and fast information to the customer
Marketing data	Collect, analyze, and report market data	Planning Department	• Accurate and complete marketing data
Sales data	Prepare sales report	Planning Department	• Accurate and complete sales data
Report on equipment sales	Prepare report on sales by type	Purchasing Department	• Accurate sales data by zone and product
List of sales personnel who have been trained	Report on sales personnel who have been trained	Human Resources Department	• Up-to-date information on sales personnel that have been trained
Report on vacant sales personnel positions	Report on open sales personnel positions	Human Resources Department	• Identify open positions monthly
Report on budget variances	Evaluate cost of operation vs. budget—prepare report	Budget Department	• Operate within budget • Accurate and on time monthly report
Budget estimate for the rest of the year	Analyze and forecast budget needs for year end	Budget Department	• Forecast year-end budget every three months

In general, though, the concept of *customer first* rather than *product out* is essential to develop. There are several ways to help people concentrate on the customer. One of the most effective is to publish and visibly display the customer's requirements. Management and employees will quickly begin to understand these requirements and will look for ways to meet them. Senior managers must push their teams to focus on the customer. When team members or managers say or do things that are not focused on the customer, their attention must be brought back to the customer.

Define the Standards

Define the standards that can be used to gauge whether customer requirements are being met. To begin identifying the processes that are in need of improvement, and to what degree, it is necessary to state how they measure up against a standard (see Table 4.7). Standards are today's best practices or specifications that are followed to meet the customer's expectations. Normally standards include specifications that can be measured. These measurements can be tracked as indicators that show whether the specification is being met. Each process needs to be measured to determine whether some "gap" exists between it and the requirement. If the product or service is being delivered to an internal customer, you may be able to negotiate a standard. For every process, however, effort should be expended on determining how it affects the ultimate (external) customer. This is because internal customers sometimes specify a standard that is below the level of quality required by the external customer. To avoid this, always keep in mind the ultimate customer. Look to the customer needs table as a resource to use in educating employees and making sure that day-to-day processes are all working toward meeting the expectations of the customer.

It may take a good deal of persuasion to convince some internal customers that their requirements are not valid or that they are in conflict with the needs of external customers. Managers, supervisors, and first level employees must try to negotiate—using facts—to convince internal customers. Facts will help overcome the emotions which generally accompany these sessions.

TABLE 4.7. Standards to Achieve Customer's Valid Requirements

Customer	*Valid Requirements*	*Standards*
Sales VP	Achieve sales quota Provide accurate and fast information to the customer	• Achieve a minimum of 50% sales on those customers that call • Respond to a customer within 3 days of a call
Planning Department	Accurate and complete marketing data	• Legible, error free, and with all market data every Monday by 10:00 am
Planning Department	Accurate and complete sales data	• Legible, error free, and with all sales data by the 3rd working day every month
Purchasing Department	Accurate sales data by zone and product	• Legible, error free, and with all marketing data including information by product, price, area, and consumer before 10 am each Friday

(*continued*)

TABLE 4.7. Standards to Achieve Customer's Valid Requirements (continued)

Customer	*Valid Requirements*	*Standards*
Human Resources Department	Up-to-date information on sales personnel who have been trained	• Complete information including courses attended and additional training needed
Human Resources Department	Identify open positions monthly	• Complete list of vacant positions by the 5th working day of the month
Budget Department	Operate within budget Accurate and on time monthly report	• Operate within .5% of budget • Complete report delivered by the 4th working day of the month
Budget Department	Forecast year-end budget every three months	• Complete analytical report delivered by the 6th working day of the month

Determine the "Gap"

Rank the importance of each requirement and determine the "gap." The ranking should be done by the person responsible for the job and checked with his or her immediate supervisor for agreement. This will help identify the areas that need the greatest attention (see Table 4.8).

Check to see that department basic functions correspond to each department product and service to make clear what needs to be done to satisfy the customer (see Table 4.9). Develop concise statements that describe what must be done to produce the product or service. Similar products or services can be grouped together to eliminate redundant efforts and to ensure collective responsibility.

A ranking must be employed to continue to home in on which processes are most in need of improvement. A good method is to rank job accountabilities using the weights that appeared in the customer needs table. If a job accountability has no relationship to the external customer, but exists only to satisfy an internal company need, judgment must be applied to rank the job accountability according to priorities. Job accountabilities often satisfy both internal and external customer requirements. In this case, one way to rank the job accountability is by giving both internal and external requirements a 50% weight contribution (see Table 4.10). Using this approach will balance the requirements of both the internal and external customer. Whether you use this method or some other, the important thing to remember is that all organizations, no matter how well-endowed, have limited resources. These resources need to be applied in the most effective way.

After priorities have been established, define the objective for each job accountability. The objective is what is expected to be accomplished by the job. Managers and supervisors should ask, "How do I know when the job is complete and correct?" Next, a measurement system or simply an indicator to check to see if the conditions are being met must be established. For highly ranked job accountabilities control systems need to be put in place. The job must be checked to see that the customer requirements are

TABLE 4.8. "Gap" Analysis

Standards	*Importance*	*Present Situation (GAP)*
• Achieve a minimum of 50% sales on those customers that call	High	35%
• Respond to a customer within 3 days of a call	Medium	4.8 days
• Legible, error free, and with all market data every Monday by 10:00 am	Medium	Acceptable
• Legible, error free, and with all sales data by the 3rd working day every month	Low	Delayed one week
• Legible, error free, and with all marketing data including information by product, price, area, and consumer before 10 am each Friday	High	Customer estimates 20% not clear
• Complete information including courses attended and additional training needed	Low	Acceptable
• Complete list of vacant positions by the 5th working day of the month	Medium	Acceptable
• Operate within .5% of budget	High	+.2%
• Complete report delivered by the 4th working day of the month	Medium	Acceptable
• Complete analytical report delivered by the 6th working day of the month	Low	Acceptable

TABLE 4.9. Department Basic Functions

Products and Services	*Department Basic Functions*
Sale of exercise equipment	Respond to customer's orders
Marketing data	Provide market information
Sales data	Provide market information
Report on equipment sales	Provide market information
List of sales personnel who have been trained	Train sales personnel
Report on vacant sales personnel positions	Employ Sales personnel
Report on budget variances	Operate department within budget
Budget estimate for the rest of the year	Operate department within budget

TABLE 4.10. Ranking Job Accountabilities

	% weighting by management	Job Accountabilities				
		Provide market information	Respond to customer's orders	Employ sales staff	Train sales staff	Operate the department within budget
Internal customer's valid requirements	50%	15 / 7.5	30 / 15.0	21 / 10.5	18 / 9.0	24 / 12.0
External customer quality requirements	50%	48 / 24.0	186 / 93.0	136 / 68.0	65 / 32.5	50 / 25.0
Combined weight		31.5	108.0	78.5	41.5	37.0
Ranking		5	1	2	3	4

Weight of each customer requirement × % assigned Weight

being met. If the process is under control, it should be standardized and checked regularly. If the process is out-of-control, improvement action must be taken until the job objectives are met or the standards are changed. Figure 4.5 is a flow diagram of the "job accountability" process.

The job accountability approach identifies the needs of the customer and the responsibility that a particular work process has for meeting these needs. It ranks the job accountabilities in order of importance, defines the objective of the job, establishes a measure to gauge the effectiveness of the job being performed, and provides a control system to determine whether the customers' requirements are being met, prompting improvement action when out-of-control conditions are identified.

If the job accountability approach is followed, it is advisable to ensure that linkages of job accountabilities exist among the various layers of management—running either from top to bottom or from bottom to top. This is not a particularly difficult task, but may take some time to accomplish as disjunctions between various layers of management are uncovered. Because organizations develop over time, new work and new functions are constantly being added. Yet few organizations ever go back to check whether the original system of department basic functions remains valid.

Assume, for example, that a position exists that has broad-based responsibility for a large geographical area (e.g., the division vice president). Reporting to the division vice president are several regional managers and staff managers. Each regional manager has several managers reporting to him or her: a customer service manager, a sales manager, a construction manager, and a maintenance manager.

Reporting to each of these managers are several supervisors who, in turn, have first-line employees reporting to them. What needs to be checked is whether there is a clear link running from the first line employees' responsibilities to their supervisors', to their managers', and ultimately to the division vice president's. If the division vice president's responsibilities are tied to the customer's requirements, the organization is focused: each unit's work is ultimately tied to meeting the needs of the customer.

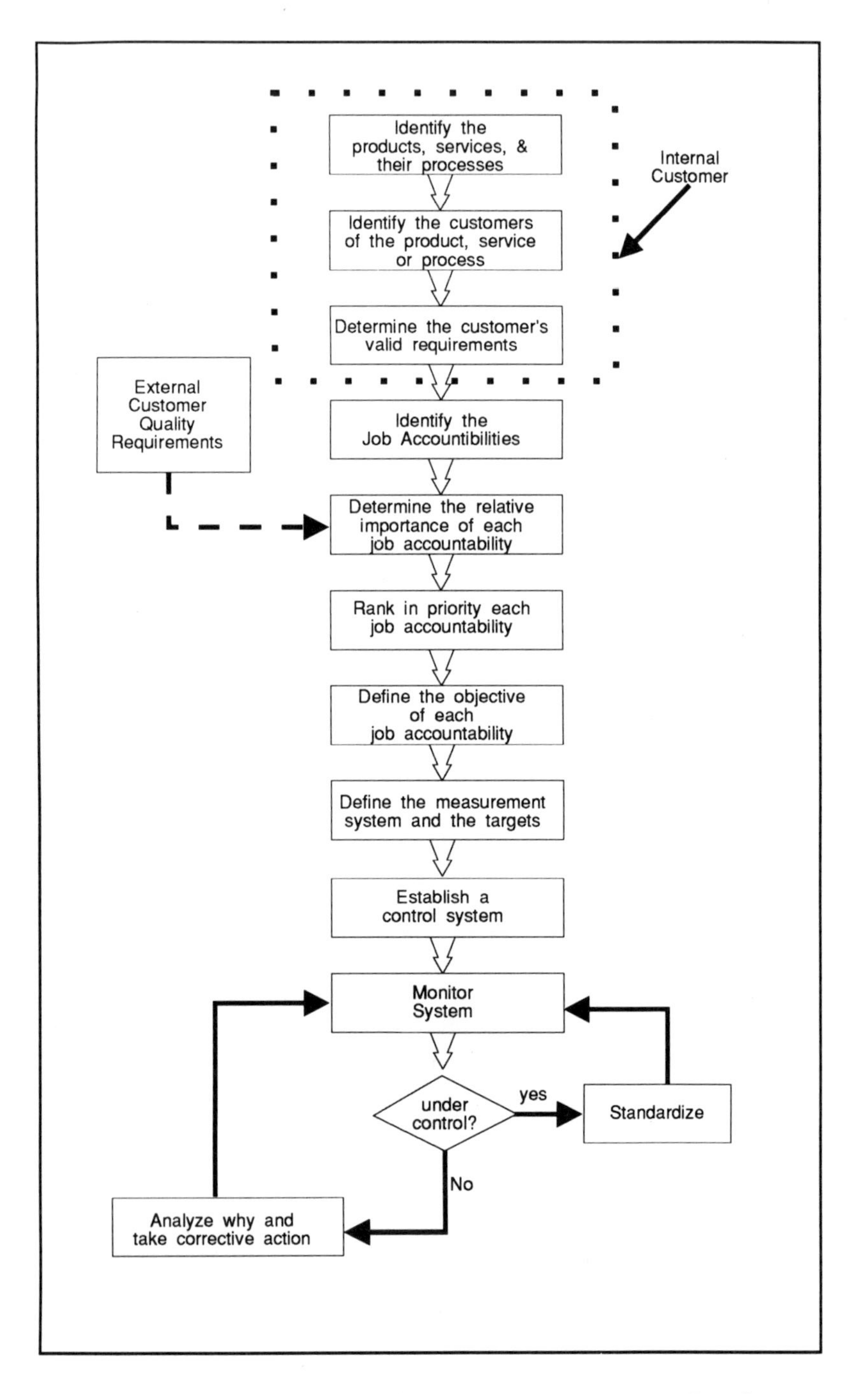

FIGURE 4.5. Selection of Daily Management Activities Based on Job Accountabilities

At FPL, there was this type of clear link up and down the line. The method was very useful in our effort to eliminate redundant work efforts. The method ensured that the most important work activities were being controlled.

CONCLUSION

A series of approaches and steps has been described that can help to pinpoint areas on which to concentrate resources, to focus the organization, to identify indicators, to track results, and to examine processes that are in need of improvement. The most important thing to keep in mind, however, is that what you want to accomplish is more important than following some prescribed method of getting there. You need to determine the best method to identify the important work activities that must be considered for improvement under Daily Management. The following general objectives are worth keeping before you:

- Identify customer requirements accurately.
- Determine where gaps exist between requirements and performance.
- Narrow down the range of possibilities to include only those areas that are most important to improve.
- Make the improvements needed to satisfy customer requirements.
- Check progress.

Daily Management is a fundamental TQM process that every organization should have in place to practice the principle of continuous improvement. It is part of an overall management system. It addresses the many problems organizations face every day in keeping requirements under control, improving deficient operations, and striving to provide "exciting" quality.

5

Team Activity

INTRODUCTION

The magic of teams and team work has captivated the hearts of many companies—companies looking for some sort of panacea to help them improve their performance. Most companies view team activity as an answer to quality issues—a way to get everyone involved in improving products and services. Company executives have been lured either by their staffs or by consultants into believing that, if you form teams, you can revitalize a company. It sounds simple; it seems like magic. But it is not!

Most companies start their improvement efforts with teams and team activity. After several months or years of activity, however, management looks at the investment it has made in time and training and is often disappointed with the overall results. Several good examples and applications might be noted, but when the bottom line is examined there is no strong result that can be attributed solely to team activity. This is usually the fault not of teams, but of management and its failure to understand how to make teams effective. It is the failure of management not to provide direction and guidance to teams. It is the failure of management not to get actively involved in the activities of the teams. It is the failure of management not to set the example and work in a team manner.

At FPL in 1981, at the direction of our chairman, we began a full-fledged effort to implement teams. We went from having no teams to eventually having 1,800 teams. Because I had always been concerned about making improvements and generally increasing productivity, I saw the team activity as a means of achieving these goals.

During that period I had responsibility for a line organization of about 7,000 people. I had decentralized a number of activities and responsibilities to get the resources closest to the customers we were serving. The company had grown to the point where it became ineffective to try to make all decisions from corporate headquarters. The concept of team activity appealed to me and others. It seemed that if we could only get the people who worked closest to the customer to identify customer service problems and solve them, we would be a much better company.

After a couple of years, however, I and some division and district managers became disenchanted with the idea of teams. A great deal of resources had been spent on training quality improvement facilitators and team leaders and members. Thousands and thousands of labor hours had been spent at team meetings. Although the teams had made some excellent improvements, these were not, in my opinion, worth the total effort; the activity as a whole did not produce a great payback.

I remember visiting one of our local district offices in late 1983. I asked the manager if there were any teams. He proudly responded that there currently were four active teams. I asked, "How long have you had these teams?" "Two years," was his answer. I asked to see the problem solutions that the teams had produced, but the manager said there were none; the teams had not yet solved any problems. I asked, "How often do the teams meet?" He replied, "once a week." I then asked to see a list of problems the teams were working on. He said, "The teams have not yet selected any problems to work on."

I managed to exhibit a good deal of self control, but certainly some disappointment showed. I talked with members of one of the teams to find out why they had not been able to select any problems. The team showed me a list of over 25 problems, but said they were having a difficult time selecting which was the most important to work on. I helped them select a problem and encouraged them to work diligently to solve it.

Obviously in this case there had been a total failure on the part of *management* to understand its role in team activity. I wondered how many other of our locations were experiencing the same problem? We either had to step up management involvement or stop the activity altogether.

In 1984, we examined our whole approach to implementing TQM. Our senior management team realized that implementing teams was not the only thing we needed to do. We introduced Policy Management followed by Daily Management. We examined *why* teams were not effective and sought to make some dramatic changes.

To revitalize a company, management—not employees—must be the first to change how it thinks and acts. Most employees come to work wanting to do a good job. They do not purposely plan to foul up, to make errors, to be rude, or to provide poor service or defective products. They learn these habits mostly from *management*—or, I should say, from what they see of management. It is management that establishes the basic rules, including the rules for teams and team activity. Employees are often frustrated because they cannot do anything about problems they see. There is no proper vehicle for them to change the rules. They cannot change the system or the policies.

Because of this, employees often develop poor attitudes and that frustrates management. Team activity, however, when properly structured, coached, and nurtured, can be one of the most important ingredients in resolving this type of problem and improving everything else a company does. Team activity is an essential TQM process, even though, at times, it can be one of the most frustrating to manage.

Management must have a deep understanding of the following:

- The different types of teams.
- When to use and promote the different types of teams.
- The education, training, and support that is necessary.
- The time required of teams.
- The number of teams required.

- The roles and responsibilities of management in team operations.
- The tools teams use.
- The reasons why team activities may fail.

TEAM STRUCTURE AND ENVIRONMENT

Several approaches can be employed to create effective teams and an effective team environment. The size and structure of the organization will often dictate the nature of the teams and their operating environment. It may also be necessary to allow the team structure and environment to evolve as the organization's implementation matures. Care should be taken not to create an overly bureaucratic system. The purpose of teams is to improve the business and the quality of work life—not to fulfill some administrative need.

TYPES AND LEVELS OF TEAMS

There are four major types and levels of teams: the steering committee, lead teams, project teams, and natural teams. The steering committee and lead teams are administrative teams, and the project teams and natural teams are working teams (see Figure 5.1).

Administrative Teams

Steering Committee

The best place for teams to start is with senior management. Management-by-example will give a clear message to the organization that management practices what it preaches. Companies should avoid creating new organizational structures and committees to administer quality. They should use the natural organization wherever possible. In most companies there is some type of

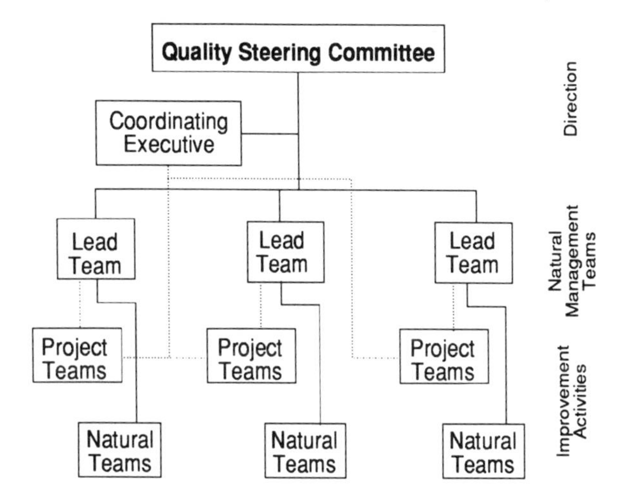

FIGURE 5.1. Types and Levels of Teams

management committee already in place. It may be called an executive committee, an operating committee, or a planning committee. A good place to start the administration and planning of quality efforts is with these committees. Some companies end up calling this senior management team a quality council, and may broaden the membership to include not only senior management, but also selected representatives from other layers in the organization. Some companies include union leaders as part of this steering committee structure.

In addition to the traditional roles of senior management committees (e.g., resource allocation and strategy development), the primary purpose of a steering committee or quality council is to plan and oversee the implementation of the corporatewide quality effort. It is this unit's responsibility to decide how and when TQM process components will be introduced, who will be trained and how, and what the training will include. The steering committee will also regularly check progress and institute countermeasures when deficiencies appear.

In some companies, the steering committee administers Policy Management. The steering committee acts as the policy-setting group that must analyze the state of the business, identify gaps in performance, establish the vision or overall strategic direction for the company, and oversee its deployment throughout the organization. Their job therefore becomes broader—involving not only overseeing, but actively participating in identifying and checking areas that are in the greatest need of improvement.

Lead Teams

Lead teams are "natural" management teams. They consist of managers and their direct reports. The objective of the lead team is to plan and to execute the business activities for their designated area of responsibility. For a company that has adopted a TQM management style, the lead team plans and oversees not only traditional business activities (e.g., budgets, marketing plans, and resource allocation), but also activities in TQM. These activities include determining how and what contribution their unit will make to corporate policy, identifying additional improvement opportunities for their area of responsibility, developing a TQM team promotional plan, and reviewing quality improvement activities.

The lead team is the natural administrative and planning body for an operating unit. For some companies, the lead team structure describes the same levels in the organization that budget flows describe—the levels where accountability is monitored. Adding TQM responsibility at this level assures that the planning activity for quality follows the traditional management planning and review cycles. Typically a lead team meets to review its operations, to compare them against plan, and to resolve any new or outstanding issues affecting unit operations. Additional tasks undertaken by the lead team include selecting areas for improvement, planning and checking the control of operations, reviewing improvement actions, planning training in operations and quality improvement, and reviewing team activities and suggestion systems.

Lead teams therefore set the example for first-level personnel by demonstrating the art of teamwork. "Do as I do" rather than "do as I say" is the operative rule here. The practice of TQM must become part of the way a company conducts its business—not just something added on to routine practices. By incorporating TQM into everyday business processes like unit planning and reviewing, the whole organization will begin to think in terms of quality.

Promotional activities conducted by the lead team are also very important, but are often misunderstood. Some think that this activity involves only banners and slogans. But banners and slogans should be used only if they help promote the overall intent of the company's quality efforts; they are never a substitute for true quality. In early phases of quality promotion, the lead team needs to think about education and training needs, how to establish and promote team activity, and the need to create employee suggestion and recognition systems (see Chapters 7 and 9).

In the planning area, the lead team needs to be alert to any barriers that arise either at the local level or at the corporate level. Barriers are rules and practices that inhibit improvements or that indicate improvement is not viewed as important. For barriers that are created through activities at the corporate level, the lead team needs to provide documentation to corporate headquarters. Corporate headquarters often does not realize that it creates barriers. Rules and regulations, procedures and practices, and instructions and standards issued through corporate headquarters are often the most common barriers encountered. These corporate dictums are almost always well-intended, yet it is difficult for corporate headquarters to be fully aware of the effects its proclamations may have on employees. If local management uncovers a corporate-created barrier, it must assemble convincing evidence, complete with examples, to convince headquarters that a remedy is warranted.

Local management also issues rules and regulations, procedures and practices, and instructions and standards. These can often become barriers to making improvements. A vigilant local-management team will be on the lookout for these types of defects and apply the appropriate countermeasures. One of the best and easiest ways to detect barriers is to observe employees' behavior and to talk openly and candidly about it with them.

Working Teams

Project Teams

The characteristics of the project team are:

- A particular problem to be solved is assigned to the team by management. The assignment can come from any level of management. If the team is assigned responsibility for an improvement stemming from the Policy Management process, the assignment can come from the steering committee, a coordinating executive, a division lead team, or the local lead team.
- Members of the team are normally selected based on some special expertise that a member brings to the team.
- The team is normally dissolved after the problem is solved.

Project teams are well-adapted to solving problems identified through Policy Management. Policy Management problems normally involve more complicated corporate or interdivisional issues that require varying levels of expertise as well as knowledge of the different aspects of the business. Because of this, project teams are almost always cross-functionally composed (see Chapter 11). This gives a team the necessary and sufficient human resources to attack a complex problem and implement the means to resolve it.

Managing project teams requires careful coordination to avoid duplication of efforts and resources. Without coordination, different project teams may devote energy to working on the same problem or the same component of a complex problem, when instead they could be concentrating efforts on different parts of the problem. It takes a coordinated effort to attack as many of the root causes of a problem as possible and in the shortest amount of time to gain the largest impact for the organization. This is particularly important when an organization is large, diversified, or geographically dispersed.

Early in the implementation of Policy Management at FPL, we identified a critical improvement opportunity through the use of customer surveys. The customers were telling us that we had to dramatically improve the consistency of service we provided (i.e., keep the lights on). We thought we had been doing a good job, but further analysis indicated that there was substantial room for improvement.

Senior management undertook to deploy our policy (and a target) to the organization, which stated that, "We want to improve customer satisfaction by reducing service unavailability". As part of that policy, we set a target of reducing service interruptions so that they averaged only 32 minutes by 1992. Each organizational unit began to analyze the reasons why it had to interrupt service to its customers. Without exception, each unit concluded that the major reason for interruptions was damage or other problems caused by lightning. (This should have come as no surprise, because Florida is the lightning capital of the U.S.) Each unit then deployed a project team to address the problem of lightning. This resulted in tremendous duplication of efforts, with several different teams trying to get at the same root cause.

The coordinator of this policy soon realized what was happening. He had overseen the deployment of a policy and a target, but without coordination of the teams' activities to achieve the end desired. He knew he needed to act as the mediator and make sure that everyone was working in the same direction, but he did not recognize then that the approach taken resulted in resources being wasted unnecessarily—the same thing was being done over and over. He ultimately realized that using this approach would take years to produce a significant overall improvement. He discovered that different project teams were coming up with different solutions for the same problem, resulting in some conflict among the teams.

Finally, to resolve the situation, the coordinating executive asked his staff to perform a more detailed first-level analysis to determine whether the lightning problem could be broken down into probable root causes or subproblems. In this way, each project team could attack a different aspect of the same general problem. For instance, one team was assigned responsibility for addressing grounding standards, another problems with grounding equipment, and another the placement of lightning arrestors. The coordinator proposed this to the various teams and, even though they did not report directly to him, each team seemed to realize that this made good sense. The results were very successful. In three years, there was a 70% improvement in reducing service interruptions caused by lightning.

Project teams are also useful at the local level where there are critical business issues to address. The same general rules apply. Management assigns the problem and designates the team members. Management brings together the talent and resources necessary to resolve the problem. After the problem is solved the team is dissolved, unless parts of the problem remain. Project teams should be managed like any other project assignment. A schedule, as well as a periodic review procedure, should be established to ensure that the team is making progress and any barriers inhibiting it are removed.

Natural Teams

The most popular and widely used teams are "natural" teams, sometimes called quality circles. In contrast to project teams, natural teams have the following characteristics: the team members volunteer, the team members select their own problems, and the team continues to exist after the problem is solved. Companies normally begin their quality improvement efforts with natural teams for several reasons. Some believe that by giving employees the opportunity to participate in improvement activity, the quality of the products and services will automatically improve. My interpretation of this is that such companies believe that it is the employees who are causing the quality problems. These companies fail to understand that to improve quality, one must first improve the management system and management thinking.

Another group of companies begins their quality efforts with natural teams because they expect that team activity, particularly with natural teams, takes the longest of any TQM process component to implement. I find no fault with this reasoning—natural teams (or quality circles) do take a long time to implement. But it is fruitless to begin this activity if no effort has been made to change management's attitude and practices. As long as one holds to the premise that management's thinking and actions must be changed before implementing natural teams, companies can successfully begin here (although I do not fully endorse it). Too many companies believe that having natural teams is all there is to having a quality system. For these companies, a team program will pay little or no dividends.

The risk of beginning your quality efforts with natural teams is that you may frustrate both employees and management if the proper training is not in place. If, for instance, you have an autocratic supervisor and you begin team activity in the workplace, the supervisor may not want to listen to or endorse a team's solution to a workplace problem. The supervisor, in all likelihood, was taught that employees need to be controlled, that they can be lazy, and that his or her role as supervisor is to tell employees what to do.

There is a proper time to introduce and promote natural teams, because they are an invaluable and inexhaustible supply of continuous improvement. They provide hundreds or even thousands of smaller problem solutions that, when added together, can represent major improvements. There are times when these natural teams may even provide a major breakthrough for a company. The team effort represents a means or system to tap the intelligence of those who know the day-to-day work and who know how it could be improved. Natural teams are a way to improve the overall quality of work life for employees. They are a means for management to show that it has respect for employees.

The proper time to introduce natural teams is when management has put sufficient training in place to teach the management ranks how to create a work atmosphere that stimulates employees to think. It is better to begin after management identifies the most important problems facing the company, after this has been clearly communicated to employees, and once management asks employees to help in resolving the problems. It begins when management is willing not only to listen, but to *do*. It begins when management has broken down established corporate barriers to help employees implement their own and management's solutions. The dangers of beginning before such conditions are in place are significant. One creates false hopes, promises

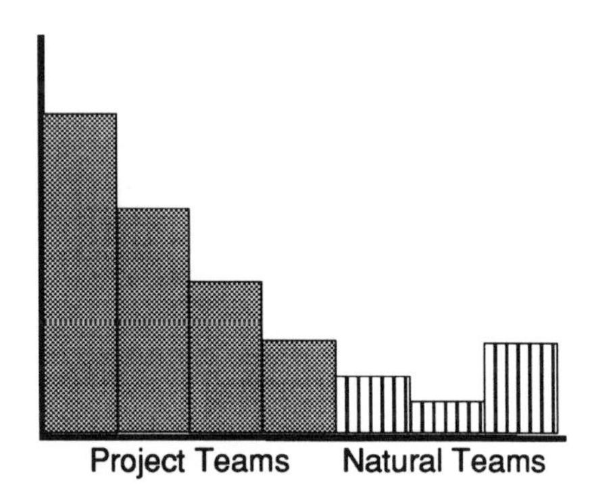

FIGURE 5.2. Assignment of Teams

that cannot be kept, anxiety, distrust, and skepticism. It is almost better not to start at all than to start before management is ready to accept a new way of doing business.

One final way to contrast project teams and natural teams is to think of a general problem and its component parts as represented in a Pareto diagram (see Figure 5.2). The higher bars indicate problems to be solved by project teams and the lower bars indicate problems for natural teams (i.e., the vital few as contrasted with the trivial many).

SYSTEMS TO SUPPORT TEAMS

Teams need support structures if they are going to survive. The support structures can be simple and inexpensive; some are optional, others are mandatory.

The most important support structure management must adopt is an education and training program. Without proper training on the use of quality tools and the skills necessary to work effectively in a team environment, team activity will not be productive. Another important structure to put in place is a review process. A systematic review method should be established to check the progress of the team, to check that root-cause analysis is conducted, to give guidance, to approve proposed solutions, and to provide a means to continue strengthening the training. In addition, if properly conducted, a review process is a high form of recognition. One of the major failures of many companies is that their process requires management to check on a team's progress only when it is time to secure approval for implementing the team's solution. If management finds fault with the team's solution, both management and the team get discouraged and no improvement is seen. To avoid this, management should check with the team at each step of the problem-solving process.

A recognition system is a must. I have seen both inexpensive and expensive systems that are successful. The most important thing to keep in mind is that employees want management to implement the team's solution if the solution solves the problem. This is the highest form of recognition. Some companies put the team's name on a plaque and place it in the vicinity of the improvement or improvement results. If, for example, the improvement involves a standard or procedure change, the team's name appears in the standards or procedure manual. Credit must be given where it is due.

Other recognition events include breakfasts, dinners, banquets, and the like. One company president told me that having the team's picture taken with the chairman of the board was the most effective recognition they tried. Another company, to show its appreciation, sent its best teams to special conventions. All of these events can be useful to promote your quality efforts, but according to a survey we conducted at FPL, the most important recognition was implementation of the team's solution, followed by formal recognition of team members by their immediate supervisors. Gifts, prizes, and money are not necessary, but recognition in some form is a must (see also Chapter 9).

Another support mechanism is a team tracking system. Companies that have good computer networks and communication terminals should consider implementing a system that can relieve the team of some administrative work (e.g., keeping track of team meetings and recording and circulating team-meeting minutes). Tracking systems should be designed to be useful for teams. One powerful use of a tracking system is as a reference source for teams. A well-designed system can help teams locate other solutions that have already been implemented or it can assist in finding other divisions in the company working on the same or similar problems. Using this type of administrative support for teams can save time and resources, helping to replicate and to improve solutions from other teams and speed up the improvement cycle. If a tracking system is implemented simply because extensive administrative work is required of teams, it is probably an indication that the system is overly bureaucratic. Tracking systems are implemented to make the teams more effective, not to fulfill unwanted and unnecessary paperwork requirements by corporate headquarters or local management.

MAINTAINING ACTIVE TEAMS

In addition to training, the time allotted to team meetings will be a major investment. Natural teams will normally meet under one of two conditions. The first is when a serious problem or defect arises in the workplace and the team gathers immediately to solve the problem. This type of team activity must be encouraged to prevent defects from occurring. Members of the team work together every day and are skilled in detecting deviations from specifications. If a problem arises, production stops until the cause of the deviation is found and corrected. The second type of team meeting occurs on a regular basis to identify other problems and resolve them. These meetings typically take place for one hour a week.

The first type of natural team activity requires all the time that is necessary to solve the production problem the team faces. Typically, the problems faced by natural teams affect the daily operations and must be solved immediately. Natural teams will also need time to put in place remedies to prevent the recurrence of the problems they solve.

The second type of natural team activity also requires time to identify areas for improvement. Management should play an active role in helping teams to select an improvement "theme" without dictating exactly what they should select. Teams that have little or no direction from their management often flounder and fail; this type of activity can be very expensive and nonproductive. But when properly trained and guided, this sort of team activity can provide very significant improvements.

Unfortunately, there is no magic percentage or number of teams to strive to attain. Management, however, must be discouraged from establishing participation rates as an objective. Such activity-based indicators as the percentage of employees on teams should only be used to give senior management a pulse check on how well lower levels of management are encouraging employees to participate. Each company will ultimately have to determine for itself what makes sense as far as the number of teams is concerned. Team activity must make good business sense or it can be counterproductive.

WHY TEAM ACTIVITY FAILS

Teams fail for a number of reasons, and new reasons turn up every day. As previously mentioned, many companies believe that team activity is a simple process that can be launched quickly and with great success. It is this general lack of understanding about the complexity of team activity that creates most of the failures. From my experience, there are several common reasons why teams fail:

- Bad group dynamics.
- Lack of tools.
- Improper reliance on facilitators.
- Lack of direction.
- Non-companywide deployment of teams.

Bad Group Dynamics

It seems so simple—just get a group of people together who can make a contribution to defining and solving a problem. If you get the right people together, isn't the problem half solved? Yet for teams to be effective they must possess some essential ingredients: quality awareness, knowledge, commitment to quality, and personal acceptance of team members. Quality awareness and knowledge involve the ability to spot problems and use the proper quality tools to make improvements (see Chapter 8). Commitment and acceptance (or "respect") within the group are necessary because without them the most useful quality tools in the world will not be applied effectively. It takes all of these ingredients to create a functioning team.

If you have ever had the opportunity to sit on the sidelines and carefully observe people in a group setting, whether it be at a cocktail party or in the work place, you may have noticed how group members who do not know how to behave properly in a group environment can disrupt the rest of the group. First there is Lydia No Listen. Lydia is really a nice person once you get to know her but she cannot concentrate on what people are saying. Her mind wanders. Then there is Tom the Talker. He is Lydia's cousin and has some of her listening problems, but he doesn't listen because he is always talking. There is also Ida the Interrupter, Cindy the Cynic, Paul the Put Down, Dennis the Disinterested, and a host of other interesting personalities. They may be found in any organization. They are great as individuals, but can be poor team members.

Management must recognize that individuals acting in a team setting may exhibit behavior that is dramatically different from one another and from their own behavior in a more individualized setting. Luckily all is not lost. Teamwork is a taught skill. The skills of listening, of participating, of contributing, of respecting one another and one another's ideas and, most importantly, of arriving at consensus, can all be taught. For team members to work effectively together they must learn all of these skills. Management at all levels must understand that it cannot just put a group of individuals in a room together and instantly create a team, simply because that is what is desired.

Study the successful coaches in baseball, basketball, volleyball, or any other team or team-related sport. You will find instances where teams do outstanding jobs even though they might not have the best of individual talent. There are other examples where an organization has incredible depth and a variety of talented individuals, yet the team does not win games. The difference here is that while one group acts as a team, the other is merely a collection of individuals who formally belong to the team but who do not participate. The difference is that the coach for the successful team has taught the skill of *team* activity—the synergy and power that make the team a team. Management, too, must be the coach in the case of organizations. Management must study the art of team activity and coach the team on how best to work together for the benefit of all.

Management and team members must be taught methods to develop consensus. Consensus can be reached more readily if *facts*, together with good human relation skills, are used. If consensus is not established, those people in disagreement may end up waiting in readiness to pounce on the first minor failure so they can say, "I told you so." Consensus involves understanding, respect, and ownership. Even a less-than-perfect solution can work effectively as long as the team members concur regarding the solution. If the solution ends up failing, the team can go on to dig deeper into the problem and find out where and how things went wrong.

Lack of Tools

I have seen many organizations that understood the need to train employees in how to work in teams. The organizations understood the power and problems of group activity, and yet even when they did something to bring about team activity, the teams turned out to be ineffective. The reason is often that the teams had little or no training in the use of quality tools—which is like sending a worker to the job site with no tools to perform the work needed or with inadequate tool training. Can a carpenter work effectively without a hammer or saw? Can he or she work effectively if unable to use these tools? The situation is no different with a process-improvement team assigned to problem solving. The team might eventually solve a given problem through trial and error, but the time needed to do so could be greatly shortened if the team were given the proper tools and knew how to use them.

All tools are not equal; and all tools do not need to be given to everyone. Too often I have seen a team using a 20-pound hammer to drive a pin. I have also seen organizations become so enthralled with quality tools that they teach hundreds of people sophisticated statistical tools only to find that these tools are never actually used.

In most instances, the seven basic quality tools will solve around 90% of the problems facing a company (see Chapter 8). Four of the tools—the graph, the check sheet, the cause-and-effect diagram, and the Pareto diagram—alone can solve about 80% of the problems. This is where your efforts should be concentrated.

Improper Reliance on Facilitators

Another major mistake companies make in implementing and carrying out team activity is to create a whole new category of specialists called "facilitators" and to allow them to act as an independent (or "parallel") organization. There are varying definitions and uses of a facilitator. In one company I visited, a facilitator was a person who had the skills to keep a meeting running on time. In another, a facilitator was a highly skilled statistical expert. And in still another, the facilitator was trained in conducting team activity. The facilitator role to be discouraged is one created simply to bypass the existing organization to implement quality, because this role in essence assumes responsibilities that management alone should assume. This type of parallel facilitator organization is expensive, a waste of resources, and if allowed to continue, shows management's failure to assume its responsibilities. Facilitators can provide a useful service if and when they are properly used (e.g., in the role of technical advisors). Unfortunately, most organizations use facilitators in an inappropriate manner. Such companies probably have received some expensive advice on how essential facilitators are for building successful teams. This approach, however, can and will inhibit the development of TQM within most organizations. Relying exclusively on expert facilitators takes those who are really responsible for quality (i.e., management) off the hook. It is too easy a way out.

In some cases there is a place for creating parallel structures or organizations that run alongside the main one, and many have advocated that this is a good way to break traditional methods of management—a means to establish a more creative organization. I do not particularly endorse this type of thinking or behavior, because it can be wasteful and counterproductive. The task of TQM is to transform the entire organization, not simply add on additional units or overhead. If it seems that your company might benefit from having facilitators working alongside traditional management, think about saving time and money and restructuring the original organization instead.

The facilitator organization initially created at FPL clearly falls into my idea of what companies should avoid. Early on, our chairman was convinced that teams were the real answer to quality. He recommended that teams be formed, that training programs be developed, and that a group of facilitators be selected to direct the activities of the teams. He informed the organization that we were introducing a new way of doing business: Quality Improvement Program (QIP). We were going to form teams, and no one needed to worry about this because a facilitator would be provided to implement and coordinate them.

There was a subtle message here: do not interfere with the teams—they are not your responsibility. The job of quality was going to be the facilitator's. The organization understood. At our Nuclear Department, a separate quality organization emerged from the quality assurance efforts there. It became clear that quality matters were the responsibility of the Quality Assurance Department. Because the rest of the company was initially following this organizational model, everyone knew and understood that quality efforts were to be conducted through inspection and reports, as per the nature of the parallel setup.

After a while, however, first-line supervisors voiced dissatisfaction with the teams. They said that teams were a waste of time. They wrote memos. They objected to someone—a facilitator—coming in once a week, taking a group of their employees away to a meeting, and returning them without necessarily accomplishing or improving the day-to-day tasks of the job. The supervisors were being held responsible for the outcome of the work, but resources to perform the work were being taken from them. Because of this, in 1985 we began to phase out our facilitator organization and make supervisors responsible for all team activities. We did so to send a new message. We had to let supervisors know that quality was *their* responsibility and that employees and teams were their tools for improving quality.

I also believe that there can, in some cases, be a need for a small group of facilitators in a large organization. They might be put in place to help management plan its quality efforts, to help promote quality activities, and to act as a resource for teams when difficulties are encountered. A group of highly-skilled individuals who have advanced statistical training will usually be needed to assist teams working on complex problems. Also, a few individuals will be needed to keep abreast of new developments in the application of quality tools. They will essentially act as the quality R&D department. In this way facilitators can assist management in planning quality improvement activities. But they should never be held accountable or responsible for the final quality results. Only management can be held responsible for quality. Quality specialists are simply a tool for managing effectively.

Lack of Direction

The most important reason teams fail is because management fails to give teams proper direction. Giving the proper direction is, of course, more easily said than done. But teams need to understand management's priorities. They need to understand where the largest "gaps" in performance occur. They need to understand their customers' requirements. They need to understand product or service deficiencies from a customer perspective.

Companies that have done a good job in implementing Policy Management have provided their employees and teams with the kind of direction that is needed. Under Policy Management, teams are offered specific guidance, they work on the most significant projects, their intentions are directed, and they can draw on a unified method. Their cumulative efforts add up to greater positive effect for customers.

Management will set the direction and policy in the broadest terms. Management should also identify the means to carry out the policy. Using Policy Management, the means become the policy for the next layer in the organization, and this layer goes on to define new means in making the policy actionable (see Figure 5.3). By aligning the activities of the teams with the policies of the company, a great deal of activity becomes concentrated and directed toward carrying out corporate policies. The teams better understand what must be accomplished and they can direct their efforts to that end.

Using Policy Management does not mean that teams should not be allowed to select their own problems to work on. Depending on the type of team, the selection process will vary. But

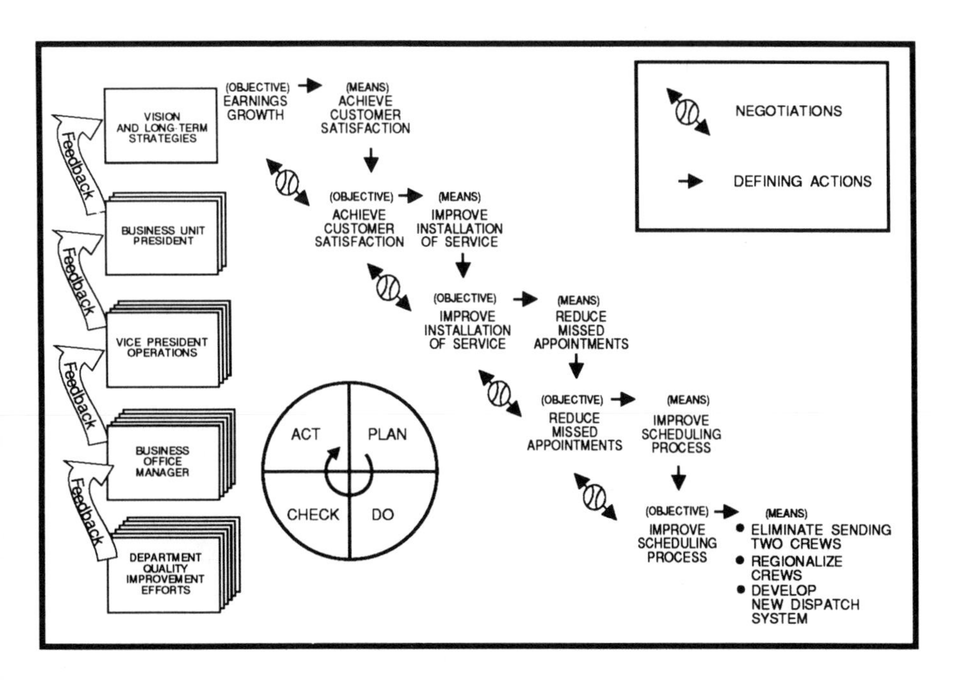

FIGURE 5.3. Policy Negotiations

management cannot know all of the problems that should be worked on. Teams can help identify improvement opportunities that may not be of the highest priority, but are nevertheless important.

Non-Companywide Deployment of Teams

I was once on an executive visit to a remote part of FPL's service territory. During the visit I had a chance to review a first line employee team solution to a nagging problem. The problem related to the installation of a cluster bracket. This bracket had 70 pieces that needed to be assembled and it weighed 90 pounds. The bracket frustrated the crews because it was cumbersome and minor injuries occasionally occurred in assembling or installing it.

The team's solution was to create a new design that reduced the weight by 78%, to only 20 pounds, and reduced the number of pieces by 91% to 6. The life expectancy of the new bracket was increased to 40 years instead of 20—a 100% increase—and the installation cost was reduced by 38%. What was also impressive was that the team had applied industrial-engineering techniques to determine the labor component needed to install the new bracket. Needless to say they were very pleased with the new part.

When the team finished demonstrating the new bracket to me, I was very excited and congratulated them on doing a great analysis and achieving such outstanding results. The team members were pleased to see my reaction. After a brief pause, however, one team member observed, "We are glad that you like our solution, but you should know that the general office has rejected it." My heart sank. I knew we still had a great deal of work ahead and a great many people to convince that management methods must be changed.

This story illustrates the effect that staff or others who are not part of team efforts can have on the effectiveness of a quality program. Despite the team's best intentions, their efforts were undone by a simple "no" from those in authority who were not part of the solution. This is something to guard against. Effort should be made to see to the *companywide* deployment of, or at least respect for, teams and team activities. (The bracket designed by that team is now the company standard.)

CONCLUSION

Teams and team activity are an essential component or process in implementing TQM. Before management attempts to implement team activity, it must understand the purposes of and types of different teams. Management must put in place the necessary perquisites to foster team spirit. Management must develop a work atmosphere where teams may flourish and survive, where improvement solutions are acknowledged, recognized, and implemented, and where the brainpower of the entire organization can be expanded.

6

Vendors, Suppliers, and Quality

INTRODUCTION

As a company starts to implement a total quality approach to doing business, it may seem that the task ahead will never end. And it well may never end! Determining customer requirements, assessing internal business problems, implementing Policy Management, Daily Management, and team activity, and developing such support components as a comprehensive education and training program and a suggestion system will tax the organization's ability to deal with change.

Companywide efforts, however, no matter how intensive, still may not be enough to make the critical difference in improving the quality of your products and services. This is because many companies, if not most, must also rely on outside suppliers and vendors to carry out their normal business operations. Suppliers and vendors can have a significant impact on customer satisfaction, on overall costs, on product or process cycle-time, and on performance, safety, delivery, and overall company image.

Companies with mature quality management systems have realized the importance of vendors in their overall business success. These companies have developed vendor quality programs designed to foster quality concepts and practices *outside* the company, which may lead to a dramatic reduction in the total number of suppliers. Such companies maintain only a few suppliers that can always be counted on to delivery high-quality, low-cost products and services. These TQM companies realize that their vendors and suppliers are really their *partners* in creating the product or service, and so they undertake to work closely with them for mutual benefit. Quality vendors and suppliers are *part* of your company's business and they should be treated as no less than that.

Assume you decided that you are going to start a new company based on the traditional partnership form of business. You of course would want to be extremely careful about the partners you choose. You no doubt would seek to cultivate a long-term relationship based on mutual trust and respect. You would not want, under normal circumstances, to change your partners every month or every year; nor would you want to have an excessive number of partners—none of whom knew one another well. The partnership model is apt because the same type of thinking should apply when selecting suppliers.

Dr. Deming, in his book, *Out of the Crisis*, advocates having only one supplier for a particular part. He writes, "How can a supplier be innovative and develop economy in his production when he can only look forward to short-term business with a purchaser?"[1] Suppliers need some assurance that if they make investments, the investments can be amortized over a reasonably long period of time to allow the suppliers to recoup their initial expenditure. Many companies tend, however, to believe that it is the suppliers that should take all the risks. They believe that the suppliers are the ones that should make the capital investments and that the suppliers should do the R&D so that they and the company can remain competitive. But suppliers will more readily make the necessary capital and R&D investments for the benefit

[1]W. Edwards Deming, *Out of the Crisis* (Cambridge, MA: Massachusetts Institute of Technology, Center for Advanced Engineering Study, 1982), p. 35.

of themselves and the company when they have a sound basis for knowing that the company will stick with them for a long enough a time to allow them to recover their costs.

It was formerly the practice of FPL to re-bid certain types of contracted support services every year. These particular services had been re-bid every year for some 25 years. I was displeased with the amount of time some managers were spending on this yearly ritual, and I requested that the purchasing department let the bids for a five-year period instead. The reluctance to make this change was so great, it was almost like breaking some cardinal rule of nature. Eventually, however, a compromise was arranged in which contractors would be allowed three-year contracts. When we examined the subsequent bids we found that contractors were able to reduce their costs by as much as 20 percent because they could amortize their mobilization and equipment costs over three years instead of one. Previously, because they never knew from one year to the next whether they would be the successful bidder, they submitted bids that were designed to recover all their investments within one year. Under the extended-contract system they could plan more effectively and concentrate better on the quality of the work. There were many other examples like this of longer-term relationships resulting in lower costs and higher quality.

Dr. Deming goes on to discuss the problem of product *variation* that multiple suppliers can and do create. He says, "Lot-to-lot variation from one supplier is usually enough to give fits to manufacturing. It is reasonable to expect that variation between lots from two suppliers will give even more trouble."[2] Having multiple suppliers for a single product or service compounds the problem of variation. Such companies as Motorola and Xerox have made significant progress in reducing the number of suppliers with which they work. Xerox reports a 10-fold reduction in this respect, and Motorola has notified suppliers that the company is making significant changes from its historical practices. General Motors has also recently embarked on this path.

---

[2]Ibid.

Change is not easy for anyone to accept. Even the most progressive companies have experienced resistance to change. Implementing a vendor quality program stands to create significant resistance both within and outside a company. Internally the resistance will stem from those who fear that long-standing personal relationships with suppliers will be lost. It is often difficult for people to accept that by having fewer suppliers, everyone's work will be simplified and corporate overheads will be reduced. Others will feel that by limiting suppliers, the company will no longer have a hammer to hold over the heads of other suppliers to keep costs down. They expect that suppliers will try to take advantage of their vulnerability and raise prices indiscriminately.

On the outside, suppliers will resist because they fear losing their current level of business. Many would rather retain a small portion of a company's total business than risk losing the business altogether in new bids. Few suppliers will view it as an opportunity to gain greater market share.

A great deal of time, therefore, must be spent selling the concepts both internally and externally. Ultimately some will win and some will lose. But it does not have to be that way if all the suppliers would improve their overall quality (i.e., quality, cost, and delivery). Yet this is highly unlikely because many suppliers will not be willing to make the investments and long-term commitments required.

CLEAN YOUR OWN HOUSE FIRST

Before any company starts waging war with its suppliers, an intensive internal review of in-house standards and relations with vendors needs to be done. Evaluate how suppliers are currently dealt with and what kind—and quality—of information they are provided. One cannot complain unless one's own house is in order. The investigation will probably show that many problems attributed to your suppliers in fact begin with your own company as a result of inefficient and ineffective management systems.

A good place to start is in the accounts-payable department. Sometimes financial managers can get a bit overzealous and establish stringent cash management programs, creating problems for vendors. The attitude often is, "if a supplier wants to continue doing business with us, it will have to wait to receive its payment. They need us, and they know we have other choices." This, however, is no way to begin a long-term relationship. Such a practice can ultimately cost your company more money because the supplier will have to add to its prices the cost of carrying the unpaid account.

In addition, look at the procedures and practices by which the vendor is actually paid. An accountant by training, I nevertheless fail to understand why companies inevitably require invoices for everything they purchase. This seems a sure sign of bureaucracy. Seek to check how much paperwork is collected, processed, and stored. The cost of such paperwork can be substantial. It is often, moreover, an *unnecessary* cost incurred by the company and its suppliers and passed on to customers. There would no longer appear to be the need for cumbersome and redundant paperwork in paying one's vendors given the widespread use of computers and modern purchasing, inventory management, and manufacturing systems.

Check on the average time it takes to pay suppliers and on the timing of payments. Company financial officers may say that they are helping to maximize income by postponing payment until the last minute. But this only creates a false sense of security. Suppliers will again probably only add the cost of carrying the account to the prices it lists. Such a practice does not build up partnership trust.

If a company is producing a product and each product requires two component parts from a single supplier, why not simply count the number of finished products and send the supplier a check? Most likely the receiving department fills out a receiving report in triplicate and sends it to the accounting department. The accounting department then sorts the receiving reports, files them, and matches the receiving report with the invoice required from the supplier, and matches this to the initial purchase order. Whenever a mismatch occurs (which is likely to be often under this type of system), invoices must be sent back, phone calls made, memos written, and various other inefficient and costly practices must be conducted. You may be surprised at the number of mismatches that occur and how infrequently they are analyzed to determine why or how this happens. A system of paperwork like this is archaic, costly, and time consuming—resulting in increased costs and the potential for conflict with your suppliers. Pricing issues need to be settled and agreed to before anything is ever shipped. Often great delays in payment result and costly overheads incurred when pricing is not properly established well in advance.

But what if the supplier sends more parts than what actually ends up in the finished product? Several things may be wrong if this condition arises, and almost all of them are likely to be the fault of the company rather than the supplier. A company's production and planning systems may have failed to recognize a change in production schedules, resulting in improper notification to the supplier. If, however, it is determined that the supplier is at fault, it will simply have to wait to be paid until the overstocked parts find their way into finished product or are returned. The supplier should probably also be sent the bill for warehousing or returning the unwanted parts.

I recently spoke with a manager of a data processing company whose business, in part, is to act as a payroll processing service bureau. The company processes the payroll for many companies. Years ago they decided they would limit their business to data processing only and would contract with another company to actually print and deliver the pay checks. Companies that request the complete payroll service have a series of quality characteristics they require, including accurate, clear, and timely checks. The printing and delivery company—the outside vendor—obviously plays an important part in meeting these requirements.

The payroll service company requires the printing and delivery company to send them an invoice based on the number of payroll checks finally printed and delivered. This seems a somewhat redundant step because the company already knows how many payroll checks will be printed and delivered based on the data supplied to the vendor. Practices of this nature generally evolved during a time when sophisticated communication means were not available. With today's technology, however, such practices can be eliminated.

Many Japanese automobile manufacturers have instituted more streamlined, or "lean," practices. They pay the supplier of steering wheels, for example, based on the number of cars coming off the end of the assembly line. If a car is produced, obviously it should have a steering wheel. Why go through the costly and unnecessary paper work to fill out a receiving report, ask the supplier to send a bill, and then match up the paper work? Even if computers were used to expedite this mundane work, an unnecessary cost would be incurred.

Another area to review is your company's purchasing practices and processes. When bid evaluations are made, how much of the evaluation is based on quality characteristics? Does the company's system include an evaluation of reliability, durability, and delivery in addition to cost? Keep in mind that low *initial* cost is a different measure than low cost. Rework, inspection, failures, and warranty costs are all part of total costs and should be included as part of the company's purchasing practices. Unless the system includes these types of evaluations as part of regular procurement practices, it is probably cheating the company, its vendors, and its customers.

One common purchasing practice is to play one vendor off against another. This practice can easily lead to distrust and suspicion, and can prevent building long-term relationships. Vendors must be treated as your company wishes itself to be treated in the marketplace—with honesty and integrity.

Another place to review is any department that develops and issues specifications, including the purchasing department. This is an area that can make a great difference in the quality of the product or service provided. Specifications are your means to express and circulate the quality characteristics required. If the specifications are not clear, obviously the product or service cannot be properly produced.

One of the most common equipment failures we experienced at FPL involved line transformers. On a visit to Kansai Electric Power Company in Japan, I had lunch with one of the Kansai division managers and asked him about the failure rate for the company's line transformers. He hesitated and told me that he did not want to answer the question without first checking his data. I pressed him, saying I was not interested in a precise answer but only a rough estimate of the magnitude of the failures. With great reluctance he said he believed they had only had one service failure during the last year. Later, when we returned to the office, he verified that the information he gave me was correct.

I was astonished by the information. At FPL, in a division of equal size, we could expect several hundred failures during a stormy Florida weekend. The Kansai division faced some of the same environmental challenges that many of FPL's divisions faced: frequent storms, high volume of lightning, and high humidity. I asked to see a copy of the specifications for a typical line transformer. Again I was astonished. The specifications were about a half-inch thick, as compared to our own two- to three-page specifications. For us, it was our commercial terms and conditions that seemed to carry more weight—based on the volume of documents. Kansai left no room for doubt about what it required. The company had worked with its suppliers over a number of years to improve equipment performance and reliability, and the fruits of this effort were stated clearly in the specifications in the form of technical and quality requirements and characteristics.

If one does not specifically write a requirement, the vendor cannot meet the company's needs. Specification-writing skills are an essential ingredient if quality products and services are to be produced. Specifications do not have to fill a half-inch thick document and they do not have to be a bureaucratic nightmare, but they must be thorough, clear, and complete. Vendors cannot be blamed for a company's own shortcomings.

ELEMENTS OF BUILDING A VENDOR QUALITY PROGRAM

As we at FPL began to appreciate the need to expand our quality program beyond the company, we started investigating companies that had been working at improving their suppliers' quality for some time. We looked for companies that gave preference to vendors that delivered products or services on time, with few defects or deficiencies, and that provided highly reliable products on a just-in-time basis. On one occasion, I met with the president of a communications equipment company noted for its highly reliable equipment, but with little manufacturing capability. Essentially, his company designed the equipment, purchased component parts, and assembled them. When I asked what kind of quality program they had developed, he told me that the most important part of their program was their vendor quality program.

He noted that over a period of several years the company had dramatically reduced the number of its suppliers and had only kept those that had proven process capability to deliver high-quality components. I asked him how he convinced his suppliers to adopt quality-related processes. He responded that it was simple. He had told them that they should do it "as a matter of greed." He had called in all the suppliers and told them he intended to dramatically reduce their number. If any wanted to remain working with the company they would have to demonstrate, through the use of data, that they had the capability to produce quality components as specified by the company. In return for demonstrating their capability, they would receive substantially larger orders and for longer periods of time.

Today you can find many companies following a similar practice. One of the most notable is the program of Motorola, a 1988 winner of the Malcolm Baldrige National Quality Award. Motorola makes it clear to every supplier and vendor, including those that supply janitorial services, that it expects them to adopt quality practices that will meet the standards of the Baldrige Award—or else they can expect not to do business with Motorola. Ford Motor Company is also noted for its Q-101 Standards that suppliers must meet.

Smaller companies may not think they have sufficient purchasing power to accomplish this—and most likely they do not. But there are ways that even small companies can get the attention of a supplier. They can, for instance, band together with other small companies to gain strength in numbers. I have seen this practiced effectively with local governments that band together to place pressure on their suppliers. Another way is to find a new supplier. There are many good suppliers who value their customers no matter how small they may be.

One thing I was not fully satisfied with in FPL's vendor quality program was that it appeared to be too prescriptive. I kept getting reports from suppliers that our people were telling them not only what the end results should be but exactly how to accomplish them. Since leaving FPL, I have met with company suppliers and seen firsthand that at least some FPL personnel were unnecessarily prescriptive.

Companies often make the mistake of requiring their suppliers to adopt the very same program, or same type of program, that the company itself has adopted. This is both unfair and unreasonable. Each approach must be tailored to a supplier's particular needs and circumstances. A vendor quality program *per se* is not the objective. The real objective is quality *results* necessary to improve customer satisfaction. Your own company's approach may not fit with the cultural characteristics of its suppliers, and this should be taken into account.

The better strategy is to require the vendor to demonstrate, through the use of data, its process capability. Periodically, the company should audit the supplier to make sure the data received accurately reflect the results needed. Alternatively, the two companies could develop inter-company goals to improve on specified areas of quality. Joint *teams* may also be commissioned in this regard. In any case, both parties will benefit from sharing both information and improvement activities. The vendor's prices will likely be lowered and both its and your own company's profits likely increased.

Another feature commonly seen in vendor quality programs is a graded or multi-staged certification process. Implementing a quality management system takes time. Simply deciding it is the right thing to do will not make it happen. Vendors and suppliers, like your own company, need time to adjust. Establishing a staged or graded certification process allows you to recognize vendors' ongoing efforts as they progress in their quality journey.

FPL, for example, adopted an approach that had many merits. The company's first requirement was that the vendor already be supplying an acceptable product or service. A vendor then needed to develop and submit an improvement plan, followed by the identification and completion of a specific, mutually agreeable improvement opportunity involving current business. In addition, a self-evaluation by the vendor needed to be completed. Once these activities were satisfactorily carried out, the vendor reached the first stage of certification and was designated a Quality Vendor. For attaining this distinction, the vendor was given preference during bidding.

FPL also had two other stages or grades of certification. The second level was that of Certified Vendor. At this level, the use of statistical process control needed to be demonstrated, a self-evaluation had to be completed, and a process capability (C_p) of >1.0 was required.[3] The third and final stage or grade of certification was that of Excellent Vendor. Such vendors needed to demonstrate a process capability of >1.33, have applied specific techniques to improve the reliability of its products, and demonstrated that TQM was its management system. At each level of achievement the vendor was, in theory, to get a greater preference in receiving business from us.

I say "in theory" because in only a few instances did vendors that demonstrated these quality results actually increase, to any great extent, their share of business with FPL. Nor was there any significant reduction in the total number of vendors as a result of FPL's vendor quality program. In fact, vendors who had repeatedly supplied the company with unreliable equipment continued to do business with it. I cannot say with certainty why, exactly, this occurred but I suspect that there were those at our end of the business who continued to believe that low-bid prices were everything or who had built relationships with vendors over many years and did not want to see them disrupted. It could also have been due to the immaturity of the program. In the end, I think that the vendor quality program *as practiced* was probably discouraging to some of our suppliers: it took too long to see significant results and it did not particularly eliminate poorly

---

[3]Process capability concerns the ability of a process to produce product within specification. The measure is expressed as C_p and an acceptable process is indicated when C_p is greater than 1.0 or, ideally, greater than 1.33.

performing vendors. To avoid this kind of situation, company personnel should begin with a clear picture of what they would like to see and when they expect to see it. Such information must be communicated to all suppliers as quickly and as clearly as possible. Many companies in the U.S. have been effective in doing this. Milliken, a Malcolm Baldrige National Quality Award winner, is another outstanding example.

The certification process is an excellent method to employ if one remains committed to it and one wants vendors to know that the company is serious about eliminating those that cannot provide the level of product or service quality required under a TQM system. Eliminate a few and the others will quickly get the message. Dealing with fewer vendors will help reduce variation and allow the two companies to work in partnership for longer-term improvement. I have never believed that any contract negotiation should result in one side having an advantage over the other. Too often I have seen companies push vendors to the limit, or beyond the limit, ending in costly disputes and litigations. Building relationships in court is no way to proceed! Contracts must be made mutually beneficial.

Both the Deming Prize and the Malcolm Baldrige National Quality Award include criteria to evaluate the quality of your supplier relations and how your company has incorporated vendors and suppliers into its quality efforts. In the case of the Malcolm Baldrige award, companies applying for the award must demonstrate:

- Principal quality requirements for key suppliers.
- Principal indicators the company uses to communicate and monitor supplier quality.
- Methods used to ensure that the company's quality requirements are met by suppliers.
- Current strategies and actions to improve quality and responsiveness (delivery time) of suppliers.[4]

---

[4]*1992 Award Criteria, Malcolm Baldrige National Quality Award* (Gaithersburg, MD: National Institute of Standards and Technology, 1991), p. 22 (item 5.4).

Vendors and suppliers are as important to your company's overall quality results as your own management system and employees. Making suppliers part of your business, developing long-term relationships and contracts, identifying and establishing joint improvement objectives, sharing quality process-improvement techniques and practices, and paying in a timely and efficient manner will produce lasting rewards for both you and your supplier.

THE JUST-IN-TIME SYSTEM

One key benefit that can be derived from long-term relationships with suppliers is lower inventories. The "just-in-time" (JIT) system pioneered and developed by Toyota in Japan demonstrates what can be achieved when such long-term relationships exist. The JIT system cannot be implemented simply by writing just-in-time specifications into your contracts. Toyota did not do it overnight. It took many years working with its suppliers to perfect the system.

Many seminars are held around the country that encourage companies to implement this system. The results are not always encouraging. There have generally been more failures than successes in the U.S. because companies fail to understand what must be done to establish an efficient and effective JIT system. The danger in trying to adopt such a system before *both* the company *and* its suppliers have well-established control processes in place is that both businesses can suddenly be brought to a halt, causing chaos.

JIT is intended to produce lower inventories and create more smoothly running production processes. A company must already have a predictable production schedule. Without a predictable schedule, adequate requirements concerning volume and other characteristics cannot be furnished to the suppliers. Production processes at both the company and the supplier must demonstrate exceptional quality control. If one's processes are out of control, a rigorous production schedule cannot be met. Specifications must be spelled out clearly and followed to the letter. No breakdown in communications about what is required can occur. The supplier must play the role of the "swing": it must constantly adjust its production schedule to meet the order-requirements from the company. If all such features are present, you can think about implementing JIT. Otherwise, both organizations must work on improving each and every process that runs between them.

CONCLUSION

Giving the very best efforts to improve internal practices and systems may not be good enough; shortfalls can occur when suppliers have an affect on the product or service produced. Few companies exist that have no or a limited number of suppliers. In planning its long-range quality improvement strategy, a company must consider how and when it will involve its suppliers. Adopting a vendor quality program is essential if a company is serious about maintaining the highest levels of quality.

A vendor quality program will often have a dramatic effect on the internal organization and existing suppliers. The internal organization may resist and most certainly the suppliers will resist. The objective of a vendor and supplier program is to improve the quality of the products and services received, improve delivery time, reduce cost, and improve safety where it applies. Some suppliers will not want to change and others will fall short in their efforts. The end result will be fewer suppliers. Corporate attention can be devoted to the remaining suppliers, thereby building a longer-term relationship for the mutual best interest of both parties. No company can adopt such a system without making some reductions in the number of its suppliers. Companies have obligations to those remaining that not only show the willingness to quickly adapt but also have demonstrated their capability to deliver. These obligations include showing a desire to engage in long-term contracts so that suppliers feel secure about their potential for realizing returns on investments. Companies must also pay their suppliers on time. The final result of the effort should be a partnership in which both companies can grow and prosper.

Remember that vendors and suppliers can have a significant impact on quality. Vendors and suppliers affect customer satisfaction, initial cost, life-cycle cost, performance, reliability, safety, delivery, and company image.

7

Education and Training

INTRODUCTION

Dr. Kaoru Ishikawa, the well-known Japanese quality-control expert, observed "QC begins with education and ends with education."[1] Education and training is definitely an area where management must devote its time and attention. A major commitment of resources must initially be made to the development and delivery of training and educational materials for the organization. The amount of resources will depend on the level of training required, the resources already in place, and the time period for the initial training. The training program does not necessarily need to increase total education and training expenditures. A *reallocation* of resources can usually serve the same purpose. As with any major investment, a valuable return will and should be expected. Yet, often, companies launch massive quality training programs without thinking ahead to the *application* of the train-

[1] Kaoru Ishikawa, *What Is Total Quality Control? The Japanese Way* (Englewood Cliffs, NJ: Prentice-Hall, 1985), p. 13.

ing. This is something to get a jump on early on. What are your company's expectations in this regard? What results do you expect, and when do you expect them? These two questions are important and should be well-understood before you begin.

Training is a long-term event. Not everyone needs to be trained during the first year, but everyone will probably need some training. Training is best when it is conducted as close as possible to the actual time for which it is needed and will be used. In other words, JIT principles, as employed in sophisticated manufacturing processes, may also be applied to training. Training can be conducted either by in-house resources who have themselves undergone TQM training, by outside professionals, or by a combination of both.

The scope of training must be sufficient to effectively implement Policy Management, Daily Management, team activity, problem solving, and any other system that would improve the company's operations to meet customer needs. The training should be designed to provide necessary and sufficient skills to the employees who will be using the training. For instance, senior management needs in-depth training on the concepts and components of TQM and Policy Management, but only an overview of Daily Management. In contrast, first-level supervisors and managers should receive thorough training on Daily Management's application, but do not need to be trained in the methods to evaluate and develop corporate policy.

WHERE TO BEGIN: SENIOR MANAGEMENT

Start where the biggest effect can be quickly realized (i.e., with senior management). A seminar to familiarize senior management with the essential concepts and processes of TQM is a good beginning place. Senior managers need to know and understand that TQM is a way of running one's business and they must learn how to apply TQM concepts to their business units (see Chapter 2). Senior management training should be designed to make it clear to each manager what his or her role is in the implementation of TQM.

All too often senior managers fail to take the time to conceive and prepare their own plan. They tend to delegate this chore and ask staff to prepare an implementation plan. When something goes wrong with the plan, they blame the staff. An effective means to avoid this situation is to set aside the last day of the seminar to have senior management develop an implementation plan. By having senior managers participate directly in developing the plan, a consensus can be gained on the type of approach to use, the TQM process components to be adopted or altered, the schedule of implementation, and everyone's roles and responsibilities. When senior managers devote themselves to this effort, the implementation inevitably will be smoother as the plan becomes *theirs*, and not something handed to them by staff or a consultant who may not know the unique characteristics of the company. Much more senior management acceptance and commitment can be gained in this way.

In addition to seminars, senior managers should also form study teams to visit companies that have successfully implemented various aspects or components of TQM. During such visits, the two companies' implementation plans can be compared to see what has and has not worked for the host company, and what may or may not work for one's own company. Valuable lessons can be learned in this way.

Basic Statistical Tools: Training and Review

The education of senior management most likely will continue for *several years*. At each stage of the implementation of TQM, a deeper level of knowledge and practical experience will be required to bring out the full potential of the processes and structures being introduced, as well as to confirm the evolving roles and responsibilities of the players. Several types of training are particularly useful for senior managers. The most fundamental is a course on quality control problem-solving tools and techniques as taught to working teams. Senior managers must have a solid, practical understanding of the seven statistical tools of quality. These include the line graph, the check sheet, the histogram, the Pareto diagram, the fishbone diagram, the control chart, and the scatter diagram (see Chapter 8). Such a course should include both the proper use *and* common misuse of these statistical tools. Do not fall prey to the idea that those with weak statistical skills or with executive seniority should be exempt from learning these basic tools.

The task of the senior manager is to process information and make sure that any proposed problem-solutions treat and overcome the root cause of a problem and not just its symptoms. Managers in the TQM organization will be acting as advisors and coaches to teams. They must understand the application of statistical tools so that when teams offer problem-solutions without verifying root causes, managers can recognize this and respond accordingly. Management's job is "fact control" and the art of coaching. Practicing PDCA, involving a regular review process, is one of the best means to teach and maintain fact control. Senior managers need training in the proper way to participate in and conduct review sessions centered around facts, and also in coaching participants in their use. These review sessions should always be constructive. The way a person asks a question inevitably establishes the tone or framework for the kind of information one receives in return and the kind of analysis that subsequently is performed. The focus should be on facts, not emotions, and teams usually need to be coached in this direction. *Every* manager should have a solid working knowledge of the basic quality-improvement tools and techniques as well as of the problem-solving and review process.

It may be difficult to assemble senior managers for several consecutive days to deliver the in-depth training needed. If this is the case for your organization, an alternative is to schedule one half day or one full day a month for either individual or small-group training until the course is completed.

I have seen situations where the management and review process produced information that previously had been hidden and, when revealed, shocked senior managers. In one case, people reacted emotionally and criticized a manager in front of his peers. This type of "hidden" information was never again revealed in the sessions; it went into the archives of the unknown.

When conducting review sessions, care must be taken to appreciate the factual nature of the information being presented without being critical of the presenter.

The review process should, on the other hand, never allow faulty analysis to go unnoticed. Questions should be asked that will cause the presenter and everyone else to know that the analysis needs to be strengthened before it or the proposed solution can be accepted. Constructive critiques are essential as the organization gains experience in applying the quality-improvement tools and in using the logic of the problem-solving process.

OTHER STATISTICAL TOOLS

In addition to the seven basic statistical quality tools, managers should have a working understanding of both the "seven new tools" and a few other advanced problem-solving techniques. The seven new tools are the affinity diagram, relations diagram, systematic diagram, matrix analysis, matrix data analysis, process decision program chart, and the arrow diagram (see Chapter 8). Again, the best way to learn them is to use them. The seven new tools will be of great help to the organization in analyzing the voice of the customer, identifying internal business problems, assessing competitive information, and in establishing policy. With the exception of one of these tools (matrix data analysis), the seven new tools do not draw as heavily on hard data. Rather, they involve management experience and the use of the more creative part of the mind.

A number of more advanced statistical tools are available for more complicated problems (e.g., fault-tree analysis, failure mode and effect analysis, design of experiments, Weibull analysis, and value analysis). These tools are generally used in less than 10 percent of the cases and should only be employed to solve more complex problems. Training in advanced tools for senior management should be simply designed to make managers familiar with them and their application; there is no need to become particularly skilled in their use. One need only know when to call in an expert trained in advanced statistical tools—which is essentially when the application of the more basic tools does not control a problem.

TQM TRAINING: BUSINESS SYSTEMS AND MANAGEMENT

Individual senior managers may think they understand the fundamental business and management system that governs the operation of their company. In my experience, however, although individually managers may have a grasp on the system, when assembled together it is clear that they hold dramatically different views. Everyone in a TQM organization should be playing with the same game plan. Therefore, in addition to the statistical tools of quality, senior managers need a clear understanding of the essential structures and processes of TQM. Policy Management, Daily Management, team activity, and vendor quality must all become a way of doing business and be incorporated into the management system of the company. Senior management sessions designed to lay out, critically discuss, and review the existing business and management system, in the context of TQM concepts and goals, therefore need to be scheduled early on.

At FPL these TQM sessions were very important. Over a period of several months, the officer team met in the evenings to review, critique, and modify the fundamental business and management systems of the company. We reviewed not only the new TQM components we were putting in place, but also the purchasing and control system, safety systems, financial planning and budgeting systems, and an array of other core business systems. Such sessions were typically very revealing. We discovered some of the more cumbersome practices that had developed and become part of the overall system over the years. I believe this was the first time in the company's history that any officer group had taken the time to thoroughly scrutinize the company's management system. As a result, every officer walked away with a much better, and collectively-shared, understanding of how the company was run and what it would take to change it.

One activity to carry out early on is to have someone skilled in flowcharting draw a high-level "wiring diagram" or business map of the company's basic business processes (see Figure 7.1). The picture should depict the planning, design, manufacturing, operations, marketing, sales, and customer service business processes. It should also show the feedback loops that exist to prevent recurrence of problems. The diagram will undoubtedly produce an interesting and revealing picture to launch management-system review sessions. It may also serve as a vehicle to track and check on the changes made to the system.

Senior management training involves a combination of managers playing student and then taking charge of the rest of the organization's training. Senior managers must not only learn about and critically examine their business systems and how the organization works, but also seek to change these by providing ongoing training. Training and education is not a one-time event; it is a continuous process.

MIDDLE MANAGEMENT AND FIRST-LINE SUPERVISORS

In addition to senior management training, middle managers and first-line supervisors need a thorough, practical knowledge of the statistical tools and problem-solving techniques. The basic statistical and problem solving training must be supplemented with a more extensive tools-and-techniques course focused on use. Employees working under these managers and supervisors will be employing the tools on a daily basis, and if middle managers are to carry out their role as coaches and overseers, they will need a good understanding of the correct application of the tools. Managers and supervisors will also need training in promoting team activity, managing teams, and in coaching techniques.

The best time to begin the basic training for middle managers and first-line supervisors is after senior management has completed its initial training and has established the policies of the company. Training should again be JIT (i.e., it should not begin until it is needed and it should be put to use immediately after it

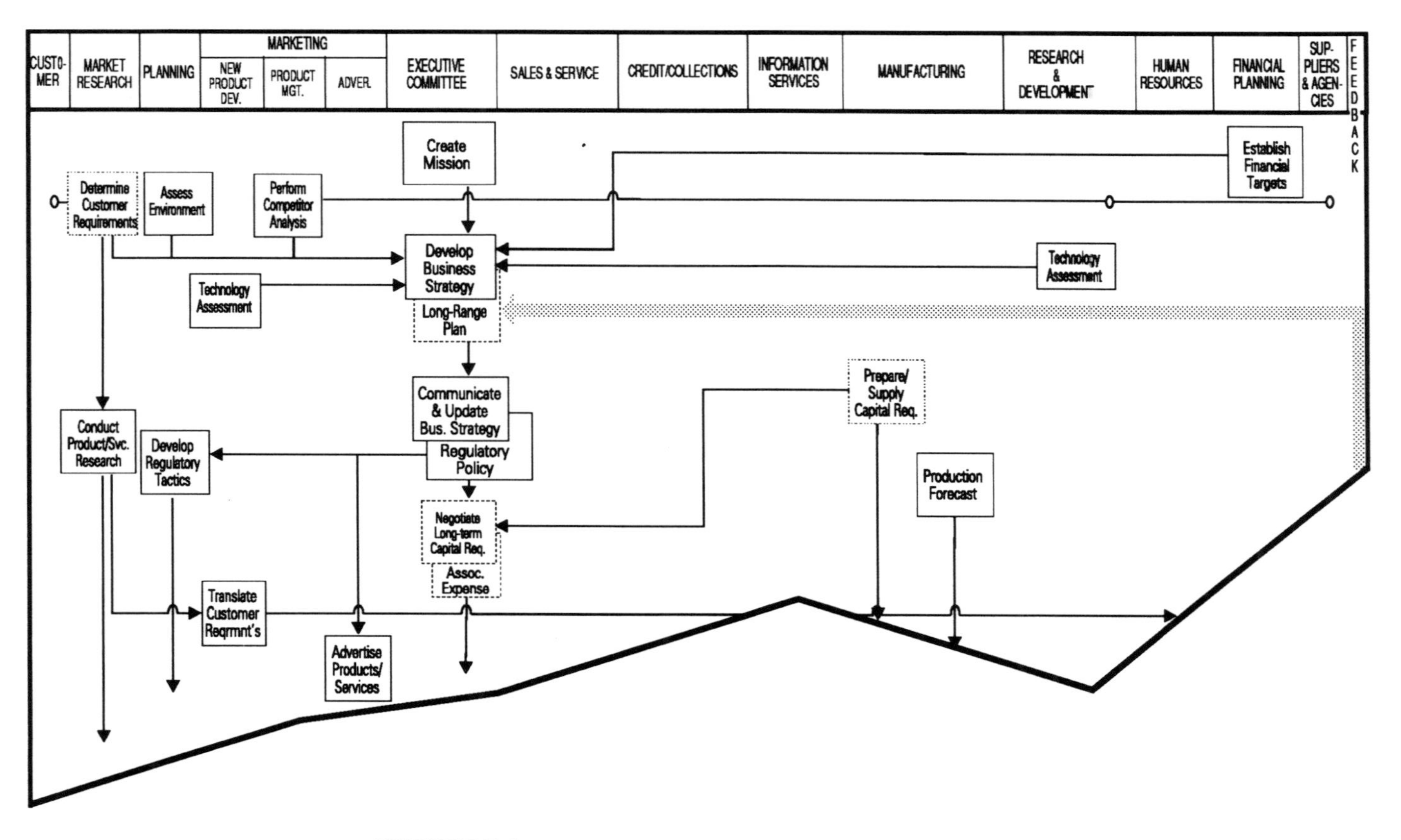

FIGURE 7.1. Management Systems "Wiring Diagram"

is conducted). Too often companies train without having thought about the practical application of the training. This creates frustration among many employees and a kind of "mental atrophy" can develop when the knowledge is not applied.

One reason Policy Management is so important is that it is an effective means for integrating management's training and application of the tools and techniques with the processes and structures of TQM. Policy Management serves to identify company problems that management alone can and must solve. Before employees are asked to improve the company, management must carry out its own quest for improvement, and Policy Management is the best vehicle to use. Only then can middle managers and first-line supervisors, along with selected staff, begin forming the initial project teams to address specific improvement opportunities. After participating in Policy Management project teams, these individuals will have a greater understanding and experience in how to coach and assist working teams that they will then supervise directly.

The organization will have to address what to do with managers and supervisors who exhibit highly autocratic styles. These managers cannot successfully participate in a company that adopts TQM. This does not mean that individuals with this style cannot be changed. At FPL, one of the divisions—and division heads—that was most successful in implementing TQM had a reputation as a hard line, "get the job done *my way*" organization. As the senior management of that division began to learn about TQM and see results, their management styles changed dramatically. Thus, through the leadership abilities of two key managers trained in TQM, the organization was transformed in a relatively short period into one that exhibited a great deal of appreciation for the skills and abilities of its employees. It ended up being the most improved division and having the best employee-participation record in the company.

Middle managers and first-line supervisors are the day-to-day promoters and monitors of quality within the organization. Senior management cannot expect widespread application of TQM principles and practices without getting middle managers and supervisors deeply involved. Because this level of the organization is so critical to the overall success, and because it will impact the employee population, middle managers and supervisors need special training in human-relations skills, group dynamics, and team coaching. Team leadership training usually incorporates these fundamental skills and may be combined with, or added to, team problem-solving and other TQM training.

EMPLOYEE TQM-ORIENTATION AND TEAM PROBLEM-SOLVING TRAINING

A general employee and new employee orientation program should also be developed to educate new and existing employees in the basics of TQM, the plan of implementation, and in what is expected of them as members of the company team. The orientation needs to be done as soon as is practicable (i.e., after senior management finalizes its plans). Employee training responsibilities should not be relegated to the human resources, quality, or corporate communications departments—although these departments can and should provide support for the activity. The TQM-orientation training should be performed by the manager or supervisor responsible for the day-to-day activities of the employees. The orientation may be done verbally, supplemented by a written description of the plan. Having each supervisor and manager conduct this activity reinforces their own participation in the education and training program and mobilizes the rest of the organization in the overall transformation of the company's culture.

Whether they are project teams or natural teams, training for employee team members in problem-solving tools and techniques and in team dynamics can be accomplished in a variety of ways. Some advocate a cascading approach to training. This method involves each successive layer in the organization training the next level of people below it. The advantage here is that the training received by those responsible for performing the next round of training is reinforced. There is probably no better way to learn than to put something into practice and then to teach it. The disadvantage is that some people are better teachers than others. Teaching is a skill not everyone can master to the same degree. Situations can arise where a poor teaching performance by a manager or supervisor can adversely affect his or her ability to further the implementation of TQM. It is good policy, then, to add a "train-the-trainer" session to the company schedule. Although the cascading approach has the benefits of forcing managers and supervisors to learn the material, the method does not necessarily provide the best quality training and other alternatives are available.

One alternative here is a classroom environment where skilled instructors do the training (or train trainers). The advantage of this approach is that a consistency in content and delivery is largely built in. If this method is used, natural employee teams might best be taught as a unit. People who work together can then take greater advantage of the training by discussing, inside and outside the classroom, how they plan to apply the training on the job. The approach can also help tackle certain group-dynamics problems.

At FPL, we chose to conduct the training by including a mixture of employees from different departments. This method was used to minimize the impact on a given unit's ongoing work activities. We managed to accomplish the goal intended, but there were too many instances where the training was either never fully used or used only after a number of other employees in a department had completed the classes. This caused a postponement in the application of the training and delays in creating tangible results. I do not recommend this method of training.

I advocate a method of training that requires the immediate use of the skills taught. To accomplish this objective, a method (and there are successful variations of this) that splits the training into segments or phases may be used. The first segment should be devoted to providing an overview and introducing the basic concepts and skills to be mastered. If, for instance, problem solving is being taught, enough material should be covered to give participants sufficient knowledge to be able to identify real problems and begin a first-level analysis of them. Participants may then return to the second segment of training with their proposed analysis and a suggested solution. These results can then be reviewed by the group. From a company point of view, a return on the training investment will be realized almost immediately.

The material taught in the classroom will therefore take on greater immediacy and depth as it begins to be applied in the organization and as participants review problems, analyses, and solutions collectively. This application-and-review process is one of the best means to teach and maintain "fact control."

Scheduling training for employees engaged in the day-to-day operations of the company is an ongoing problem. Companies need to devise their own methods to ensure that the training is done at a time that is needed without having an adverse effect on servicing the customers' needs. Whatever method is used, ultimately on-the-job reinforcement of the training is essential. Do not waste resources on something that will not produce real results.

TRAINING PLAN

When FPL began its TQM training in 1981, there were very few, if any, English-language course materials available. We developed our initial training courses by translating Japanese training materials and by hiring a consulting firm to put the material into a useable format. Often we misinterpreted or misapplied the material, creating rework. Numerous classes were given, but the training did not always achieve the results desired. The consulting firm was good at rewriting and editing but added little in terms of course content because its employees were not specialists in TQM.

Today, of course, there are any number of excellent training courses, seminars, and published materials available throughout the country, covering virtually every aspect of TQM. Many companies have even licensed their training courses and some have modified them for use by others. Developing one's own course material will take time and can be expensive. If your company has the resources and time, self-developed material can be useful in that it can be readily adapted to your firm's particular corporate style. This choice, however, will no doubt cause some delay in generating real improvements.

Whether you develop your own training material or acquire it from the outside, you must have a general plan for training.

Training the right people at the right time with the right material is essential. Although not intended to be a comprehensive curriculum, Table 7.1 offers some guidance on how to arrange the training. Ultimately, your plan will need to make sense in terms of your own company and its needs.

SPECIALISTS

As the implementation matures, it will be necessary to develop a few highly trained individuals or in-house "specialists" in TQM. The number needed will depend on the size of the organization, the number of different work locations, and the nature of the business. The training of such specialists should come in advance of the need, yet care should be taken not to introduce the training too soon, because people may become enthralled with the newer tools and try to use them inappropriately. The specialist should be someone who is very good in engineering or mathematics and with good interpersonal skills—perhaps a recent college graduate whose math skills are still fresh and who can more quickly absorb the training. The specialist will be called on to assist administrative and working teams with the evaluation and analysis of complicated problems.

This is one area where FPL initially made a mistake: we trained too many specialists and we trained the wrong kind of people. The first specialist-training class consisted of managers who had line responsibility. They were a bright group, but because they had day-to-day line responsibilities they never had time to apply what they learned (if they applied it all). It took us several months before we realized the nature of the mistake and began to select people who were more likely to be able to apply what was taught. We also trained far too many specialists—more than the company could effectively use. This resulted in frustration for everyone.

In addition to at least one specialist in statistics, you will need a few specialists in the use of unique and powerful quality tools—above all, quality function deployment (QFD). Whether you are in the manufacturing or the service sector, QFD is a powerful tool to help you deliver the product or service your customers

TABLE 7.1. Training Plan

	Phase I	*Phase II*	*Phase III*	*Phase IV*
Senior Management	TQM Basic Concepts Problem-Solving Tools and Techniques Policy Management	Business and Management Systems Advanced Tools Concepts Application and Review Process	QFD Concepts JIT Concepts Daily Management Concepts	Quality Assurance
Middle Management	TQM Basic Concepts Problem-Solving Tools and Techniques Policy Management	Team Sponsor Training Advanced Tools and Techniques Application and Review Process Daily Management Concepts		Quality Assurance

(*continued*)

TABLE 7.1. Training Plan (continued)

	Phase I	*Phase II*	*Phase III*	*Phase IV*
Supervisors	TQM Basic Concepts Leadership Skills Problem-Solving Tools and Techniques	Team Sponsor Training Application and Review Process Daily Management Techniques	Advanced Tools and Techniques	Quality Assurance
Employees	TQM Orientation Problem-Solving Tools and Techniques Team Training	Suggestion System		
Specialists	Basic Statistical Tools QFD 7 New Tools	SQC and Advanced Statistical Tools Quality Assurance	Reliability Analysis JIT	

expect (see Chapters 2 and 3). QFD can help organizations reduce cycle time in delivering their product or service. It can also help make your product or service more robust. Training in QFD should be done early in the development of TQM. The results will be very useful in helping companies evaluate improvement opportunities from a customer's perspective. Specialists in reliability techniques may also be needed if your product requires improvement in dependability, or has a long life cycle or critical safety requirement.

If your business activities involve the accumulation of raw material inventories to produce a product, a specialist in JIT technology will need to be trained. Application of JIT can result in significant cost-savings for a company by reducing inventory levels or even entirely eliminating the inventory requirements. Such techniques require sophisticated planning systems that are linked to suppliers' production systems. Normally, depending on the nature of the business, only a few highly-trained specialists will be needed.

CONCLUSION

Education and training programs are vital to the success of any quality approach. It must begin with senior management. Senior management must be fully trained and must also have a clear understanding of what training other employees and managers are receiving. Senior managers should be the architects of the training program.

Basic training in problem solving, statistical techniques, and team activity are a minimum requirement. The timing and intensity of the training program must be designed to meet business needs. Management must realize that training is not a one-time event, but a continuing process. Training programs should be designed to ensure the training is applied as close to the time that the training is received as possible, and that a return on the investment realized. A few specialists in advanced techniques may be required to assist in solving complex problems. They should be limited to a number sufficient to meet the business needs of the company.

8

Problem Solving

INTRODUCTION

In the early stages of FPL's quality-improvement program, I had heard how ordinary Japanese workers were using statistical tools to solve problems and to conduct their daily work. At first I thought this must be an exaggeration. After making several study trips to Japan, however, I became convinced that statistical tools were indeed being usefully applied by Japanese workers and could also be employed by the average U.S. worker and understood and appreciated by top managers. It would only take a little statistical training.

Statistics was never my favorite subject in college. I took statistical courses mainly because I thought they might prove useful someday in the business world. I even attempted a graduate-level statistics course to see if the relevance might become clearer as the courses became more advanced. But I was not converted, and felt that statistics were designed for people who needed to study, for example, experimental yields of corn for varying levels of fertilizer, or estimated incomes based on the number of acres and the count of cattle. I was exactly right, of course, but I have come to appreciate the usefulness and power of basic statistics for other applications!

The secret to using statistics in problem solving is to keep things simple. At FPL, we began teaching our employees the seven basic statistical tools in 1983. People seemed to pick them up and use them readily. In the beginning, it seemed that employees applied the tools very well. But it also seemed to take an inordinately long time to fully review the employee work and their use of the statistical tools. The tools were simple enough, but often the analysis of the problems tended to ramble.

Kansai Electric Company in Japan was very gracious in helping us implement a total quality approach to management. They offered to send employees over to our company for extended periods to help us better understand TQC. One of the first employees to arrive was Mikuto Suto. He was very quiet and low key, and when he spoke he always showed impeccable logic. He kept telling us that we needed to organize our analyses into quality improvement (QI) stories. We thought this sounded like a good idea, but what was a QI story?

THE QI STORY

The Japanese are generally not so forward as to tell one to "Do this!" Instead, they suggest something and let one discover for himself or herself what to do. Several employees, after reviewing the basic instructions, attempted to put together a QI story, but Mr. Suto kept shaking his head and offering them a little more advice. Finally, he must have become frustrated with our lack of understanding and created a QI story for us.

One of our district offices had been trying to solve a certain problem for over a year. The case report was nearing an inch thick. I had always found it difficult to convince people working for me that two-inch reports did not impress, and I encouraged them to look for ways to present information in clearer and more concise ways. But Mr. Suto, after going through the data, managed to reduce the voluminous report to two simple pages using sketches, graphs, and charts with little annotated arrows. It was a complete "story board" showing both the problem and the work that had been done to solve it! The story was clear, accurate, and concise.

Two pages! The QI story was something I needed. It told so much in such a small amount of space; it was logical and it was relatively easy to teach to anyone in the company. In Mr. Suto's story, deficiencies in the team's analysis were also made clear. Other company officers and I were amazed, and remarked how clever Japanese quality control techniques were. It was amazing that Mr. Suto had been able to simplify things to a level that even an aging executive (like me) whose last math course was taken nearly 30 years before, could understand!

A QI story generally addresses the following questions:

- What is the problem?
- How do you know?
- How do you measure the problem?
- What is your object or target for improvement?
- What is the root cause of the problem?
- What do you propose to do to solve the problem?
- What specific solutions have you tried?
- What results did you achieve?
- If solved, how will you ensure that the problem will not recur?
- What are the remaining problems?
- What is going to be done about them?

The QI story is an excellent way to organize problem solving in a logical manner, laying out the problem, the analysis, and the solution (see Figure 8.1). It is a graphic language, and can be a much better communicator than the written word. Simple, exact, brief, comprehensive—these are just a few of the words that describe the QI story process. It can accommodate virtually any type of statistical or analytical tools used in problem solving and provides maximum flexibility.

Although it is called a QI *story*, it is in fact a systematic problem-organizing and problem-solving process. The QI story is a procedure for laying out, confronting, and solving problems. Some companies use a five-step process, some six, and some seven. (FPL used a seven-step process.) Personally, I prefer a

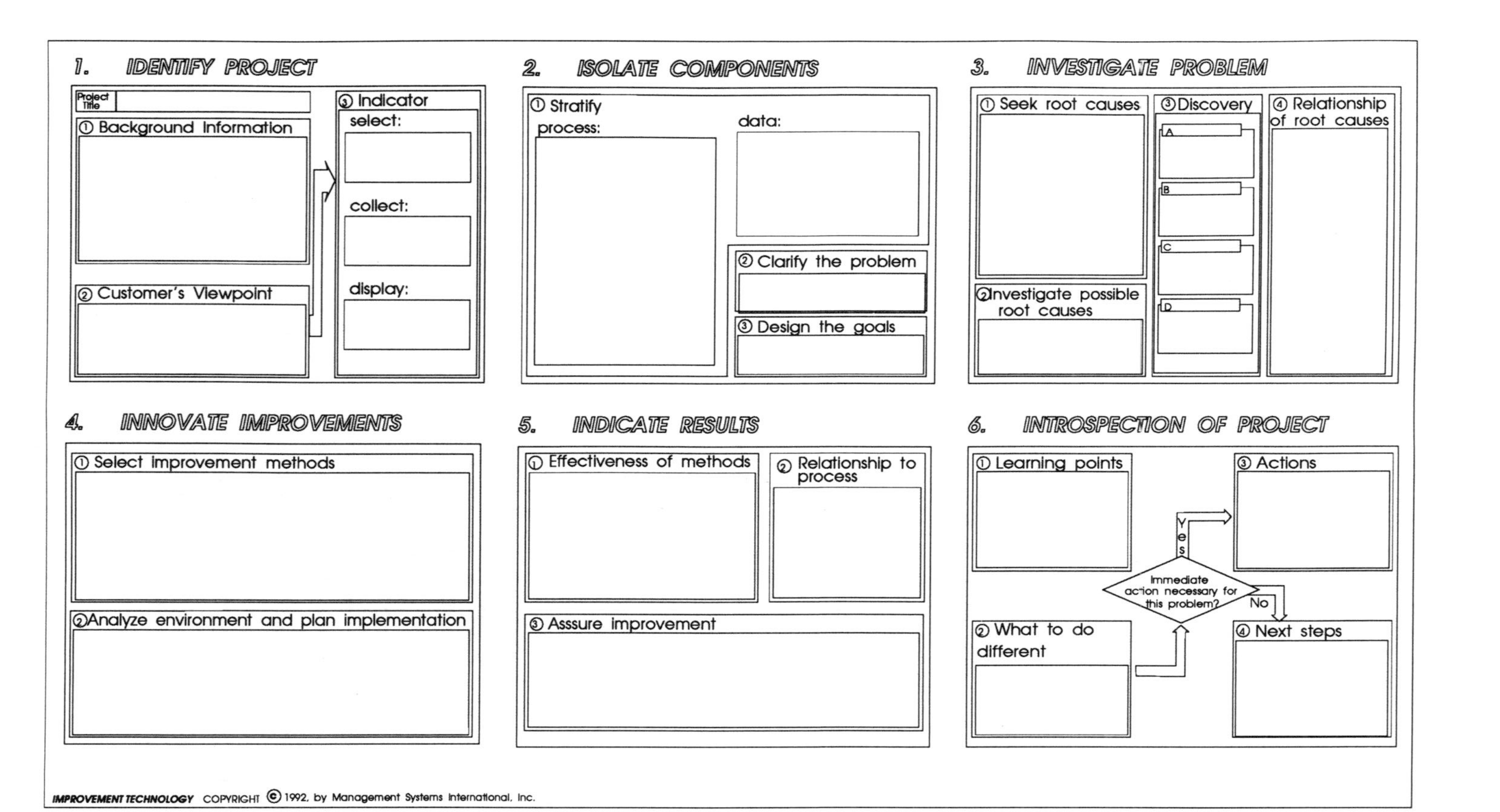

FIGURE 8.1. QI Story Template

six-step story board that combines the first two steps—reason for improvement and current situation—of the model used by FPL and other companies.

The number of steps used is not as important as making sure that the team has clearly focused on the problem to be solved. The problem-solving process as organized through the QI story must include verification of the root causes of the problem using facts, not gut feelings. It must contain a method to organize the data and a means to identify solutions. Next, it must include a check on the results of applying countermeasures and be capable of showing that it was the countermeasures, and not some other factor, that created the stated results. Finally, the process should drive continuous improvement by identifying any remaining problems and what will be done about them, including any lessons learned from the measures already taken. This is to ensure that those working on a problem have gained something valuable from the experience—something that can be applied the next time a similar problem turns up.

A QI story is therefore a "template" that provides a disciplined, step-by-step approach to solving problems. When completed, the steps provide a complete "story board" that can be used to easily communicate the problem and the solution. Figures 8.2 through 8.7 show an example of a completed template displaying the nature of the problem, the analysis conducted, the root causes identified, and the results achieved.

In addition to team members, senior management must also have a comprehensive knowledge of the problem-solving process and a clear understanding of the most useful statistical tools. Using a consistent problem-solving process will have the effect of producing a *common language* for the entire company to rely on in making improvements. The QI story may be the best and most comprehensive means of communication for all levels in an organization. It can be effective from entry-level employees to the chairman of the board.

One important result of using QI stories at FPL was a dramatic reduction in the time it took to make presentations. Whereas normally these took two hours, now they were reduced to 15 minutes—and with more precise and readily digestible in-

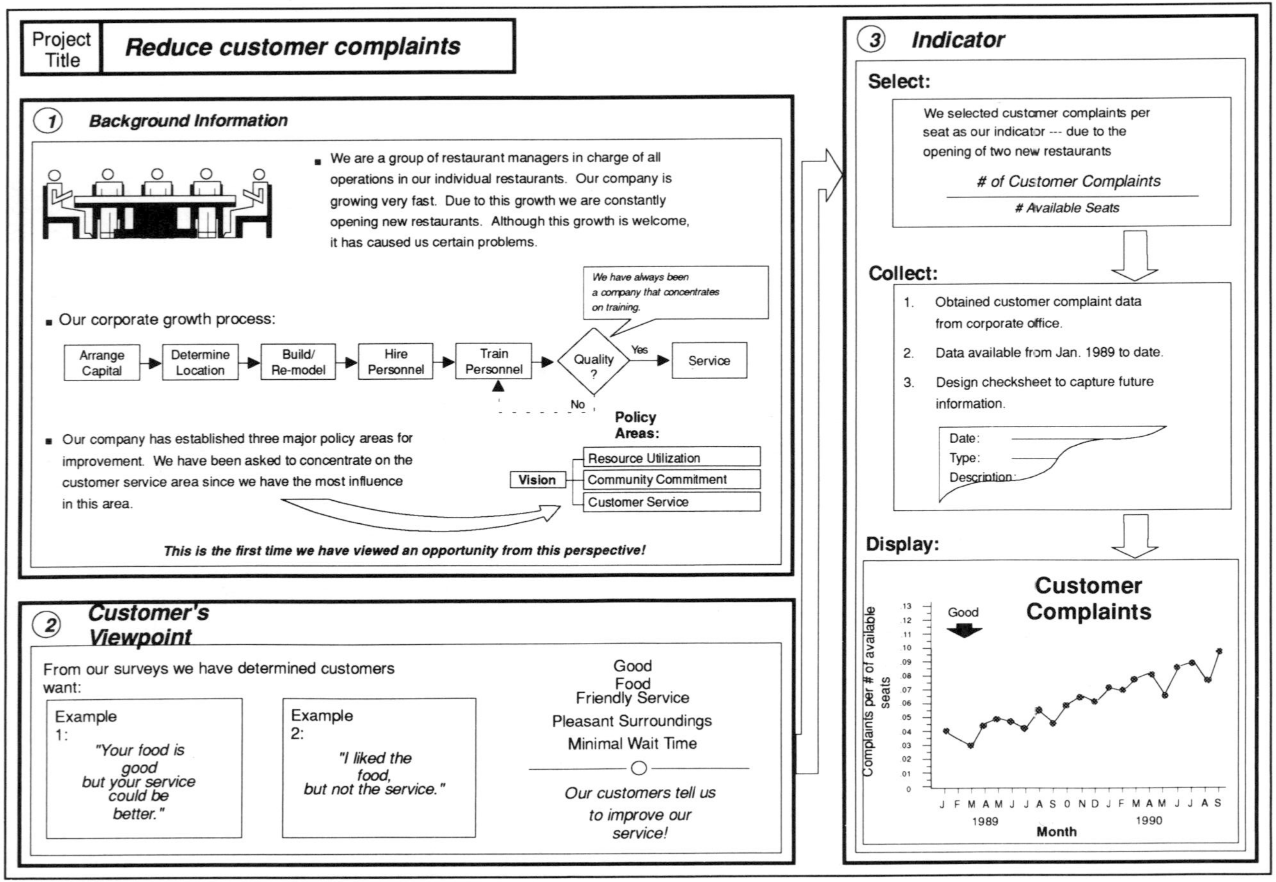

FIGURE 8.2. Step 1 — Identify Project

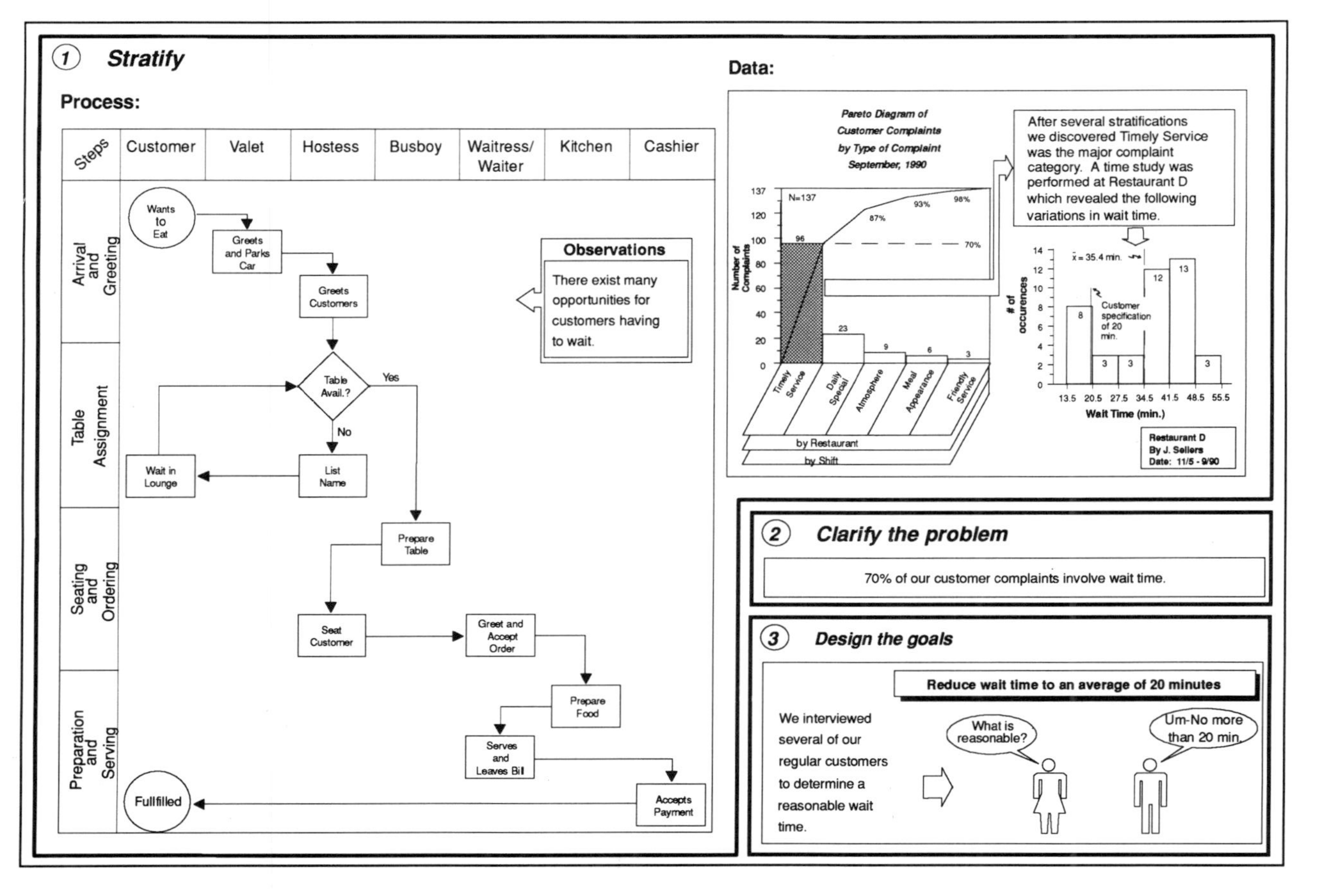

FIGURE 8.3. Step 2 — Isolate Components

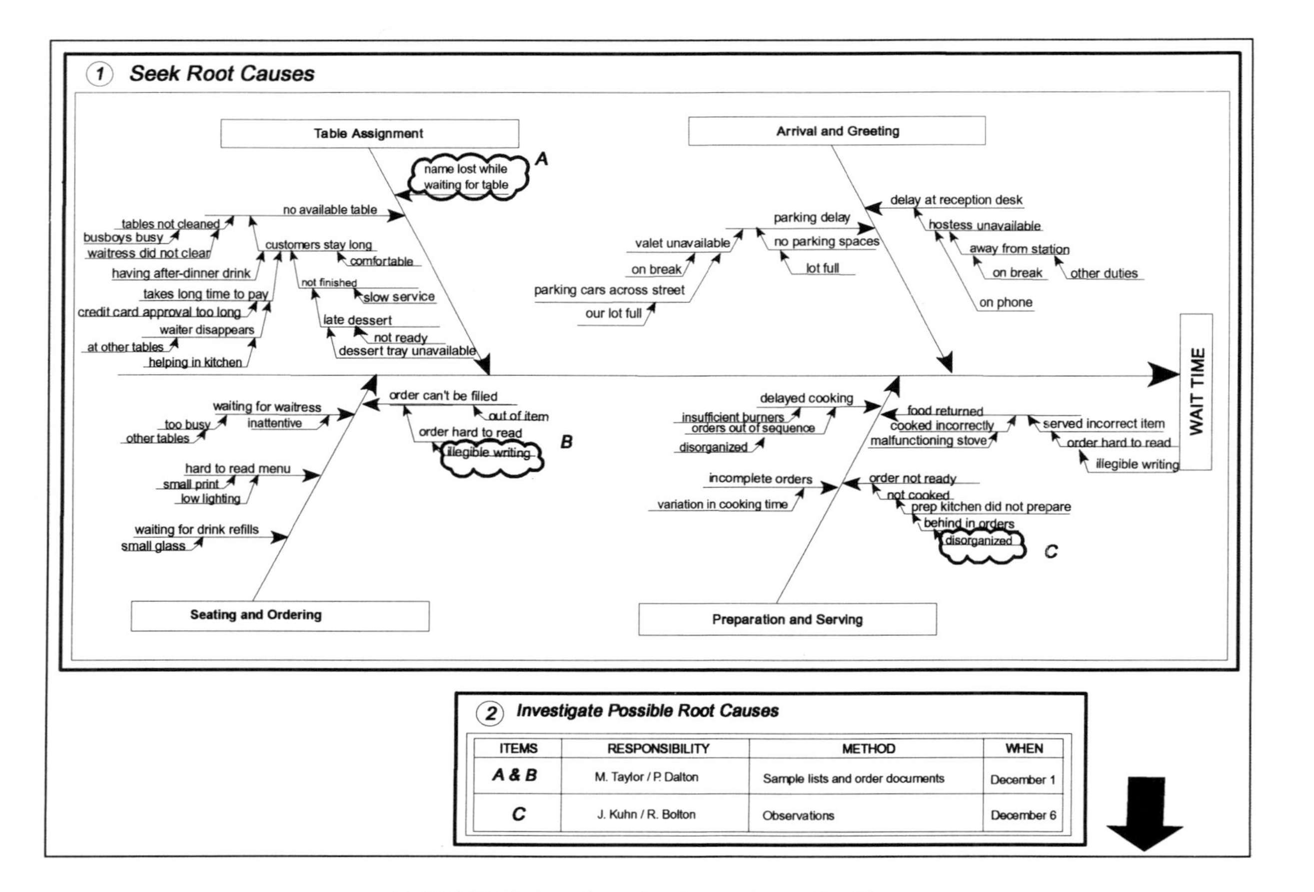

ITEMS	RESPONSIBILITY	METHOD	WHEN
A & B	M. Taylor / P. Dalton	Sample lists and order documents	December 1
C	J. Kuhn / R. Bolton	Observations	December 6

FIGURE 8.4. Step 3 — Investigate Problem

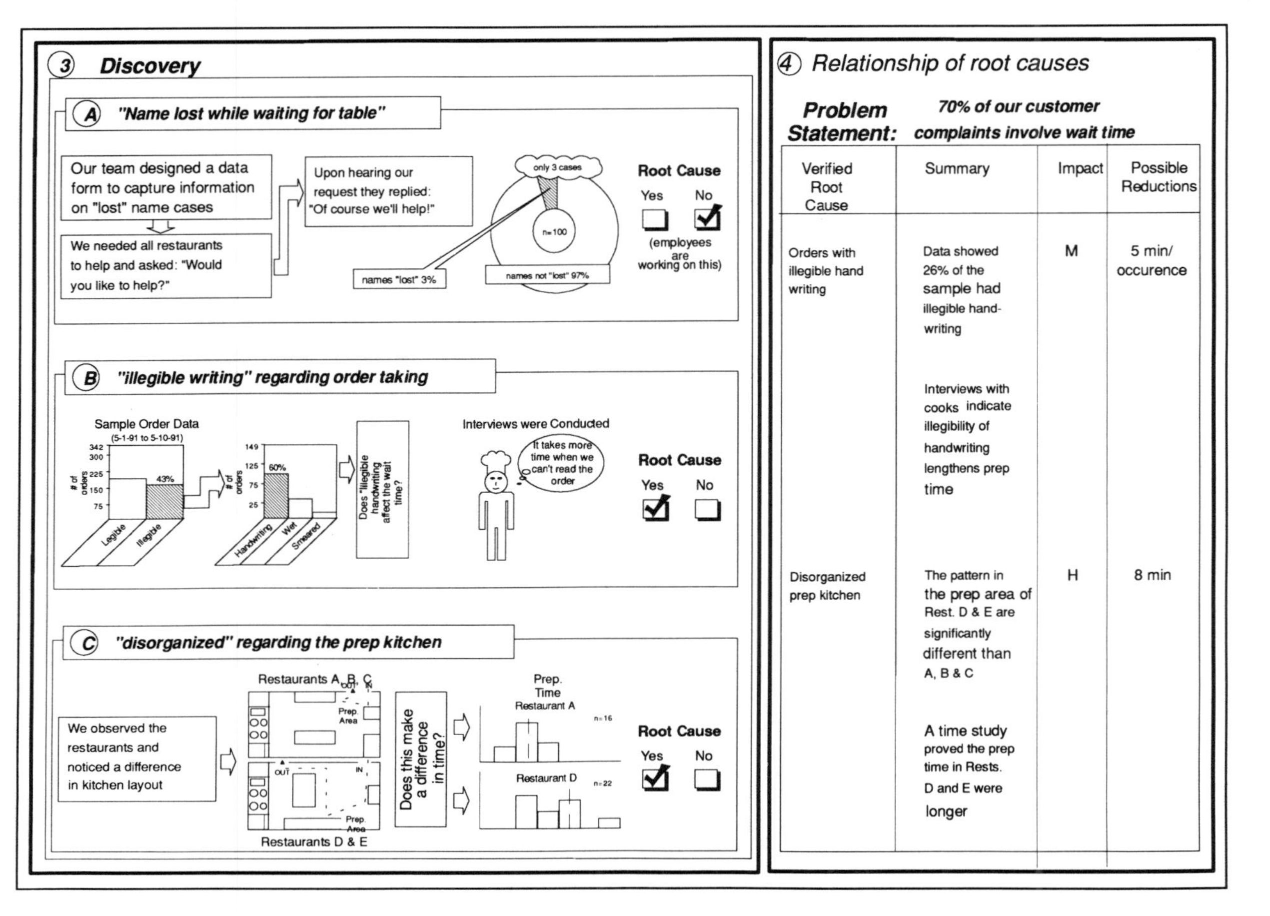

FIGURE 8.4. Step 3 – Investigate Problem (Continued)

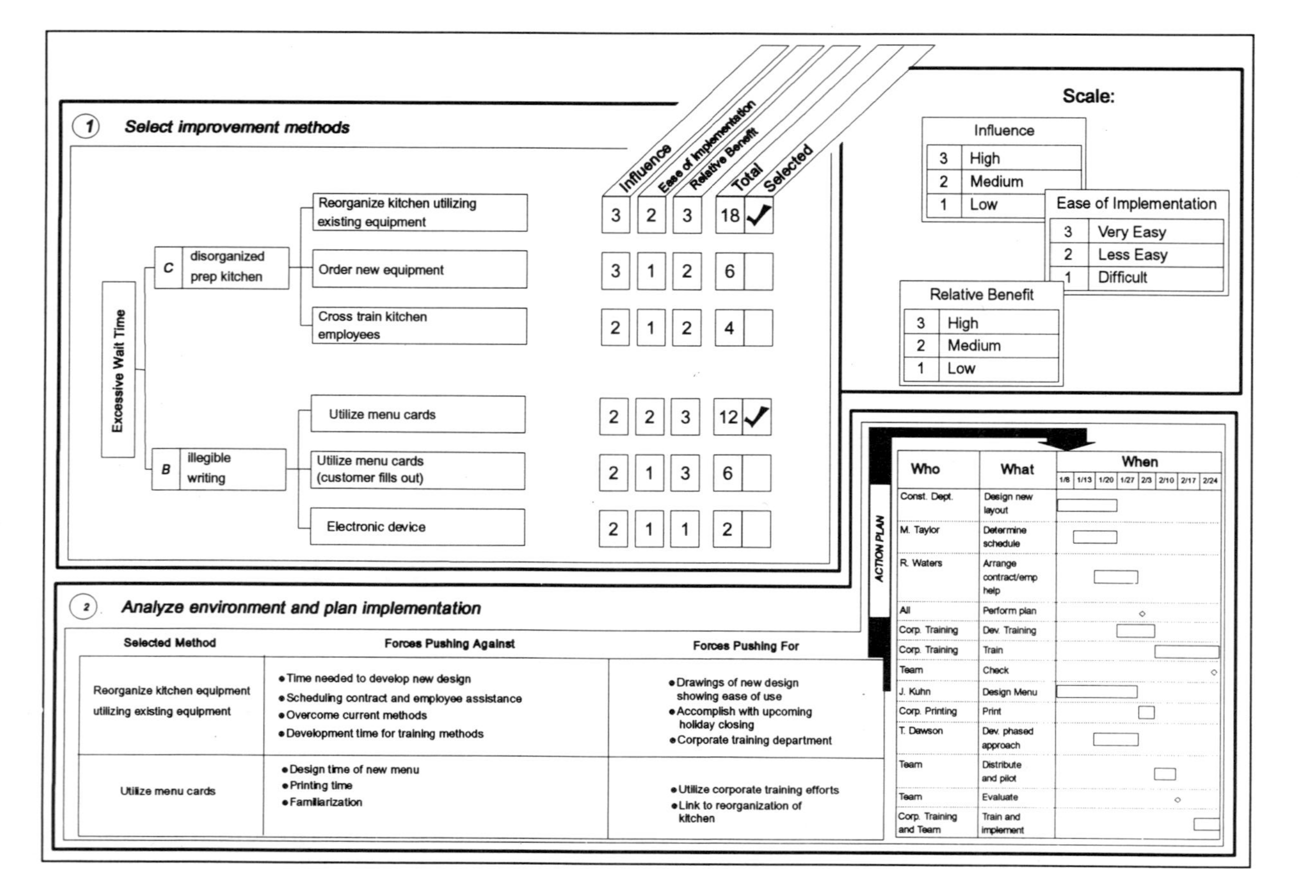

FIGURE 8.5. Step 4 — Innovate Improvements

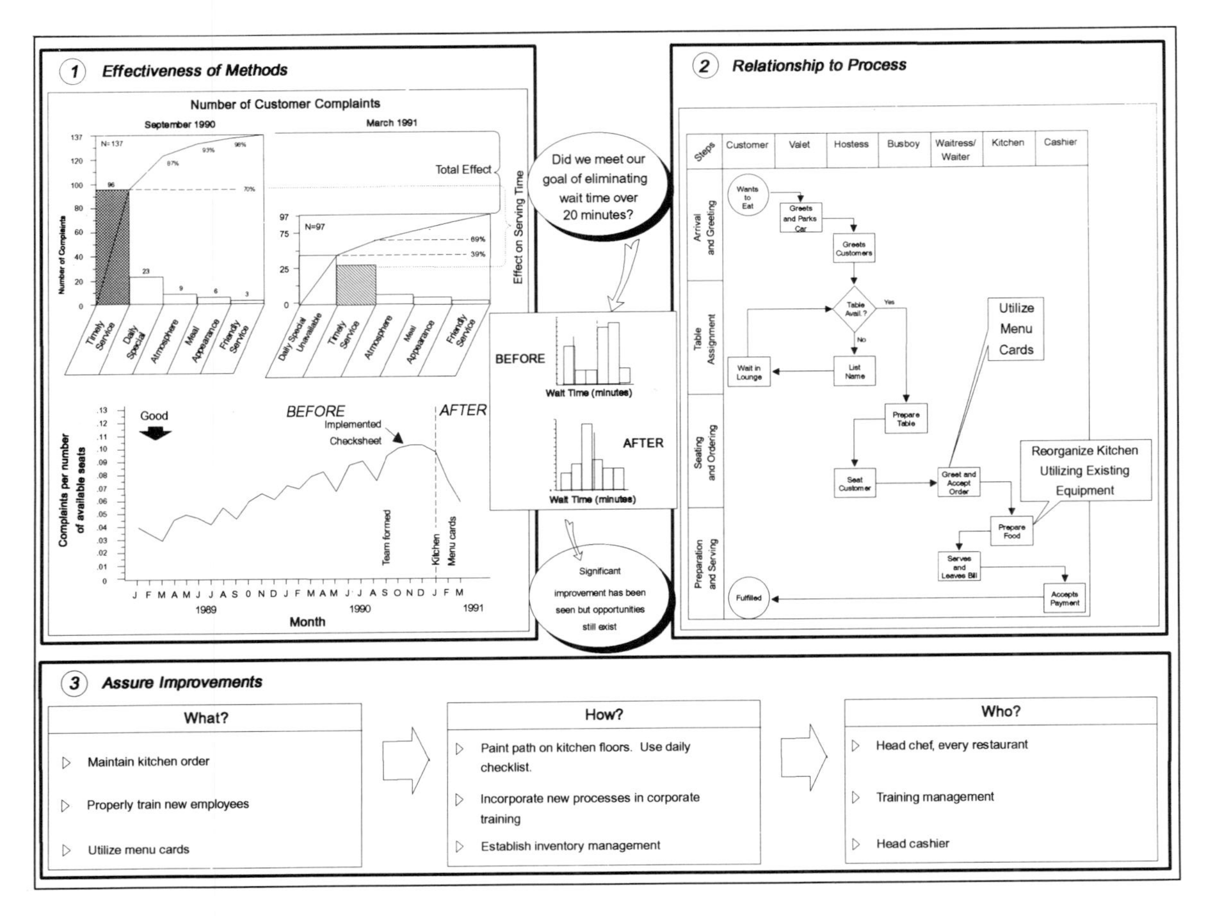

FIGURE 8.6. Step 5 – Indicate Results

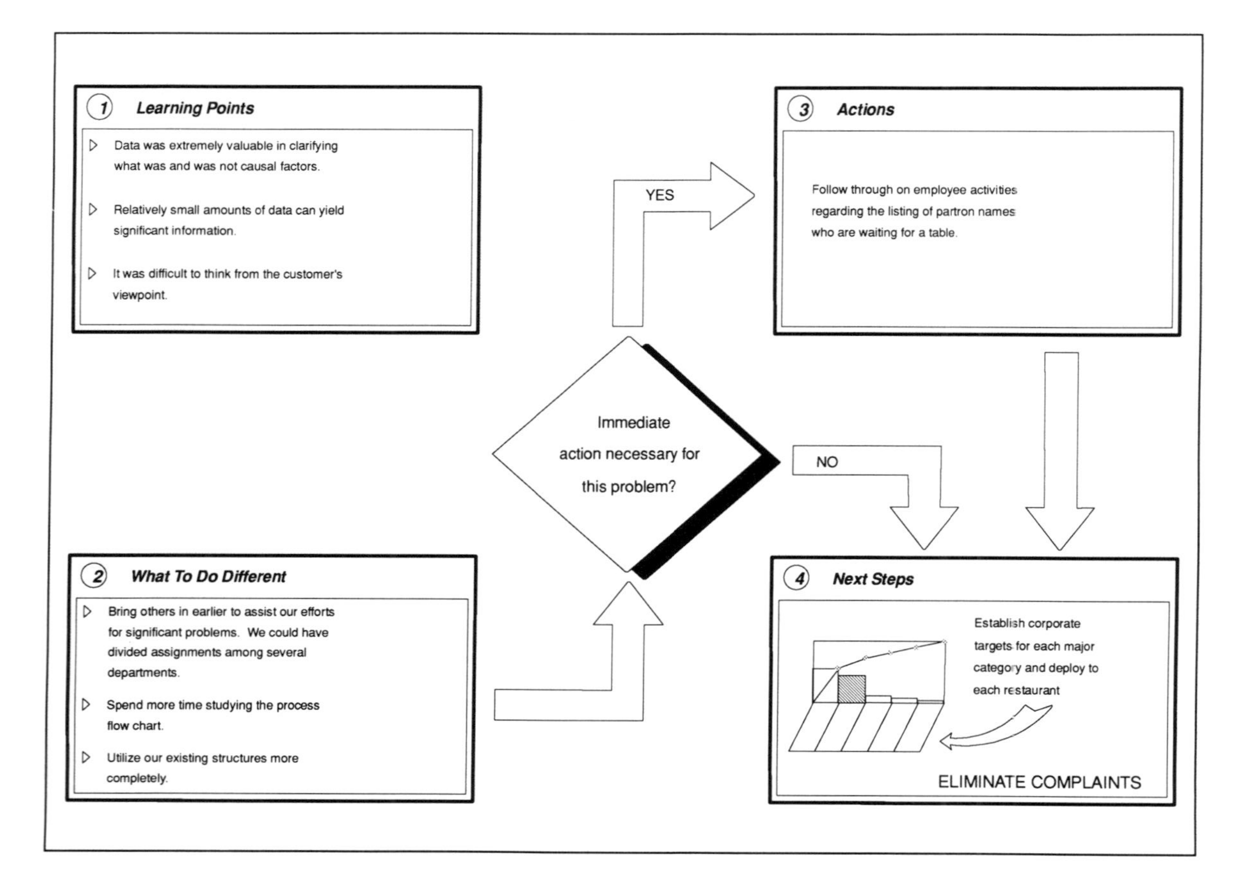

FIGURE 8.7. Step 6 — Introspection of Project

formation. The QI story is worth adopting for this reason alone. It can save executive and working teams valuable time and make meetings more productive.

Another welcome result was the improvement in communicating highly complex technical matters clearly. With the adoption of the QI story, I developed a better appreciation of the problems facing our Nuclear Department. In the past, I had had difficulty following some of the mysterious language used by the department. But after adopting the QI story, our technical departments could no longer faze me with their technical jargon. They were forced to put complex matters in terms understandable to everyone.

Cautions

There are some forewarnings and cautions for management when it comes to using the QI story format. Some people may become so enthralled with the format that they lose sight of its purpose. The purpose is to organize problems and solve them at the lowest cost. Use the QI story to organize problems that require performing an analysis and applying countermeasures. (A suggestion system may be used to solve simpler problems.) Be aware, however, that there is a tendency for teams to jump to countermeasures without discovering the root causes of a problem or without adequately evaluating alternatives. In reviewing QI stories, managers must keep this in mind and be on the lookout for it.

Some managers complain that a disciplined and systematic problem-solving method restrains people's creativity. Any method that does this has something fundamentally wrong with it and should be discontinued. Problem solving must foster creativity, and identifying and applying countermeasures is a good means to do so.

The QI story review session is also the time to look carefully at the *cost* of implementing countermeasures to ensure that the lowest cost solution is achieved. Sometimes more expensive countermeasures may be suggested. But this is the time to perfect the definition and application of countermeasures. Never be satisfied with high-cost countermeasures. Be creative! Redesign the process for implementing the countermeasure. Drive down the cost.

Another thing to guard against is when a countermeasure seems that it should be applied to a widespread problem. For instance, at FPL we had been trying to solve a problem concerning service interruptions caused by lightning. A complete analysis was performed and a very good solution was identified. The vice president in charge of the area, however, told me the solution would take 10 years to implement and it would cost millions of dollars. We consulted with some visiting Japanese quality experts and eventually discovered that lightning was not striking *everywhere*, even though the problem was widespread. The countermeasure we identified could therefore be applied exclusively to those areas with a high concentration of lightning. One of our engineers even used a lightning mapping program to plot the historical frequency and intensity of lightning. As a result, the countermeasure was applied to an area less than one fifth the total area we originally had thought would need attention, and the problem was virtually solved 18 months later. (We realized that we needed to retrofit the countermeasure to the areas that had the highest probability of lightning failures, and our long-term maintenance program could take care of the remaining areas where the lightning protection did not meet the new standard.)

In the case of expensive or extensive countermeasures, creativity must be stretched to its limits to ensure that minimum resources achieve maximum results. Remember, the goal of your quality activities is to reduce overall costs, not increase them. In the case of countermeasures that need to be applied to extensive areas, reexamine the reasons why. Countermeasures need be applied only to those areas that will solve the problem.

There are several good cost reduction techniques that can be used. Industrial engineering methods, value analysis, process improvement, and a host of other techniques are compatible with the QI story format. Once a countermeasure is identified, teams need to look for ways to minimize the cost of the countermeasure. The job is not complete until alternatives for minimizing costs are explored.

Questions such as: Is there a way to reduced the cost? Is there a way to improve the process? And does the countermeasure need to be applied everywhere? must be asked and answered. Teams are often very excited when they discover a solution to solve the root cause of a problem, and they often neglect looking for ways to reduce the cost of the countermeasure. Guidance and coaching from supervisors can help team members look for lower-cost solutions.

Every company has more problems than it can possibly solve. Some kind of systematic approach must be developed to reduce the magnitude of the problems you have. The process should be one that can be used by as many of your employees as possible. The graphic-language process of the basic statistical tools used in conjunction with the QI story will improve the ability to communicate between and among layers of management in any organization.

TYPES OF PROBLEMS

Most problems can be classified into three types: zero problems, decrease problems, and increase problems. It is important that managers understand this simple classification because the techniques used and objectives of the problem-solving process are different for each. There are some types of business problems for which statistical techniques may not be appropriate (e.g., legal problems, although I have seen statistical methods applied effectively to legal problems). Managers must recognize the different types of problems they are confronting. They must quickly recognize when someone has used a zero problem-solving technique to solve a decrease problem, or vice versa.

Zero Problems

The objective of solving a zero problem is to completely eliminate the problem—even though from a practical viewpoint you may not always be able to do this. Conditions that create zero problems should not exist. The conditions are not in the company's

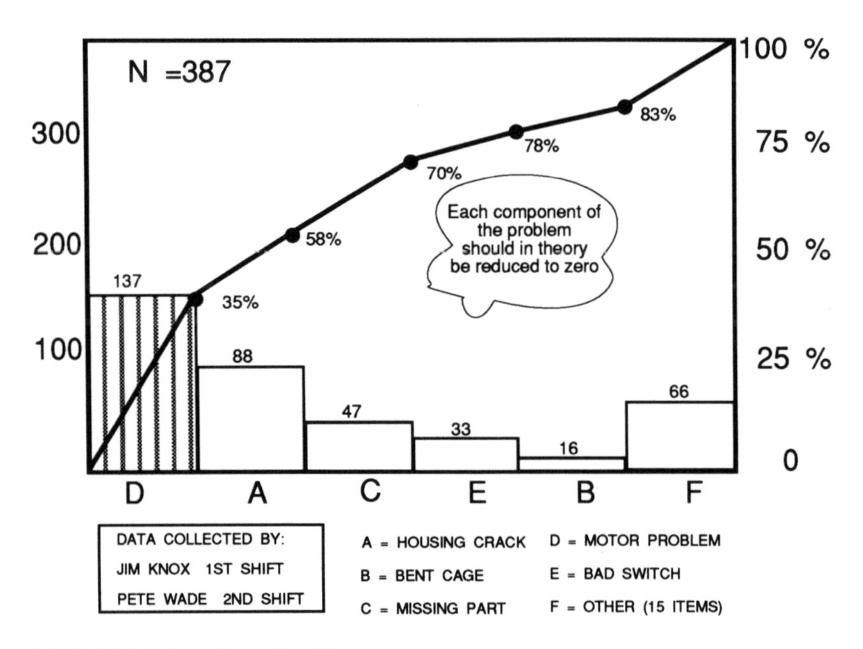

FIGURE 8.8. Zero Problems

and customer's interest and are almost always wasteful and costly. Defects, complaints, missed appointments, incorrect answers, missed deliveries are all "zero problems" that require elimination. To eliminate zero problems, you must systematically address each and every cause of the problem. For each cause there may be several different countermeasures that should be applied, depending on the number of root causes found.

In Figure 8.8, the defects need to be eliminated. To bring the defects to zero, each of the causes must be analyzed and countermeasures developed. (This could even take several years to accomplish!)

Before initiating a total quality program, one manufacturing company I visited had been measuring defects for their principal product in parts per 100. Several years into the implementation, the defect problem remained but the company was measuring defects in parts per 10,000. When I last visited the problem was still present but the company was now measuring defects in parts per *million*. This shows that when to "stop" solving a zero problem depends on your customers' requirements. If the problem relates to safety, you will most likely never stop working on the defect.

Decrease Problems

Unlike zero problems, the objective of solving a decrease problem is to reduce its magnitude rather than to eliminate it entirely. Decrease problems will most likely involve costs or other financial considerations, and time. Reduction of production costs, reduction of design time, and reduction of delivery time are common examples of decrease or reduction problems. You cannot totally eliminate costs, delivery time, or manufacturing time, but you can reduce them. When analyzing cost or time, the tendency is to arrange the data as they would be arranged for a zero problem (i.e., the highest component followed by the next highest). Although this may seem logical, it is not.

If the analysis continues in this manner, there is a high probability that the most important component to be reduced is being ignored. Just because a component cost has the highest value does not mean that the greatest reduction can be achieved in this component; in some cases there may not be any reason to reduce the highest component cost. All too often this faulty method of analysis is used by companies when they have a cost problem. The financial department produces an ABC type of analysis (a traditional ranking method) and management decides arbitrarily to cut costs in those areas that appear to contribute to the highest cost.

To solve a decrease problem effectively, the problem must be converted to a zero problem. If the analysis is directed at reducing cost or time, the necessary and unnecessary components must first be found. The data can then be arranged in the highest to lowest order, and analysis to seek countermeasures can begin. Benchmarking, value-added analysis, and other industrial engineering techniques can be used to help solve the areas identified for improvement.

In Figure 8.9, each component of the cost must be analyzed to determine the necessary and unnecessary costs, and a Pareto

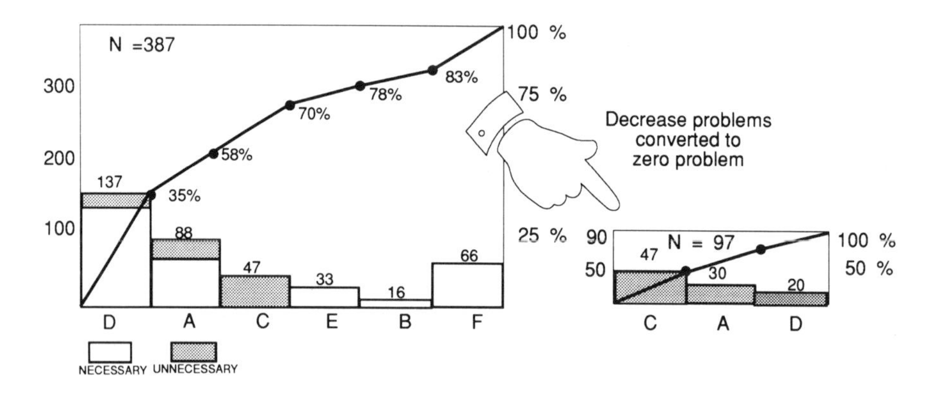

FIGURE 8.9. Decrease Problems

diagram constructed for each. Standard projected-versus-actual costing techniques, and traditional industrial engineering techniques are both ways to evaluate necessary and unnecessary costs. The first step in attacking this type of problem is to eliminate unnecessary costs and then examine how you can improve on necessary costs.

Increase Problems

Sometimes a quality problem does not involve defects, rejects, complaints, cost, or time. The objective of an increase problem is to increase something. Increasing sales, increasing production or yield, and increasing closure rates are among the types of problems classified as increase problems. In my opinion, increase problems are among the most difficult to solve. Sometimes an enormous amount of analysis is required, data are often difficult to obtain, and experiments are often required to test solutions before they are applied. In many cases, components of increase problems are caused by defects. When this type of root cause is identified, zero problem analysis techniques can be applied.

Figure 8.10 illustrates a problem in sales. In this case, to increase sales, the problem can be addressed in one of two ways: either increase market share or expand the size of the market to retain share.

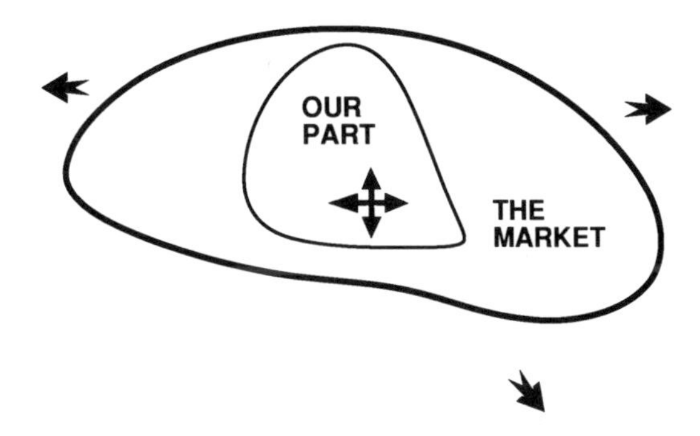

FIGURE 8.10. Increase Problems

Managers need to be aware of these three general types of problems and need to know the different techniques to use in addressing them.

THE SEVEN BASIC TOOLS

The line graph, the Pareto diagram, the check sheet, the fishbone diagram, the scatter diagram, the histogram, and the control chart are, for simple statistical tools, still very powerful. All of them can be taught to virtually anyone in your company. There are a number of books written about the use and application of the seven basic tools, and it is not my intent, here, to cover each of the tools exhaustively. (My favorite books on the subject, because they are easy to understand, are Dr. Hitoshi Kume's *Statistical Methods for Quality Improvement* and Dr. Kaoru Ishikawa's *Guide to Quality Control*.)[1] I want only to make a few observations about how these tool can assist managers.

In examining many companies' applications of the seven tools, it appears that four tools are the most widely used—and useful—in problem solving: the graph, the Pareto diagram, the

---

[1]Hitoshi Kume, *Statistical Methods for Quality Improvement* (Tokyo: AOTS, 1985). Kaoru Ishikawa, *Guide to Quality Control* (Tokyo: Asian Productivity Organization, 1982).

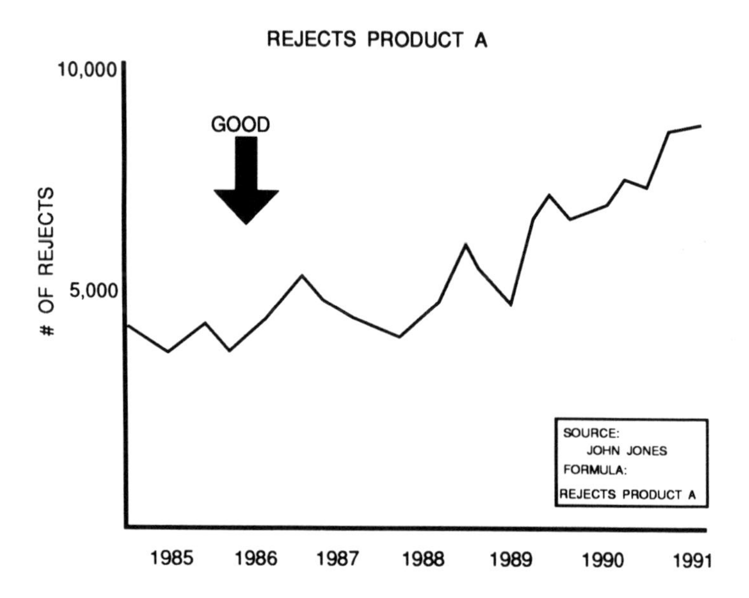

FIGURE 8.11. Graph

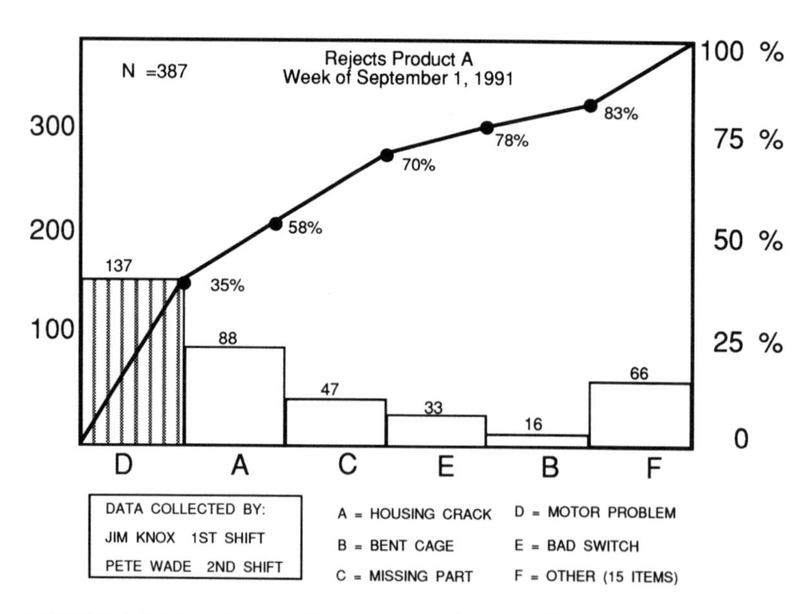

FIGURE 8.12. Pareto Diagram: A chart to Organize Data

fishbone (also known as the cause-and-effect diagram or the Ishikawa diagram), and the check sheet. I do not want to discourage use of the other tools because they are extremely helpful, depending on the type of problem one is trying to address, but I will focus on the four tools named above.

Graph

The graph is the easiest tool to teach and construct (see Figure 8.11). It quickly gives the reader a picture of desirable or undesirable *trends* in the data. The graph should include an arrow indicating which direction is "good," it should give the source of the information, and display the formula or basis for calculating the data represented in the graph.

Pareto Diagram

The Pareto diagram was created by the Italian economist Vilfredo Pareto in 1897. The diagram forces you to break down a problem so that you are working on the most important parts (see Figure 8.12). It is generally assumed that 20% of the causes of a problem will produce 80% of the effects of the problem (the 80/20 rule). You have probably seen situations in which great effort is applied to solving a problem only to find that the solutions address only a fraction of the real root causes, leaving unaddressed those items that caused the bulk of the problem.

The Pareto diagram tells much of the story all by itself. It does not necessarily "solve" a problem, but it is one of the best tools to help isolate and break down problem areas that need to be addressed. There is a great tendency, once a Pareto diagram is created, to stop there and start working on solutions. But if you are truly going to get to the root cause of a problem, you need to keep breaking it down into smaller and smaller parts to find *all* root causes (see Figure 8.13).

Teams sometimes take an inordinate amount of time to solve a problem. This is generally because they try to solve too much of a problem at one time. It is better to solve many small parts of

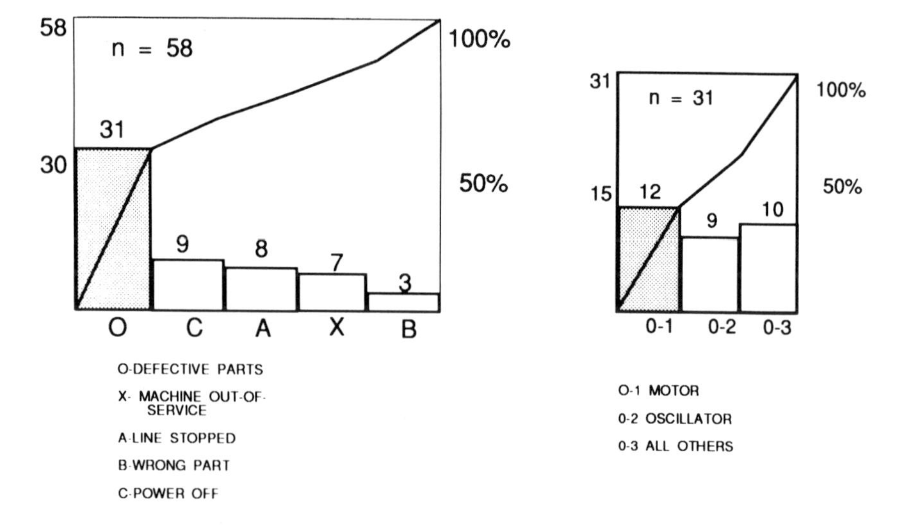

FIGURE 8.13. Total Delays of A and B Lines

a problem, where the root causes can be identified and the results can be seen earlier than they would if the entire problem were tackled at once. The Pareto diagram is a very useful tool to help divide a problem into smaller units.

Check Sheet

To construct a Pareto diagram, you need data. The easiest way to collect data is with a check sheet (see Figure 8.14). Check sheets appear to be the easiest of all the tools to use—and they are. However, a great deal of care needs to be taken ahead of time. First, you must be sure to collect the right data. Next, you must construct the check sheet so that it breaks down or stratifies the data to make analysis easier.

One of the most frustrating things that happens in solving problems is finding out that you have collected the wrong kind of information and need to go back and start all over again. For example, if a team is trying to resolve a problem about defective pumps and collects information on all the types of failures, but

A Form to Collect Data Systematically
REJECTS PRODUCT A
week of September 1, 1991

Type		A	B	C	D	E	F	Total
Line A	am	卌 卌 卌 卌 卌 卌 卌 卌 卌	卌 II	卌 卌 I	卌 卌 卌 卌 I	卌	卌 卌 卌 I	105
	pm	卌 卌 卌 卌 卌 卌 II	III	卌 卌 卌 卌	卌 卌 卌 卌 卌 卌	I	卌	91
Line B	am	卌	I	卌	卌 卌 卌 卌	卌 卌 卌 卌 I	卌 卌	62
	pm	卌 I	卌	卌 卌 I	卌 卌 卌 卌 卌 卌 卌 卌 卌 卌 卌 卌 卌 I	卌 I	卌 卌 卌 卌 卌 卌 卌	129
Total		88	16	47	137	33	66	387

DATA COLLECTED BY:
JIM KNOX 1ST SHIFT
PETE WADE 2ND SHIFT

A = HOUSING CRACK D = MOTOR PROBLEM
B = BENT CAGE E = BAD SWITCH
C = MISSING PART F = OTHER

FIGURE 8.14. Check Sheet

fails to collect the manufacturer's name or the vintage year, the data will probably have to be recollected. Teams must think about what data they need to collect, how relevant the data are, and how the data will provide information to help solve the problem.

Fishbone Diagram

Having collected data by means of check sheets, and having organized the results in a Pareto diagram, you will need to begin probing for root causes. One of the most useful and powerful tools in this respect is the fishbone diagram, or Ishikawa diagram, named after one of the great teachers of quality, Dr. Kaoru Ishikawa (and also called the cause-and-effect diagram). This diagram shows the relationship between an output, or quality characteristic, and the factors that caused the result (see Figure 8.15).

Once again, this tool appears to be very simple to use. Employees seem to like it and can begin to use it easily. I have found that this simple tool is one of the most powerful of all thc basic tools. After years of using it at FPL, few employees, including those who were highly skilled in statistics, ended up exhausting the use of this tool. All causes can be organized by major characteristics (e.g., "people," "material," "method," and "machine"), or they can be organized by processes that drive the outcome.

There will again be a tendency to jump to solutions after constructing a fishbone and before verifying the root causes of a problem. Potential root causes must be verified with facts. The check sheet and Pareto diagram can be very useful tools in this

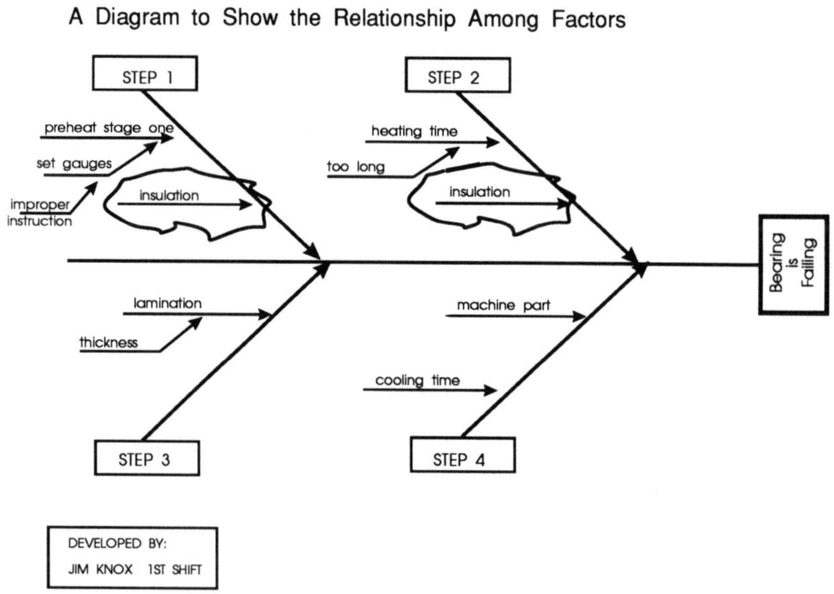

FIGURE 8.15. Fishbone Diagram

regard. If the problem is complicated, more advanced tools (e.g., fault-tree analysis, failure mode and effect analysis, and others), may be necessary to help identify root causes of a problem.

Root causes of a problem will most likely be found after asking and answering the question "why" five times. Most analyses stop after the second why and jump to remedies. The danger in this is that of addressing a symptom and not the root cause. As you review problem solutions, mentally check to see if the five whys have been asked and answered.

THE SEVEN NEW TOOLS

In addition to the seven basic tools of quality, there are also seven "new tools" of quality. I mention these tools because they can be very useful for senior management and staff, particularly employees engaged in planning activities. Once again, the intent here is only to make the reader familiar with the tools and not to teach how to use them. (An excellent reference book for more details is Shigeru Mizuno's *Management For Quality Improvement—The Seven New QC Tools.*[2]) The seven new tools are as follows: affinity diagram, relations diagram, systematic diagram, matrix analysis, matrix data analysis, process decision program chart, and arrow diagram.

Affinity Diagram

The affinity diagram, sometimes referred to as the KJ Method, is used to arrange large amounts of qualitative data into manageable groups (see Figure 8.16). This tool is extremely useful to summarize massive and complex data. It is particularly useful to establish customer requirements when unclear, indeterminate,

[2]Shigeru Mizuno, *Management for Quality Improvement: The Seven New QC Tools* (Cambridge, MA: Productivity Press, 1988).

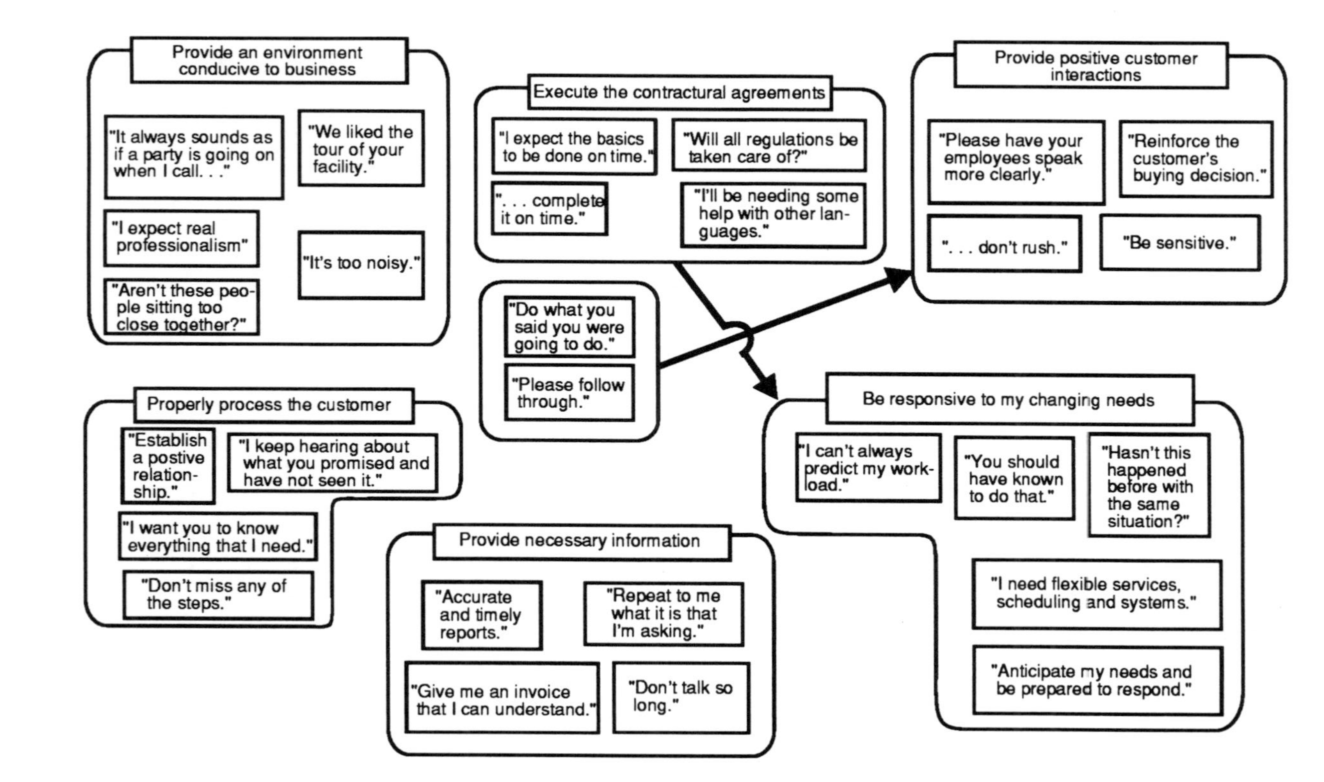

FIGURE 8.16. Affinity Diagram

or unquantifiable specifications are received from the customer. There are six characteristics associated with this tool:

- It is designed to collect facts and opinions about unexplored areas.
- The data are arranged by mutual affinity.
- Old ideas can be broken down and arranged to form a new way of thinking.
- Using the tool requires the use of nonlinear (or "right-brain") thinking.
- It is useful when organizing a planning team.
- The tool is very useful as a communications vehicle.

Relations Diagram

The relations diagram is used to clarify intertwined relationships involving complex problems or situations (see Figure 8.17). There are a number of uses for this tool throughout the organization. For senior management, the relations diagram can assist in de-

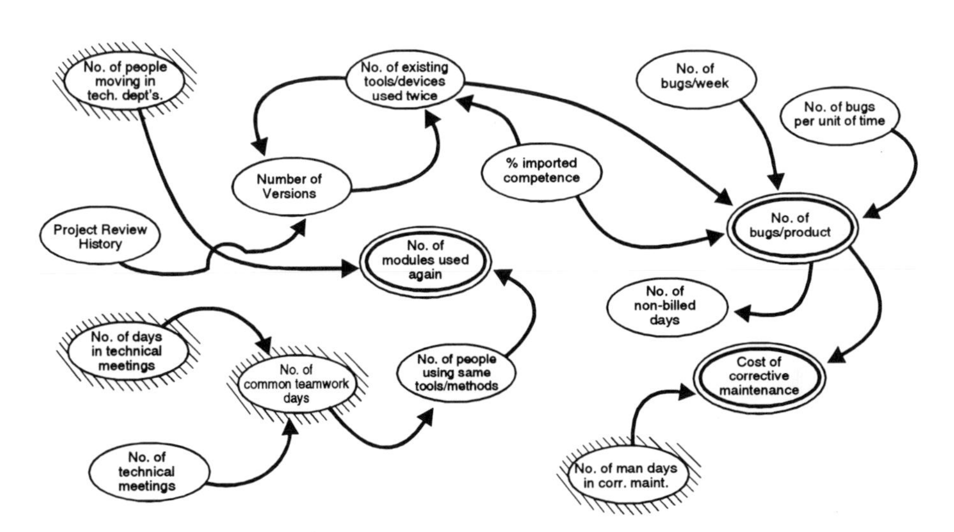

FIGURE 8.17. Relations Diagram

termining and developing policy and in summarizing customer requirements and business problems. The characteristics of this tool are:

- It is useful for organizing problems with complex cause-and-effect relationships.
- It helps with the examination of problems from a broad perspective.
- Major factors can be accurately identified.
- The diagram has no form or model restrictions.
- The diagram facilitates consensus building.

Systematic Diagram

The objective of the systematic diagram is to develop and confirm objectives and means (see Figures 8.18 and 8.19). For senior management, this tool is extremely useful to test the proper interpre-

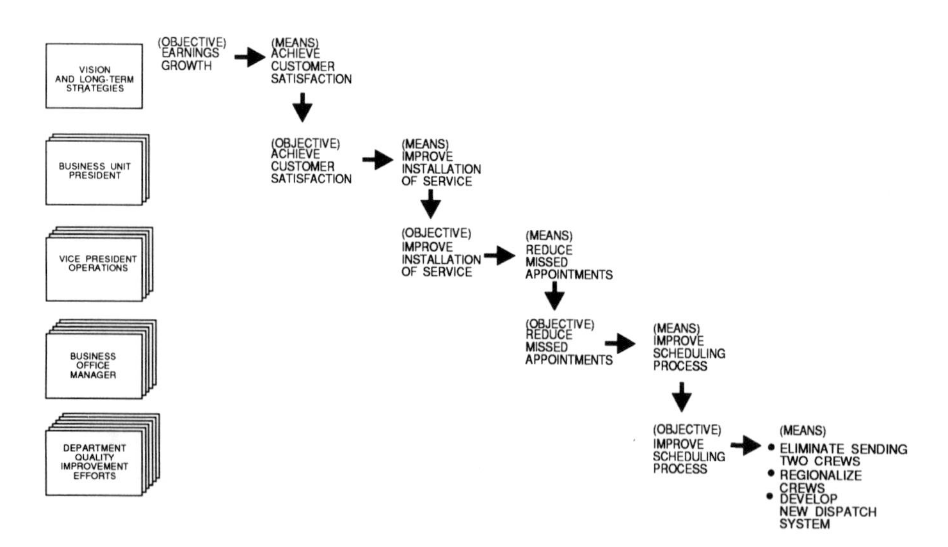

FIGURE 8.18. Identifying Objectives and Means Using a Systematic Diagram

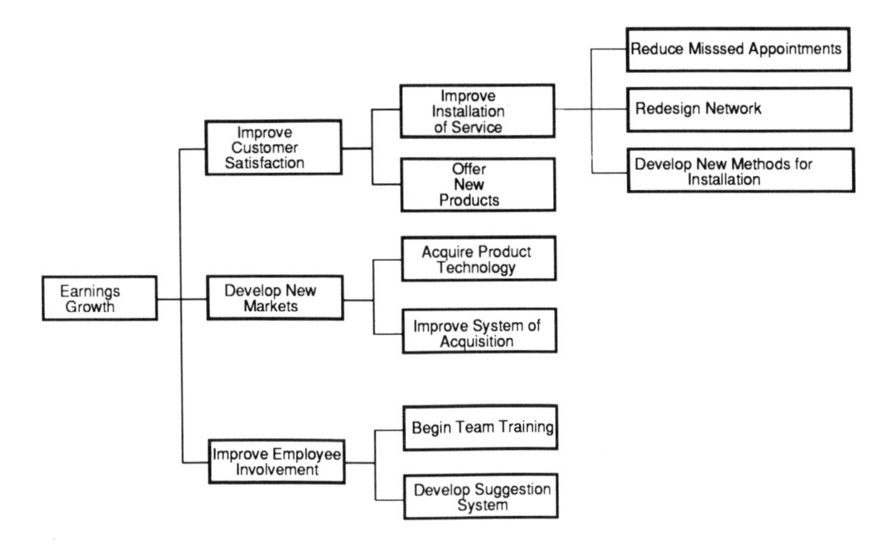

FIGURE 8.19. Systematic Diagram

tation of policy. It is a way to check how subsequent layers of management have interpreted and applied a given policy. Each layer should take the means given and use it as their objective and, in turn, create a new means. The process can also be used in reverse to examine how projects contribute to the making of corporate policies. The characteristics of the systematic diagram are:

- It identifies objectives and the means to achieve them.
- It clarifies departmental and control functions.
- It illustrates cause-and-effect relationships.
- It assists in the coordination of the development of quality improvement when used with the process flowchart.

Matrix Diagram

The matrix diagram is used to analyze the relationships between different factors, to clarify areas of importance (see Figure 8.20).

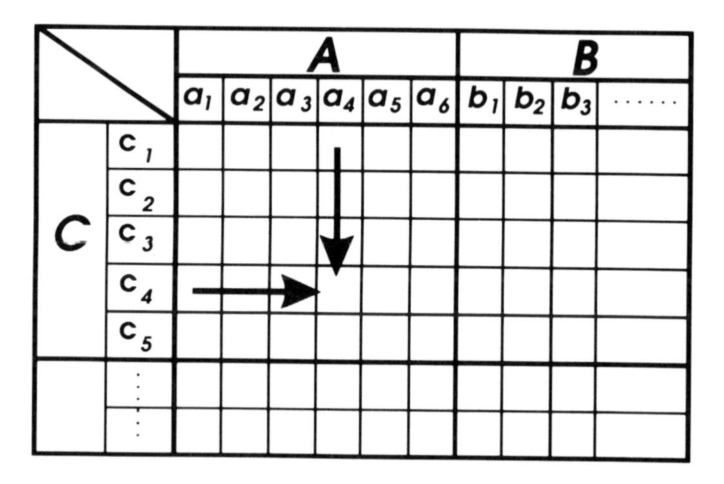

FIGURE 8.20. Matrix Diagram

This tool can be of great assistance to senior management as it begins its evaluation and selection of policies. The tool is used to look at the relationship between, for instance, the voice of the customer and the voice of the business, or in an evaluation of competitive factors affecting the adoption of business objectives. The characteristics of this tool are:

- It is designed to lay out important factors.
- It assists in understanding complex relationships.
- It allows for the study of problems from multiple points of view.

Matrix Data Analysis

Matrix data analysis is a technique to arrange the data in a matrix diagram so that a large array of numbers can be visualized and understood easily (see Figure 8.21). Once again, this tool is useful to senior management in evaluating marketing strategies, qualitative and quantitative performance, and performance as compared to customer requirements. These evaluations are extremely important when establishing policy. The characteristics of the tool are:

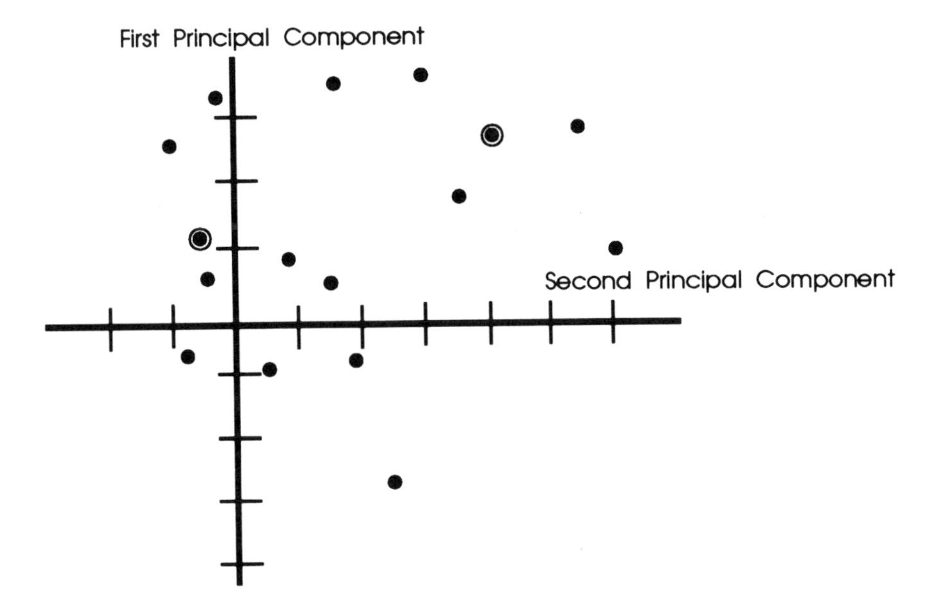

FIGURE 8.21. Matrix-Data Analysis

- It quantifies and arranges data for easy visualization.
- It is the only numerically geared tool of the seven new tools.
- It is a major technique that is used in principal-component analysis.
- Satisfaction and importance measurements from marketing data are sometimes arranged in this format.

Process Decision Program Chart (PDPC)

The PDPC chart is used to assist in selecting the best processes to use by evaluating events and probable outcomes (see Figure 8.22). It is also useful in contingency planning, particularly in evaluating failures or undesirable outcomes. The characteristics of the chart are:

- It highlights difficulties that can occur during a process.
- Several approaches for a desired outcome are considered.

- It allows adjustment for a selected approach as new information becomes available.
- It assists in dealing with events that are dynamic in nature.
- It assists in comprehending the actions of the system as a whole.

Arrow Diagram

The arrow diagram is a tool to establish an appropriate daily plan for a project and is used to review its progress (see Figure 8.23). This is probably the most widely used tool among managers who control projects. Its roots can be found in a number of operational tools used by business, including PERT and CPM. The characteristics of the arrow diagram are:

- It graphically displays a plan.
- It assists in reviewing a plan during the planning stage.
- It can accommodate changes in the plan or conditions.
- Delays can be communicated accurately and promptly.
- It assists in getting an overview of large projects.
- It helps prioritize control processes.

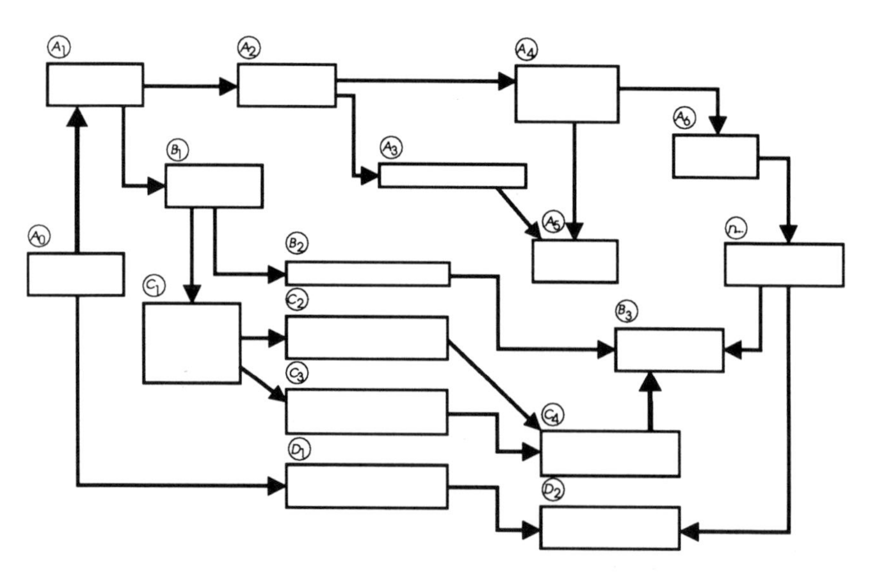

FIGURE 8.22. Process Decision Program Chart

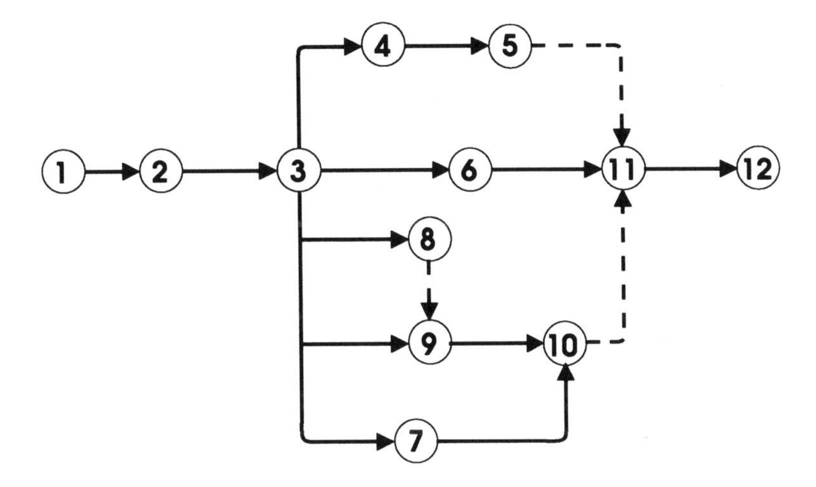

FIGURE 8.23. Arrow Diagram

ADVANCED TOOLS

Senior management also has some responsibilities when it comes to more advanced statistical tools such as fault tree analysis, regression analysis, design of experiments, and failure mode and effect analysis. Senior management may not need to be as knowledgeable about these tools, because they are used for more complicated problems and generally after a quality program has matured. But managers must make sure that there are a sufficient number of trained specialists available who are skilled in the use and application of advanced tools. As team problem-solving abilities mature, senior management will need to understand what tools are available, how to recognize them, how to determine when they should be used, how to identify their misapplication, and when to call in an expert. Courses designed to familiarize senior management with such advanced statistical tools should be considered.

CONCLUSION

Without a systematic problem-solving process, Policy Management and Daily Management activities cannot be effectively performed. The seven basic tools, the QI story, the seven new tools, and advanced statistical tools provide any company with an effective "tool box" for solving business problems and improving products and services, thereby improving customer loyalty and satisfaction. Besides solving business problems, a systematic approach provides the means to improve communication among all layers in the company. Select a problem-solving method that is suited for the business operations and the culture of the company, and use it rigorously. Teach employees the methods and the tools, and a great, untapped reservoir of improvements will be the reward.

9

Suggestion Systems

INTRODUCTION

At least one of the objectives in a total quality approach is employee involvement in the improvement of business operations. Companies that have adopted a TQM way of doing business typically institutionalize some sort of team activity. Teams, teamwork, and team activity provide a means to get people to work together and instill an atmosphere of cooperation. Teams members are taught the value and power of synergy, together with learning the statistical tools of quality and a systematic problem-solving process. Teams, particularly natural teams, are also taught methods to generate improvement opportunities, such as by "brainstorming" ideas for improvements or identifying problem areas in the workplace. Such brainstorming sessions produce lists of opportunities for improvement.

Not all problems, however, require the depth of analysis of a disciplined problem-solving process, and may not require the use of statistical tools. Solutions to problems can sometimes be very obvious and problems can be solved quickly. Unless there is a ready outlet to identify and solve these types of problems, however, teams may end up using detailed and disciplined problem-solving processes unnecessarily. I saw this time and time again at FPL, and it led me to become disenchanted at times with the team process. It often seemed that what the teams were doing amounted to overkill.

This misuse of teams and problem-solving methods was caused mostly by management. To encourage team activity and justify team training, management set some rather arbitrary goals by emphasizing the number of solutions developed. The rationale was that, by emphasizing these goals, managers and supervisors would be encouraged to increase team involvement. Managers and supervisors were held accountable for these goals and included them as part of their annual review. They responded to the challenge by forcing teams to complete the seven-step problem-solving process, even if the problem was relatively insignificant and the solution was obvious. This was understood to be a form of management by fact. Obviously, we had lost sight of what we were trying to achieve: we were encouraging activity for activity's sake rather than the quality of the results.

The company also had a suggestion system that almost seemed to discourage suggestions. We had unwittingly, over time, established barriers, hurdles, and systems that would discourage even the most persistent employee. We did not properly understand the role and the importance of a suggestion system.

In most companies, some individuals may not always do well in a team environment, but are full of bright and exciting ideas. They can still make a valuable contribution to the improvement of your company, as long as management provides an effective and efficient mechanism for them to put forth their ideas within a corporate culture that encourages this process.

Companies that have developed a total quality approach to management have recognized that there is a need to supplement team activity. First, a mechanism needs to be in place to handle those team-identified problems that require little or no analysis, and that can be resolved quickly and easily. Second, an outlet must be provided for individuals to participate outside the team setting. A good suggestion system, then, will satisfy both of these needs. A suggestion system is an essential structure that needs to be present in a TQM approach to management. Suggestion systems definitely support the process of continuous improvement.

LESSONS FROM JAPAN

Every time I visit a Japanese company, I am astonished by the number of suggestions that are submitted and adopted. Japanese companies tap organizational brain power at every turn. In the case of FPL, we eventually became a little embarrassed by both the participation rate and the total number of suggestions submitted. We thought we had been teaching respect for people and their ideas, but at times these words more accurately described what was intended and not what was actually happening.

The company had had a suggestion system since 1925, and many executives believed it was as good as any other. Between 500 and 600 suggestions a year were being received. When FPL first adopted its quality program, the suggestion level did not change much. With an employee population of 15,000, it appeared that we were not doing as good a job as we could of encouraging employee participation, nor had we developed an atmosphere in which employees could feel that management listened to them. We apparently had not changed our basic management style at all; we did not practice what we preached. Less than 2% of our employee population was participating, while other major companies whose suggestion systems we had studied, Maytag Co., for instance, with an employee population one-third the size of FPL's, had a 95% participation rate and four times the number of suggestions!

When we finally began an overhaul of the suggestion system, we put together a pilot program for a new system, but it was a half-hearted attempt that was declared a failure early on. There were field managers within the company who had been using the new system and were just beginning to report significant increases in the number of suggestions received, but the new system was abandoned nonetheless. I began to believe that the status quo would be allowed to remain in place forever, which seemed doubly unfortunate in light of the exciting new TQM precepts we were beginning to use in so many other areas.

We began looking at what was being done in the area of employee suggestions systems among corporations in Japan, and researched several examples. Impressive to me was an example set by Yokogawa Hewlett-Packard (YHP), whose philosophy was that a suggestion system needed to be big enough to encourage all manner of suggestions, no matter how small or insignificant. The important thing, according to YHP's system, was to encourage employees to use their brains to think about improvement on a daily basis, in every facet of their job. And, if too many or too menial suggestions were received, they were to be dealt with as a minor side effect of a system that encouraged free thinking.

A diversified team composed of representatives of various FPL departments was set up to study the findings from Japan, along with examples of suggestion systems from some U.S. companies. The team also studied FPL's existing system using their learned problem-solving methodology (e.g., root causes and countermeasures).

The findings highlighted two major problems with the old system. Too many restrictions were being put on the types of suggestions that employees could make. The first restriction was that suggestions could not be submitted for any issue dealing with wages and benefits. This seemed reasonable enough, but many of the other restrictions did not. Employees were also restricted from turning in any suggestion concerning engineering standards. Even the personnel department, whose responsibility was to encourage and promote employee participation, had placed restrictions. In total, there were pages of restrictions. After revising the system, the only restriction that held up was the one on wages and benefits.

The other problem concerned too much time elapsing between a suggestion's submittal and the end result. The network for handling suggestions was burdened by cumbersome routing, hurdles, and veto power, not to mention evaluation and follow-up. According to corporate procedure, all suggestions were sent to the general office for evaluation. When someone sends something to the general office, it will typically take time to determine what staff department the suggestion should go to, possibly involving rerouting to another department. In addition, once it got to the proper department, the team discovered the staff might have little understanding of what employees in the field were recommending. Staff departments could not appreciate the field conditions and often were in no position to properly evaluate the suggestion. Because the suggestion system was anonymous, there was no efficient way for staff to get additional information so that a more informed judgment could be made. Often the pride of the staff department became visible. How could anyone in the field know more about the subject matter than they did? They were the corporate-level experts.

More than 50 percent of the suggestions ended up being rejected. Supervisors were unaware that their employees had submitted suggestions because the process was confidential. The anonymous system was put in place in the 1930s to protect employees who went over the heads of their supervisors. The anonymous system was probably good at one time, but had no place in the open atmosphere that we were trying to promote. If the suggestion finally received approval from the staff department, it then was submitted to a "suggestion committee" made up of higher-level managers, who often disagreed with the staff recommendation and rejected the suggestion.

To rehabilitate the system, the team recommended that all suggestions be sent first to the employee's direct supervisor, who would be in the best position to evaluate them and, if deemed worthy, implement them in the workplace. Suggestions would no longer be evaluated by staff departments unless a suggestion was first recommended and implemented by local management and then recommended for company wide adoption. Management accepted the team's recommendation.

There were a number of time-related problems the team identified. The most serious was that a suggestion took, on average, *144 days* to get through the system and receive an answer. Companies with excellent suggestions programs (e.g., Maytag) were completing the process in less than half the time. Why would an employee ever submit a suggestion if it took nine months to receive a response? The team recommended a maximum of *five days*. Management agreed.

Another of the team's finding was that, of all the suggestions submitted, less than one-half ever received a recognition award for being implemented and producing good results. This was very discouraging for the employees, and a poor record compared to companies that were considered progressive in employee involvement. Finally, the most discouraging of the team's findings was that, of all the suggestions approved by the staff departments, less than one-half were ever implemented. Why, again, would any employee waste time and energy thinking of ways to improve the company, if there were so little chance that management would implement their ideas?

Another finding was that the system encouraged employees to solve corporatewide problems rather than local-level ones. These types of problems are much larger in scope, and rarely solvable through employee suggestion systems. The team recommended that, while not actually discouraging employees from suggesting improvements on the corporate level, the new system should encourage them to look within their own workplace for improvement, where it would be easier for an employee's supervisor or manager to determine the value of the suggestion.

A number of other changes were recommended by the team as a result of the analysis. The team piloted its changes at several locations in the company, checked the results, and made further changes before bringing the final set of recommendations to senior management. In the pilot locations, participation rates went up to 32% in five months. The piloted locations turned in more suggestions in four months than the entire company had done in the previous year. The team used PDCA to improve the system further.

All the changes the team recommended were adopted. The system was fully implemented later that year and its use in the six months that followed produced amazing results: over 5,000 suggestions were submitted. And, for the first full calendar year after the new program was introduced, over 25,000 suggestions were turned in.

Based on this, several new guidelines were recommended and implemented. The criteria for evaluating suggestions at FPL were as follows:

- The suggester must demonstrate the need for improvement.
- The supervisor must indicate whether the suggestion should be (or will be) implemented, the date it is to be implemented, and the person responsible for the implementation.
- The evaluation is to be made on the basis of how well the suggester has defined the idea and whether the suggestion will improve the suggester's work area or process.
- Any monetary savings, safety considerations, and customer satisfaction criteria should be awarded additional points.

We found that the new suggestion system had a beneficial effect on the team process itself. Teams could turn in suggestions produced during their brainstorming sessions. Team members felt better because they did not have to use a rigid problem-solving process for problems with obvious solutions. They were also encouraged because they saw things happening faster.

Not only was the number of suggestions submitted amazing, but the number implemented was equally amazing. The participation rate soared to over 50% and the implementation rate went from less then 25% to 70%. In retrospect, these were not sophisticated changes. They were logical and simple problem-solutions. But everyone felt better about what was going on. There was a wealth of good ideas previously untapped because the management system had placed barriers in the way. For 1990, FPL estimated the cost savings (and cost avoidance) to be over $13 million. This reinforced my belief that management unknowingly causes most of the problems in an organization. The organization was now beginning to trust the judgment of its first-line employees and supervisors.

REWARD SYSTEM

There are a number of effective reward systems. By far, the most important consideration is to ensure that employees' suggestions are implemented quickly. The next most important is that an employee's direct manager or supervisor recognize the employee's contribution. Once these two features are in place, a number of financial rewards suitable to your company's business culture and financial circumstances may also be considered. Personally, my least favorite reward system is cash compensation, although a number of companies have had great success with this approach. Cash compensation schemes range from a percentage of the first year's savings to flat amounts. Cold cash would seem, however, to be the least lasting of rewards. It tends to encourage only those suggestions that can be measured in terms of money or savings. Using money as the measure of everything causes one to lose sight of other important improvement opportunities. Such important quality characteristics as safety, reliability, durability, and a number of others might be overlooked when money is used to identify and reward success. If you do choose a cash method of reward, however, look to compensate employees whose suggestions are not easily measured by money.

Another method used by a number of companies is the "green stamp" system. This system awards points whenever a suggestion is implemented. A certain number of points is given when the suggestion is implemented in the employee's workplace, and additional points are given if the suggestion is recommended by the employee's supervisor for wider application and is implemented in other workplaces. The points are banked by the employee, who can then choose merchandise or vacation trips from a high-value catalog. There are a number of specialty-merchandise or catalog-order companies that can assist with the administrative aspects of this type of program, including customizing a catalog for your company.

The advantage of this method is that it encourages employees to constantly think about developing and making suggestions. An additional benefit is that merchandise can have longer-lasting value than cash. I myself still have a radio I received over 10 years ago in connection with a speaking engagement. I remember exactly when I received it and the occasion. Employees are frequently reminded of their worth when merchandise is given rather than cash.

Other rewards include certificates signed by the supervisor, president, or CEO, lunches, employee-recognition parking spaces, and a host of other low-cost rewards. But you should not be concerned about the particular reward system chosen until you get the basic system right. Be sure that the system encourages employees to come forth freely with their good ideas without fear of retribution.

CONCLUSION

A suggestion and reward system is an integral part of any management system that adopts the principles of TQM. It reinforces such values as respect for people and their ideas. It strengthens the concept of continuous improvement. It helps break down traditional organizational barriers and it improves communication between employees and management. Most important, it is an inexpensive and effective means for improving the products and services you provide, as well as the overall quality of work life.

In designing or modifying your suggestion system, be on the lookout for barriers that discourage employee participation. These barriers take many forms and shapes. The underlying barrier is the attitude management has toward its employees. If there are barriers that prevent open communication, methods must be devised to overcome them. Delay implementing or revising a suggestion system until all levels of management are willing to listen to and accept suggestions.

Look for too many levels or links in the chain of required approvals. Encourage a system that focuses on improvement in the employee's own workplace rather than for global change—suggestions that the employee's direct supervisor can properly evaluate and approve. If your system requires all suggestions to be approved at the corporate level, it must be changed. This says that management does not trust its people. It says that staff controls and decides everything.

Be on the lookout for approval processes that take too long. Keep the process simple and swift (see Figure 9.1). Suggestion systems must demonstrate quick response time. Time is important

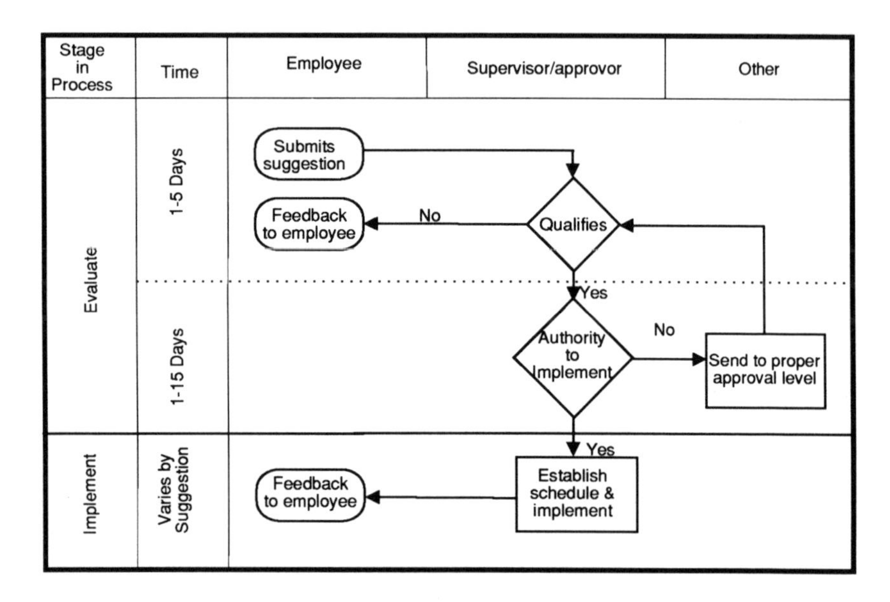

FIGURE 9.1. Suggestion Process

to show employees that management cares. It is also important because the faster one can improve the company, the better its products and services will be, and the better will be its competitive edge.

10

The Implementation Plan

> "It must be remembered that there is nothing more difficult to plan, more doubtful of success, nor more dangerous to manage than the creation of a new system. For the initiator has the enmity of all who would profit by the preservation of the old institution and merely lukewarm defenders in those who would gain by the new ones."
>
> Machiavelli, *The Prince* (1513)

INTRODUCTION

As with any important business task, a good implementation plan will help guide a company toward achieving measurable results. A quality implementation plan is a road map for the organization to effect change. The plan should establish times when tasks should be accomplished, responsibilities for accomplishing the tasks, and expected milestones to be achieved.

In creating a plan for implementing TQM, patience is the first attribute that senior management must learn and practice. A total quality management system takes time to initiate and integrate with the hundreds of existing business processes in a company. The task is to change the way you do business, the very culture of your company. Dr. Harry Levinson, a noted industrial psychologist, once told me that if you want to make a significant change in a company's culture, plan on taking 10 years. He advised that some companies try to make a cultural shift too fast and, even if the intent is good, the organization may not be ready or able to adapt to rapid change. I know of few senior managers who would have the patience to wait 10 years to see results; however, Dr. Levinson's warning should be considered when developing any plan that will have such a pervasive impact on the company's culture. For most purposes, I believe a five-year period should be adequate for fully implementing TQM.

Although patience may be the top consideration or attribute, the second attribute that senior management must exhibit is a sense of urgency. Senior managers must exhibit a burning need and passion for getting on with it, or risk failure because of a lack of attention. Organizations often respond better to change when there is clear evidence that a crisis is looming. A TQM implementation plan can be shortened when the corporate culture is extremely adaptive and responsive to change.

Most senior managers know there is no such thing as a perfect implementation plan. Plans need to be checked and revised as circumstances warrant. Senior managers also know that you need a plan to guide you. There are several points that you will need to consider before putting a formal plan together.

One of the more important issues deals with management turnover. Senior management turnover is important because inevitably senior management will either retire, die, or be replaced, and the new management may not want to continue pursuing a change in business practice that has not already taken foothold in the organization. Even if the new management process is fully integrated into the business practices, new managers will most likely want to put their own mark on the organization and may abandon what has been done. This will be particularly true if the new management was not a part of the planning for change or if it came from outside the company or organization.

Many restructurings are designed to either gain or relinquish control. All too often there is a "purging" of the predecessors' practices and policies by the new chief executive. I am surprised and dismayed when I read about massive changes in management that take place after a new CEO takes charge. Certainly there are times when major changes are warranted, but most of the time it is because the new top person has his or her own agenda and the only way to make their mark is by discrediting their predecessor's work.

Quality programs have failed because of a change of direction resulting from turnover in senior management not only in the U.S., but also in Japan. In planning the implementation of a quality management system, the CEO must consider the continuity of top management. Why waste resources training people if the next person to head the company cares or knows little about quality concepts? The organization will only become resentful and angry for having made the investment. Nevertheless, there will always be those who are overjoyed when quality practices are abandoned, because many TQM practices require a more disciplined approach to management that some people resent.

As is true with any change in management practices, systems, or processes, when implementing TQM consideration must be given to how the organizational structure needs to be modified (if at all). There are many cases where systems have failed because inadequate attention was given to the effects the system had on the existing organizational structure.

I have seen examples of new computer systems and processes being introduced without giving any consideration to the organization. Often the systems are merely tacked on to the existing organization. They are introduced without considering how the organization should be changed to take advantage of the new system, and the result is usually tragic.

As with new computer systems, so too a quality management system is a major change in management processes. The organizational structure must therefore be adjusted to gain its fullest advantage.

PLANNING APPROACHES

There are different approaches that can be used to successfully implement a total quality process in an organization. The method employed depends on the existing culture of your company, the training resources available, and the necessity and urgency to make the change.

I include here four basic approaches that I have seen used. As a word of caution when preparing a plan, do not turn over the implementation of TQM to your quality department professionals without personal supervision by senior management. The plan should actually be created and overseen by senior management to gain everyone's enthusiasm and commitment.

Top-Down Approach

The top-down approach is one of the better strategies for implementing a quality program. The method involves educating top management in ordered stages, followed at each stage by middle management, first-line supervision, and first-line employees. Each stage of the process is therefore repeated and carried out over a long period, with each group being educated in the various segments of the total plan. This is a logical approach for training, but it can take an enormous amount of time to accomplish. It builds the necessary commitment and participation from the top of the organization, which is one of the most critical factors for success.

The top-down approach to implementation can be accelerated by conducting parallel or overlapping training sessions. Much will depend on the level of resources a company is willing to devote. This modified top-down approach may also cause some confusion in the organization as one group gets ahead of the group below it. This situation should be of no special concern, as any change in management processes takes time and not all business units will progress at the same speed. The advantages of the top-down approach are:

- Leadership is clearly being directed by senior management.
- The organization grows together in their understanding of the principles of quality.
- The implementation proceeds according to the existing structure of the organization.
- Less of a separate training and support organization is needed and the method can avoid imposing an "artificial" structure.

The principal disadvantage is the time it takes. Depending on the size of an organization, this approach may take several years just to get started. If you have the luxury of time and have limited resources to devote to training and education, however, this method will probably show a higher probability of success as compared to other methods.

Squeezing-the-Middle Approach

In teaching basic problem-solving tools, team activity, and basic statistical techniques, the "squeeze-the-middle approach" can be effective. Here, middle management is left out of the loop temporarily until both senior management and first-line employees are taught the basics. Middle managers can often be the most difficult to convince that a new management process is in their best interest. This is generally because they became middle managers in the first place based on their being expert in some existing management process. If you choose this method, middle managers should be informed in advance that they are being left out only temporarily and will be included at a later time. It is also helpful to gather success stories after a sufficient amount of the work force has had a chance to practice their hand at being part of the improvement process. These success stories can then be used to promote the new management system to middle managers. Advantages of this approach include:

- Gets the organization up and running sooner.
- Gives an opportunity to more fully assess the role of middle management.
- Develops a "new language" that facilitates communication between senior management and first-line employees.

There are also some disadvantages to this approach. The middle part of your organization can become very frustrated because they will have been left out of the initial training. However, good middle managers will learn as much as they can on their own—they will not wait for formal training classes. If you choose this type of implementation strategy, you should develop a communication plan that explains your reasoning and a schedule that lets everyone know when they will be brought into the process.

Bottom-Up Approach

The bottom-up approach of implementing TQM starts quality training efforts with the first-line workers. Often there is a belief that quality problems are produced by the worker and if quality is to be improved it is the worker who must improve. Although this approach seems to be used by the majority of companies implementing TQM, I believe this method is the primary reason why so many quality approaches fail to achieve significant results. Without the complete involvement of senior management there will be little direction and significant resources will be spent on training with little return on investment. Avoid this approach and avoid consultants who promote it. The advantages are that:

- Implementation can begin almost immediately.
- Isolated improvements will be realized.

The disadvantages, however, are more significant:

- Improvement efforts will not be coordinated.
- Multiple methods will evolve with no common language or approach developed.
- Senior management will have little idea what is happening.

A BETTER APPROACH: THE LEVELIZED APPROACH

Each of the approaches above has advantages and disadvantages. An ideal plan is one that capitalizes on the advantages of the other approaches while overcoming most of the disadvantages. The "levelized approach" recognizes that senior management is the key to success, but also recognizes that senior management is often impatient and wants to see some immediate improvements without waiting for major cultural change to take place. The levelized approach retains all the advantages of starting with Policy Management while at the same time identifying quick payback opportunities. This approach also uses the concepts of JIT training so that training is done to achieve results and not simply for training's sake. The approach is divided into four phases: direction, mobilize, improve, and accelerate.

Direction

Phase I — direction — establishes the foundation, style, vision, and schedule for introducing TQM (see Figure 10.1). This phase also identifies the critical areas for improvement, the "vital few" process areas that have the highest likelihood of affecting the customer. The direction phase begins with senior management preparing a customized implementation plan, one that meets the business needs of the company. The purpose of preparing the plan is to communicate to the organization some common understanding of what is expected and when and how TQM will be introduced. In this phase, an initial road map is developed and a new language will be institutionalized that is common to all members of the organization. The tasks to be accomplished, the principles and practices to be adopted, and the assignment of responsibilities are identified and assigned.

An analysis and synthesis of business problems follows. The purpose is to objectively examine the most serious problems facing the company and to narrow them down to the most critical ones. In parallel, senior management directs the analysis of customer needs, looking for gaps in performance from a customer viewpoint. The outcome of the two analyses provides the foundation for senior management to confirm or establish the vision of the company as well as providing valuable information to begin Phase II.

Through the analysis of customer needs, the most significant business processes are identified. Immediate improvement activities can begin in the areas classified. Redesigning and streamlining of those processes that have the greatest likelihood of influencing the quality of the product or service to customers can begin, thereby creating early improvement opportunities

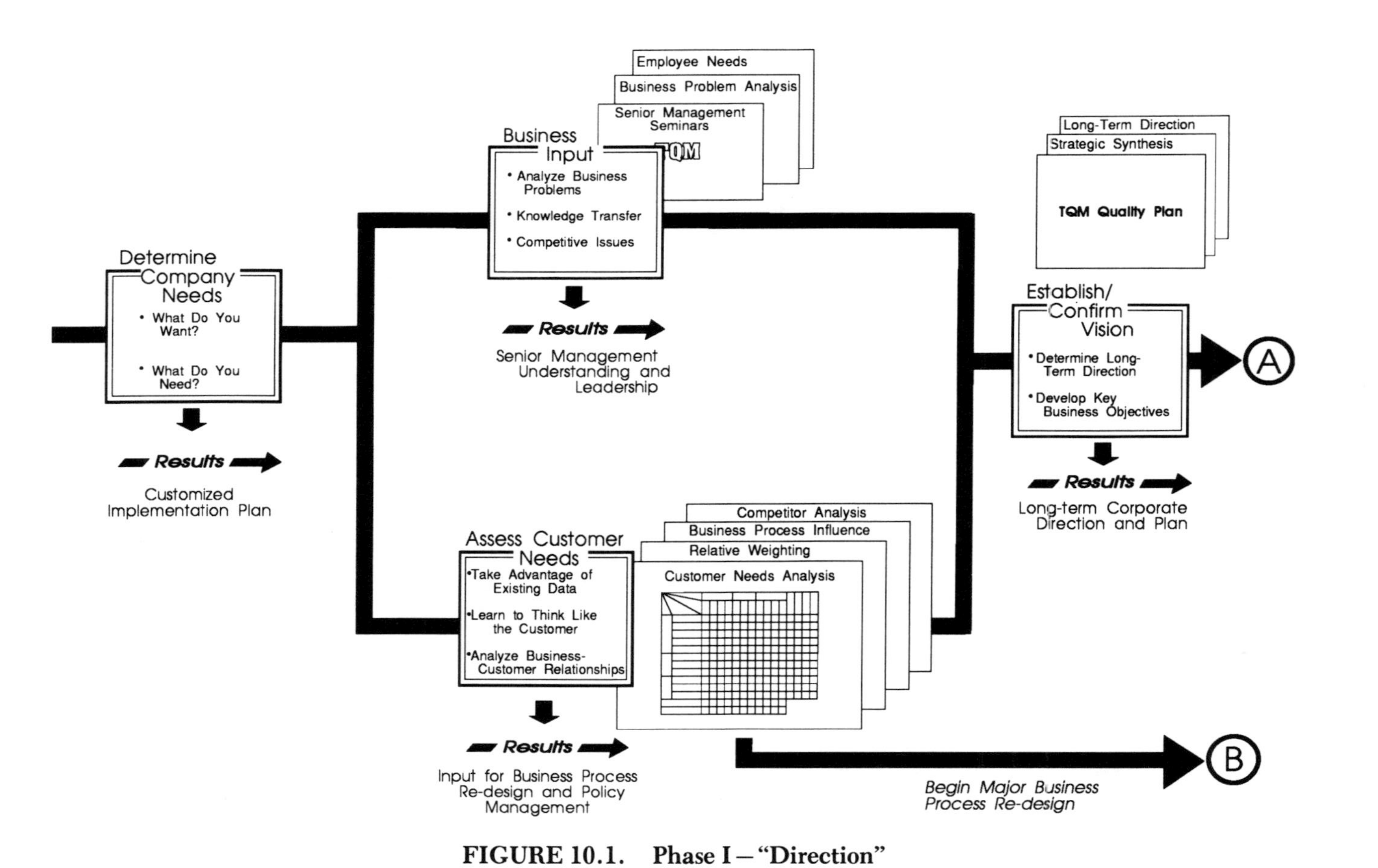

FIGURE 10.1. Phase I – "Direction"

while policy is being formulated and deployed. The method ensures that resources spent to improve processes are those that can have the greatest effect on the customer.

Mobilize

There are three major segments of Phase II — mobilize (see Figure 10.2). First, policy is developed and deployed. The results of identifying major gaps in performance from the customer point of view and of analyzing of the most serious business problems are examined and reduced to those problems that have the greatest impact on the potential success of the company. Measurements and targets are established and the policies are deployed. Contributions to each policy are negotiated with each business unit, teams are formed, and projects selected. This is one of the more critical steps in the implementation process, because deployment is intended to make major improvements in key business areas.

Second, training in a systematic problem-solving method can begin so that improvements can be made on the policy items identified. The training is JIT. Classroom work can be put to a useful test.

Third, process improvement can begin in earnest. Those business processes that have the highest impact on customer satisfaction are the best places to begin re-engineering. By restricting process improvement activities to the most highly leveraged business processes, resources can be focused to improve processes that make a real difference. This is a very different approach from that used by many companies who tend to use a "shotgun" approach, hoping that they will hit something by overwhelming process improvement with a massive amount of resources and activity.

Improvement

Phase III — improvement — acts to expand the implementation and training throughout the company (see Figure 10.3). Daily Management activities are introduced to ensure that improve-

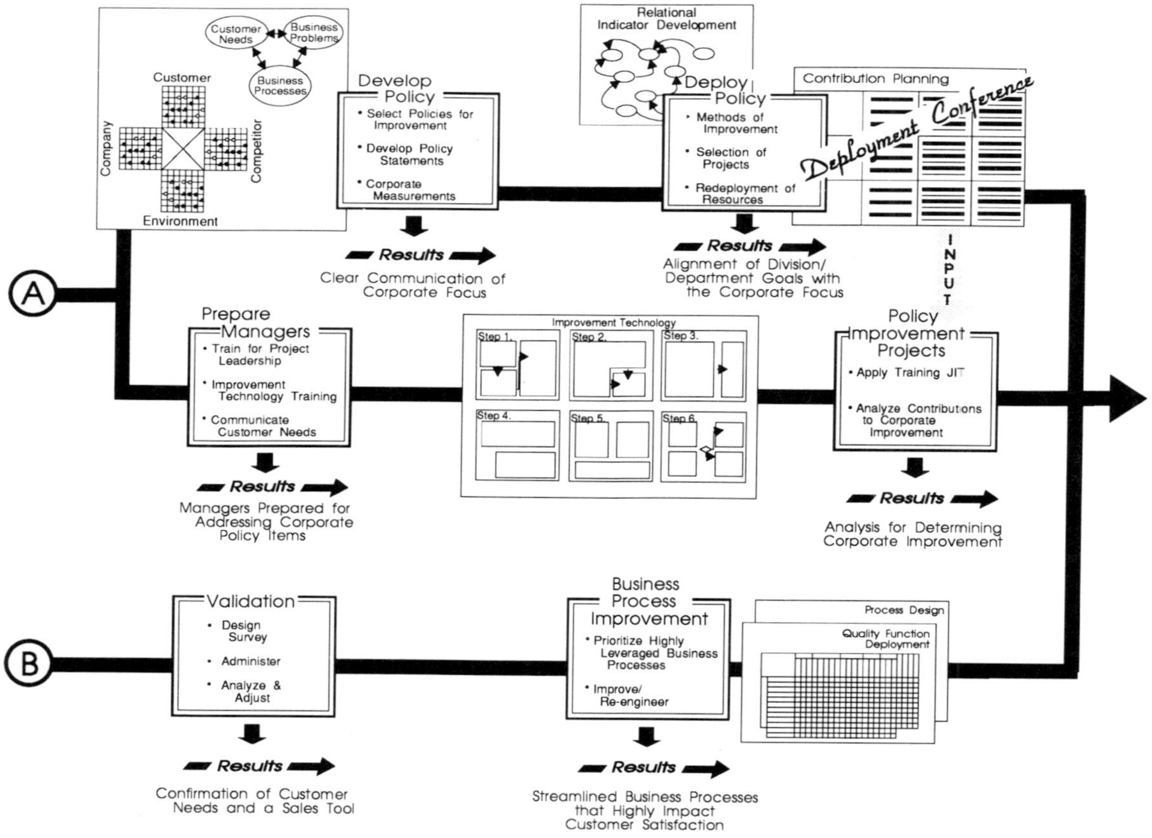

Customer Needs
Business Problems
Business Processes
Customer
Company
Competitor
Environment

Develop Policy
- Select Policies for Improvement
- Develop Policy Statements
- Corporate Measurements

Results
Clear Communication of Corporate Focus

Relational Indicator Development

Deploy Policy
- Methods of Improvement
- Selection of Projects
- Redeployment of Resources

Results
Alignment of Division/ Department Goals with the Corporate Focus

Contribution Planning
Deployment Conference
INPUT

Prepare Managers
- Train for Project Leadership
- Improvement Technology Training
- Communicate Customer Needs

Results
Managers Prepared for Addressing Corporate Policy Items

Improvement Technology
Step 1.
Step 2.
Step 3.
Step 4.
Step 5.
Step 6.

Policy Improvement Projects
- Apply Training JIT
- Analyze Contributions to Corporate Improvement

Results
Analysis for Determining Corporate Improvement

Validation
- Design Survey
- Administer
- Analyze & Adjust

Results
Confirmation of Customer Needs and a Sales Tool

Business Process Improvement
- Prioritize Highly Leveraged Business Processes
- Improve/ Re-engineer

Results
Streamlined Business Processes that Highly Impact Customer Satisfaction

Process Design
Quality Function Deployment

FIGURE 10.2. Phase II – "Mobilize"

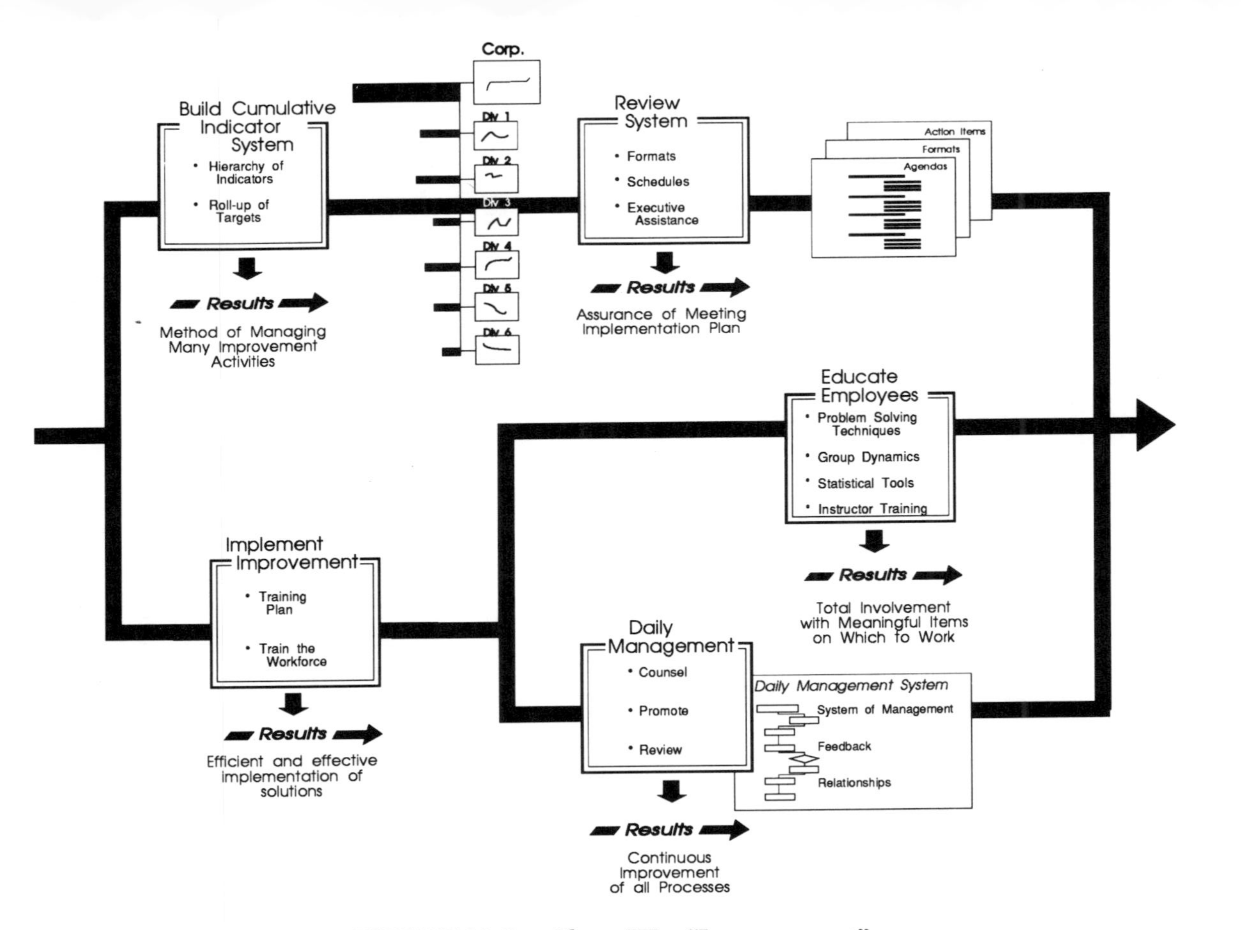

FIGURE 10.3. Phase III – "Improvement"

ment gains are maintained while keeping under control the day-to-day activities that are critical to meeting customers' needs and expectations. Team activity at all levels is actively promoted to gain support for improvement in both policy matters and daily work. The effort to convert the whole company to a TQM management style occurs in Phase III.

A system of indicators is introduced to track progress on policy. Without a measurement and tracking method, improvement activities may not become aligned. It is essential to know what progress is being made and whether the progress meets the commitments that have been negotiated. To support tracking, a systematic review or checking process is also introduced at this phase. A review system is a means to promote improvement activities, to ensure that root cause solutions to business problems are found, and to assure that the gains will be maintained.

Accelerate

If there is a business need to have a companywide quality management system, this is the point where the real push must begin (see Figure 10.4). Push to change the company culture. This is a very critical time for management to decide if they want to continue. It is a point when certain individual careers may need to change if people are not willing to participate. The accelerate phase is that time when the entire organization is working in concert with a common focus and employing the tools of quality on a consistent basis.

Phase IV—accelerate—speeds up the change process by encouraging greater employee involvement. A reward and recognition system and a suggestion system are introduced to support employee involvement in cultural change and to promote more open communication among employees, managers, and supervisors.

This is also the time to introduce advanced statistical tools and techniques. The "low hanging fruit" may be picked first and then more advanced tools may be used to help solve more complex business problems. The advanced tools may also be ap-

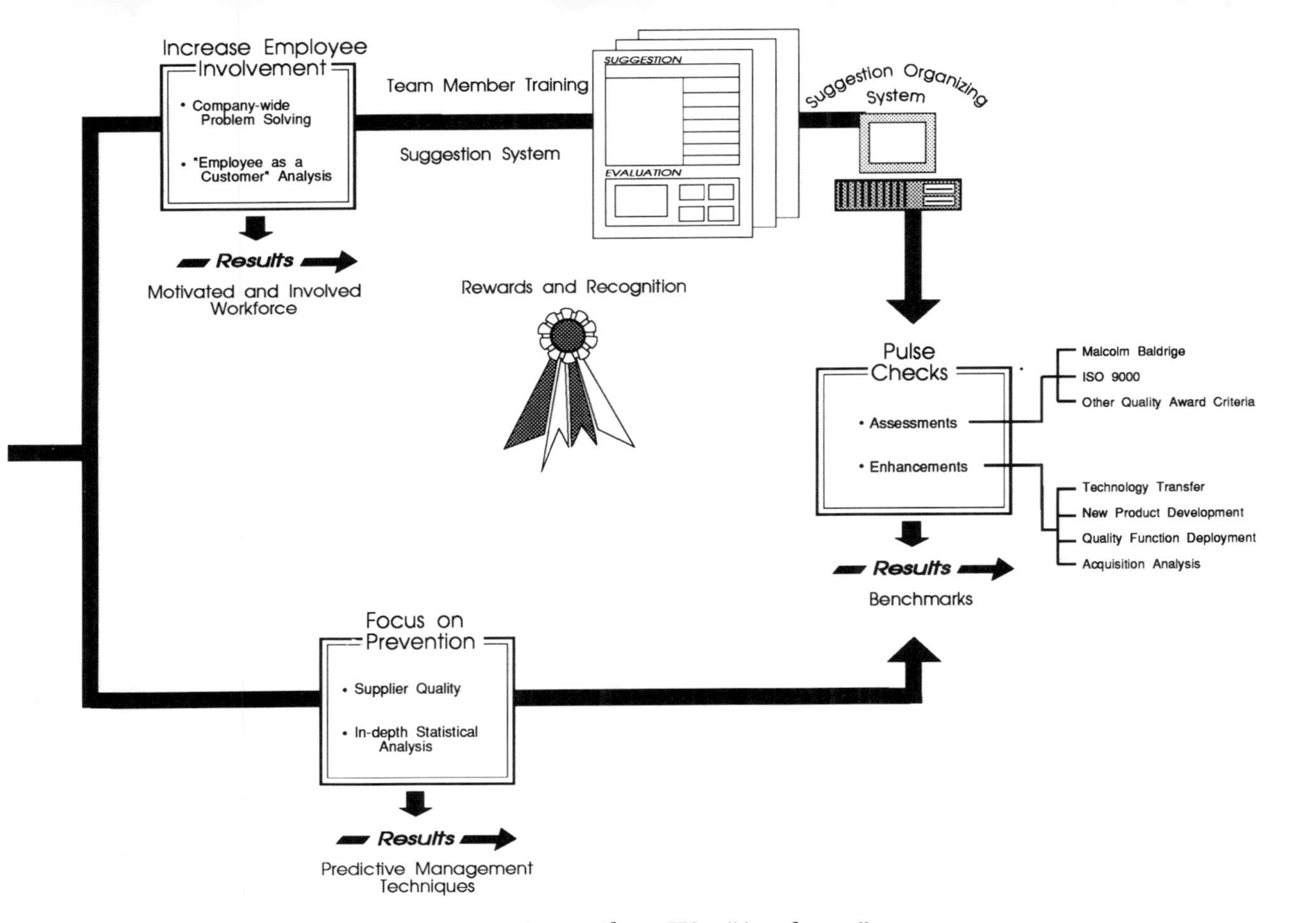

FIGURE 10.4. Phase IV – "Accelerate"

plied to special areas such as new product design or product improvement.

In addition, this is a good time to introduce a vendor quality program. Introducing a vendor program before the company itself has demonstrated a willingness to change normally fails. During this period of implementation, the company has sufficient activities underway and can say "do as I do" rather than "do as I say."

It is advisable to check on overall progress periodically. Although this activity should take place throughout the implementation, a periodic in-depth review can give the company a benchmark evaluation. From the information gained, plans can be adopted to remedy deficiencies found.

LAYING OUT THE PLAN

The four-phased "levelized" approach can provide a logical step-by-step method of implementation. The approach has the advantages of all three previously mentioned methods while overcoming many of their deficiencies. This approach overcomes the time deficiencies of the top-down approach by quickly identifying process improvement opportunities.

As you develop and refine your quality management system and plan, there will be parts of the organization that are more enthusiastic than others. Some departments will progress faster than others. There will even be pockets or even entire departments that have done little if anything. This is a natural consequence of any change in management method or style. Use success stories to convince slower departments or department heads that are not yet aboard and revise the implementation plan accordingly.

There are several ways to arrange the plan. One way is to structure it according to the major phases and specific steps that need to be accomplished. Table 10.1 illustrates one way to subdivide the plan into three broad categories: educate, promote, and develop. For instance, training cannot take place until the course

		PHASE I Direction	PHASE II Mobilize	PHASE III Improvement	PHASE IV Accelerate
EDUCATE	EXECUTIVE	QUALITY CONCEPTS BASIC STATISTICAL TOOLS	CONCEPTS OF ADVANCED TOOLS POLICY/BUSINESS PLANS	REVIEW PROCESS	CONCEPTS OF SQC
	MIDDLE MANAGE-MENT	QUALITY CONCEPTS BASIC STATISTICAL TOOLS	CONCEPTS OF ADVANCED TOOLS POLICY/BUSINESS PLANS	REVIEW PROCESS	CONCEPTS OF SQC
	SUPER-VISION	QUALITY CONCEPTS BASIC STATISTICAL TOOLS	CONCEPTS OF ADVANCED TOOLS POLICY/BUSINESS PLANS SUPERVISING TEAMS	DAILY MANAGEMENT REVIEW	PROMOTING EMPLOYEE SUGGESTIONS CONCEPTS OF SQC
	EMPLOYEE	TQM ORIENTATION	TEAM TRAINING	BASIC STATISTICAL TOOLS	CONCEPTS OF ADVANCED TOOLS
	SPECIALIST	BASIC STATISTICAL TOOLS QFD CONCEPTS	ADVANCED STATISTICAL TOOLS	SQC TRAINING	RELIABILITY TECHNIQUES ADVANCED QFD
PROMOTE	POLICY MANAGE-MENT	CUSTOMER NEEDS ANALYSIS IDENTIFY MAJOR BUSINESS PROBLEMS ESTABLISH CORPORATE VISION	SYSTEM OF INDICATORS SET CORPORATE TARGETS INTEGRATE WITH BUDGET /RESOURCE PROCESS	CROSS FUNCTIONAL COMMITTEES INTRODUCE BUSINESS PLANS REVIEW PROCESS	PULSE CHECKS
	TEAM ACTIVITY	FORM MANAGEMENT TEAMS	TEAM TRAINING	REVIEW PROCESS	TEAM RECOGNITION PROCESS INTRODUCE SUGGESTION SYSTEM
	DAILY MANAGE-MENT	IDENTIFY KEY PROCESSES	REVIEW PROCESS IDENTIFY ACCOUNTABILITIES ESTABLISH MEASUREMENTS PROCESS IMPROVEMENT	IMPLEMENT DAILY MANAGEMENT	IMPLEMENT JIT
	VENDOR QUALITY		VENDOR PAYMENT PROCESS ESTABLISH LIFE CYCLE COST STANDARDS	REVIEW PROCESS CHANGE PURCHASING PRACTICES	IMPLEMENT JIT VENDOR ORIENTATION VENDOR AWARD SYSTEM
DEVELOP	ORGANIZA-TION	PLAN IMPLEMENTATION LEAD TEAMS POLICY COMMITEE OPERATING COMMITTEE	MEASUREMENT SYSTEM	REVIEW SYSTEM SAFETY QUALITY ASSURANCE SERVICE QUALITY ASSURANCE DELIVERY QUALITY ASSURANCE	SUGGESTION SYSTEM PREDICTIVE MAINTENANCE SYSTEM
	TRAINING	SUPERVISING TEAMS QFD CONCEPTS BASIC STATISTICAL TOOLS PROBLEM SOLVING TECHNIQUES TEAM LEADERSHIP	ADVANCED STATISTICAL TOOLS SEVEN NEW TOOLS (FOR STAFF) MANAGEMENT REVIEW METHODS	BUSINESS PLANNING	QUALITY ASSURANCE ADVANCED QFD RELIABILITY TOOLS DESIGN OF EXPERIMENT
	MILE-STONES	CORPORATE VISION ESTABLISHED CORE TRAINING DEVELOPED MANAGEMENT ORIENTATION BEGIN MANAGEMENT BY FACT CUSTOMER NEEDS IDENTIFIED	LONG & SHORT TERM GOALS ESTABLISHED PROBLEM SOLVING PROCESS IN PLACE PROCESS IMPROVEMENT BEGINS	ADVANCED ANALYSIS INTRODUCED INITIATED "CHECK CYCLE" QUALITY ASSURANCE IMPLEMENTED DAILY MANAGEMENT IMPLEMENTED	FULL INTERPRETATION OF QUALITY TEAM RECOGNITION IN PLACE SUGGESTION SYSTEM IN PLACE VENDOR SYSTEM IMPLEMENTED

TABLE 10.1. TQM Implementation Plan

material has been completed, and the plan cannot be promoted without education and training support.

One could also divide the plan into target areas (e.g., management commitment, customer focus, and employee involvement), or organize it in terms of the processes that will be implemented: Policy Management, Daily Management, team activity, and vendor quality. But here the example shown in Table 10.1 will be used to illustrate how a plan can be coordinated.

Educate

In planning the education phase, the first objective is to establish what you want to achieve. Several key questions must be answered to develop this part of the plan. Who is to be trained? What should be taught? When should the training take place? Training activity should be planned to precede actual needs.

To help organize the plan, divide the training portion into groups of people to be trained. The natural organizational structure is a good basis for categorization. Most organizations have some senior management, a layer of middle management, first-level supervision, a staff group, and first-line employees. Some aspects of a total quality management system are very technical requiring more advanced skills. It would be uneconomical to train everyone in these specialized areas. As with any specialty area, there is a need to identify and train a group of highly skilled employees who can be distributed throughout the organization. Their role is to help with complicated problem solving and to provide technical assistance to the organization. The specialists will require extensive skill-based training in advanced statistics. This group of employees should be selected based on aptitude. Except in rare cases, they should not be anyone higher than a first-line supervisor. Recent graduates in engineering often make good candidates.

In the *direction* phase of education, the goal is to have the organization understand what must be accomplished. An overview of a problem-solving process is introduced. Basic statistical tools are taught and initial identification of customer needs are made. Often some quality function deployment (QFD) concepts are developed to help organize customer requirements and expectations.

The *mobilize* phase of education should focus the organization on the customer and begin institutionalizing "management by fact." During the mobilize phase your educational processes are well established. The outcome should be a corporate vision that is focused and clearly articulated to the entire workforce. This is the phase to begin specialist training in advanced statistical tools. These tools must be introduced ahead of their needs.

The *improvement* phase of the education plan will concentrate on the teaching review methods and techniques. All the fundamental training courses should be in place and the entire organization should have had at least one course on basics of quality before entering the accelerate phase.

The *accelerate* phase of education adds tools to the tool box and increases the knowledge level of the organization. This phase also trains managers and supervisors in techniques for encouraging employee participation.

Promote

Promotion means a structured approach to introducing the major components of your new management system. Promotional activities are not the same as public relations (PR) activities. The organization must be convinced that the changes are necessary and that there is a method that must be followed and there are goals that must be achieved. Communication must be clear and focused. If traditional PR-type activities help accomplish this end, they should be used. The real promotional activities involve the application of quality principles and practices.

I am not a fan of "sloganeering." Senior management involvement and participation is far more effective than slogans. However, there is room for slogans because they help the organization to understand the intended purpose of the change and the focus of concentration. Unfortunately, too many companies' quality programs are not much more than slogans, with few if any substantial processes to drive improvement.

There are many ways to organize the promotional plan. At a

minimum, Policy Management, Daily Management, team activity and vendor quality should be identified as major process components. The range of promotional activities can be expanded, depending on both the needs and resources of the company.

In the *direction* phase of promotion, focus the organization on the needs of the customer. During this phase, Policy Management must begin through the identification of gaps in performance and assessment of corporate strategy. The corporate vision should either be developed, changed, or revitalized, and key process improvements targeted.

Identify corporate and unit targets. The tracking indicators and a review process both need to be formulated in the *mobilize* phase in parallel with training teams in problem-solving methodology. Daily Management activities can begin by identifying job accountabilities. Major processes that are either in need of improvement or that have the greatest impact on quality outcomes must be identified. In addition, major processes that are already very good but, if allowed to go out of control, could result in major problems for the customer should also be identified.

Integrate the new management processes into other business processes and systems. During the *improvement* phase, integration of the budgeting and resource planning systems together with the quality management system should begin. If improvements are going to made to areas identified while introducing Policy Management, resources will need to be devoted to making the improvements.

In the improvement phase, cross-functional management should be accomplished. This is critical if there is to be a successful outcome overall. The successful companies I have studied or visited all employ cross-functional cooperation as part of their quality efforts—which is one of the most important reasons why the Japanese have made such incredible progress. These companies know that it takes an integrated organizational approach to achieve quality.

During the *accelerate* phase, all the major components of the implementation plan should be fully integrated. Clear and measurable results should be evident, and planning for the next phases of development should begin. A new corporate culture should begin to emerge, one that is focused on the customer and continuous improvement based on facts and the full use of employee brainpower.

Develop

There are three areas that one should think about in preparing the development part of a plan: organizational development, course development, and milestones.

Organizational Development

Early in this chapter, the implications of a having the organization keep pace with business process changes was discussed. There are several factors that should be kept in mind here. The organization will change as part of implementing a total quality system. For instance, if it has been a practice to have inspectors to check for defects, an objective in implementing a quality system should be to eliminate this type of organizational structure.

Processes will be discovered where transactions go through multiple departments without any apparent value being added for the customer. Such departments, sections, or subsections that do not appear to add value should be carefully examined to see if the process or system can be restructured or eliminated to improve the results for the customer. One must make sure that any organizational barriers responsible for quality defects are removed or restructured.

Often senior management will receive recommendations to change the organization in the name of improving TQM. Senior management must be very careful when such recommendations come forward. For example, one common recommendation that is often proposed is to create a parallel organization and superimpose it on top of the existing structure to improve the implementation of TQM. Quality professionals refer to these people as "facilitators." Do not be fooled into believing that facilitators are the best and only way to speed up the process of implementation. A parallel organization like this will take on a life of its own. Eventually, the rest of the organization will either come to dislike them or the organization will become convinced that quality is someone else's job and not theirs.

Resist recommendations to create a separate facilitator organization. Wherever possible, use the natural organization to implement total quality. There are appropriate uses for facilitators, but they should not predominate your decision to implement TQM. The company's own supervisors and managers should be the ones who act as facilitators.

Although I discourage the role of independent facilitator, I highly recommend that a "specialist" function be established. This function will be very important as more complicated problems need to be solved and as implementation matures. Specialists or "application experts" should be distributed throughout the organization. They will be called in by teams as problems become more complicated. The experts will be needed for design of experiments (DOE) or where complicated reliability problems are encountered. Resist any other recommendations to change the organization when the recommendations are not based on factual evidence.

In the later phases, the organization will need to adapt to new measurement methods and systems, review structures, suggestion systems, and quality assurance systems. Each can have a profound impact on the organization and its structure.

Course Development

Several years ago there was virtually no course material available—at least written in English—that a company could purchase as part of its in-house training material. Today, there are several training packages from firms specializing in training employees. If your organization decides to purchase one, make sure that the material can be modified to meet the company's particular needs. Purchased training material can greatly speed up implementation. If you develop your own training material, make sure initial courses are piloted and perform a rigorous check on their effectiveness.

There are some fundamental courses to consider. A problem-solving process, a method to identify customer needs, and some leadership training will be needed. Advanced training materials (e.g., reliability techniques and advanced statistical tools) do not need to be developed initially. The development of training courses obviously must precede their need. Each course should target the intended audience and identify the results expected.

Milestones

Planning an approach to quality should be detailed enough so that the organization understands the steps that will be taken and the intended outcome. It should not be so detailed that it causes confusion in the organization. For each phase, milestones should be established and checked as they are completed. For instance, in the *mobilize* phase teams are established and trained and a problem-solving process is in place. The effectiveness of the actions must be checked and countermeasures put in place when deficiencies are found. The milestones provide a message to the organization that results are expected.

CONCLUSION

An implementation plan is a guideline to help organize and communicate the desired results. To prepare and communicate such a plan, senior management must think about the approach it wishes to take: top down, squeezing the middle, bottom up, or levelized. No plan should be introduced that puts the responsibility for achieving quality results on anyone other than senior management. The plan must begin with senior management involvement.

Many factors must be considered in developing a plan of this nature. In preparing a TQM implementation plan, senior management must not only think about the program steps and elements, principles and practices, and timetable and milestones that it wishes to introduce, but also must carefully consider how TQM will be handled when new generations of management take over the operation of the business. The plan should be tailored to meet the specific needs of the business, and timetables should be established that match the urgency of implementation, balanced by the ability of the organization to adapt to change. The precision of a TQM plan is one that will surely be revised as the organization learns more or as the nature of business problems changes.

11

Integrating Quality into the Corporate Culture

INTRODUCTION

Some senior executives of a diversified Fortune 500 company once visited FPL's general office seeking information about the components of our quality system. After hours of discussion, one of them observed that our company operated in only one state, whereas he had the more complex job of implementing a quality process within a company that operated in over a dozen countries. He asked if I had any advice for him on how to handle such diversity.

I thought about the question for a minute, and then asked him the following question: "When you are in Italy, South America, England, or France, can you clearly identify your corporate culture as unique, or is the culture of your company different in each country?" He responded without hesitation, saying that their business culture was clearly evident in each factory and office no matter what country they were operating in.

It was obvious from his answer that the company had a business system and method that instills a uniform corporate culture. I advised him to continue doing whatever they were now doing to maintain that culture, except that additionally they should work to instill the concepts and methods of total quality.

WHAT IS A COMPANY CULTURE?

The idea of a "company culture" is one of the most misunderstood ideas in business. It leads one to believe that some mysterious force or mystical power is present in a company. The belief is that CEOs have magical power, that they can create a culture out of thin air. The way the concept is generally used also leads one to expect that each and every employee is somehow "consecrated" to the company's culture.

The reality is that corporate cultures develop over long periods of time. Corporate cultures develop from the basic philosophies embedded in the management of the company coupled with managerial behavior. Often corporate cultures become confused because management says one thing and does another.

One executive I know professes to believe in openness, trust, and employee empowerment. Yet, in spite of this philosophy—which I think he truly believes in—he consistently fails to follow it. One of his employees has even labeled him "the contrarian." His office door is closed all day. He talks about trust but does not really trust others. Few people have access to him and those who do are his inner circle of colleagues. He appears to dislike anyone who expresses a view different from his. He has implemented a highly centralized control structure and style of operation that make it virtually impossible for people to take initiative and to act. Even though openness, trust, and employee empowerment are actively promoted as concepts, it is highly unlikely in this case that such principles will ever take hold as part of the company culture. When senior managers act in a manner contrary to what they say they believe, their actions confuse and frustrate employees. People hear one thing and see another.

Corporate culture in my definition is the way the majority of employees in a company act when dealing with their customers and suppliers, as well as the way they behave toward one another. (I say "the majority" because I do not believe everyone can or should act in the same way.) Culture is an attitude, a practice, the very ethics of a business. A desirable corporate culture is the way you most want employees to act.

Today's work environment is a break from the past, and this environment continues to change. Employees want more freedom to act. They do not want to be told how to do everything. They want management to trust them. Most employees want to make a contribution and management needs to recognize that it can no longer be the sole source of decisions and improvements. So where do you start if you want to adopt a TQM culture in your company?

MANAGERS AND EMPLOYEES

The first place to start is with management accountability and a deep sense of responsibility toward employees. The attitude to foster is one that considers employees and how they are treated as the key ingredients to the company's success. This does not mean simply salary, benefits, perks, or equal opportunity—though these are important. What it means is the way management thinks about and acts toward individual employees.

Earlier it was noted that employees generally have great minds and that it is management's job to provide a forum where employees can exercise their minds. This is a necessity if one is to adopt a TQM management system. Systems and methods must be developed that demonstrate to employees that management values their contributions. Structures and practices should allow employees to present their ideas openly and free of fear. Dr. Deming says management must *drive out fear* in an organization. It must create an atmosphere of cooperation. It must develop, instill, and practice teamwork at all levels in the organization. It must eliminate internal competition because internal competition is destructive to the organization. It only promotes fear and reprisal. There is no place for this type of attitude in the workplace. And all of this must begin with senior management.

THE CUSTOMER

Another place to put emphasis while integrating quality into the company culture is through management's thoughts and actions toward its customers. How management acts toward its customers goes beyond providing them with products and services that meet their needs—this is simply a necessity, a prerequisite for staying in business. A corporate culture that is truly quality-oriented with respect to the customer is one in which employees can clearly articulate customer requirements and know the actions that they and the company are taking to improve the products and services provided. A culture must evolve where complaints and claims are treated as opportunities and not as nuisances, a culture that excites customers by doing things *beyond* what is expected and a culture that treats the customer the way each individual in the company would want to be treated if they were the customer. How can any business go wrong if it keeps its eye on the customer?

So how does management begin to demonstrate a customer-oriented philosophy? It begins by showing an active interest in the customer. Reading complaints, examining warranty claims, talking to customers directly—these are just a few of the things that can be done. When I was with FPL, I attempted to read every customer complaint. They were rich in information: the complaints identified areas for improvement and they identified areas where new services could be provided. I also tried to talk to service representatives to find out if they were having difficulties satisfying customers. I reviewed claims against the company, and these claims identified a number of areas for improvement. I talked to the organization about the customer every chance I got.

Management, then, must ensure that the gaps in fulfilling customer requirements are identified, communicated, and closed. In earlier chapters the merits of the customer needs analysis were described. This type of analysis, particularly when it is communicated by means of graphic display, provides an excellent informational vehicle.

Finally, from time to time try to *be* a customer in your company. Go ahead and use the products, receive the service, check to see if a truly customer-oriented culture has evolved.

ENCOURAGE COOPERATION

No department, section, or division has exclusive rights over the customer. Customers do not know how companies are organized and they are not likely to care. It is not important to them because they are interested only in what the company provides. So why do companies create cultures that place so much emphasis on organizational boundaries and internal competition? The Western way is to be highly competitive, so we create structures, organizations, and incentive and compensation schemes that foster the competitive spirit. Yet this spirit can be destructive!

Under TQM, management can improve the corporate culture by encouraging and rewarding behavior that promotes cooperation between and among departments and their managers. Customers receive the product and service through the organization and through close cooperation between departments. In addition, the concept of *internal* customers should be promoted to recognize that, in order to service the ultimate customer, each internal customer's requirements must also be met. This will demonstrate cooperation by example.

FACTS AND FICTION

Another factor that is of great importance in changing the company culture is the rigorous practice of management by fact. The practice of management by fact changes everyone's expectations about what is and what is not acceptable. Management by fact broadens employees' and managers' knowledge. It helps remove emotion from decisions and brings about better, more effective decisions.

For example, about two years after FPL's initial efforts in quality improvement began, we discovered a narrow but important problem area that needed to be addressed. Although I was becoming an advocate of using facts over opinions, I still wanted to give the idea a good test.

One company objective was to reduce both the frequency and duration of service interruptions. A subproblem involved the restoration of service once an interruption occurred. Yet another subdivision of the problem concerned the length of time it took to dispatch crews under various conditions.

To test the management-by-fact principle of quality, I assembled eight of the most experienced supervisors with expertise in this area. Through brainstorming, they listed, based on their experience, the reasons they considered it took so long to dispatch crews under these conditions.

The supervisors then put these causes on the list in order of priority to determine the most likely cause. Next they went out to verify the facts in support of their suppositions. After two weeks of data gathering, they returned with their findings—and everyone was shocked by the results. The causes that they identified in the field using facts and data had never even appeared on the original list they had brainstormed based on their "sense" of the problem.

Using facts, then, is another critical feature of integrating quality into the corporate culture. This will not necessarily be an easy thing to do. We each bring a set of background experiences and opinions to the work environment. We cannot and should not simply abandon these—they are the stuff of creativity. However, we must add to them the facts that support the things we feel. Management by fact must be institutionalized.

CONTINUOUS IMPROVEMENT

In his book *Kaizen*, Masaaki Imai describes both the "gradualist" and the "great leap forward" approaches to improvement. Imai says that the West relies on *innovation* for improvement—particularly technical innovation that has been the industrial West's strength. This "great leap forward" type of approach has proven successful in the West for making short-term, dramatic improvements. Japan, on the other hand, has taken the *kaizen* approach, or the idea of continuous improvement as supported by hundreds if not thousands of "small ideas." Although Imai presents the two approaches as opposites, I find them to be complementary.

If the West can continue to maintain its ingenuity and technical expertise, and simultaneously begin paying more attention to smaller improvements, I believe it can regain the market shares it once held. To gain a well-developed corporate culture that embraces quality as its cornerstone, one must instill in the organization a sense that there is no such thing as too small, no such thing as an insignificant improvement. Every process, every procedure, and every product can be improved according to the basic vision the business sets for itself.

Imai points out that the concept of continuous improvement includes, by definition, the involvement of virtually everyone in the company. Although some Japanese companies claim 100 percent involvement, my observation has been that the rate is often lower. We in the West do well to have at least 51 percent of the company's population directly involved, although we should always strive to involve everyone.

The concept of continuous improvement should prove extremely attractive to those industries that are stymied by the lack of technical innovation. Companies cannot afford the luxury of sitting idle while their research and development or engineering or computer staffs try to come up with the next breakthrough. The organization should never rest.

STRUCTURES FOR DEVELOPING QUALITY CULTURE

Some companies have gone to extreme lengths to create new organizational structures to implement their approaches to quality systems. FPL did, and I think it was probably too much. We created steering committees, quality councils, advisory groups, facilitators, and other unnatural or redundant organizational units. You will need structure as you begin integrating quality into your natural organization. TQM may cause you to change your management structure, but the change should occur as a result of an examination of the process, not as a result of adopting TQM.

Although I am not an advocate of changing the organization to implement TQM, there will initially be a need for a quality department. The department should include some specialists who will help develop training courses, assist other parts of the organization with difficult problem solving, and assist senior management in their evaluation of the management system. The quality department also can be of great assistance in helping senior management with the promotion of quality throughout the organization. Just as you have technical experts in staff advisory roles to assist the organization in technical areas, the quality department is the company's technical quality expert, but their technical expertise should be used in an advisory way. I do not believe you need to create numerous new structures within your company.

Use your natural organization to promote and implement your approach to quality. Why create another layer of overhead? Your quality consultant may encourage you to use new structural approaches, but be cautious and skeptical. If your current organizational structure prevents or inhibits you from an effective implementation, change the structure first. Avoid creating new and artificial structures because they will inhibit development of the type of corporate culture that must evolve.

CONCLUSION

Changes in the culture of a company are a natural consequence of implementing TQM. Corporate cultures develop over time and can be traced to the behavior and values of senior management. Senior management will need to apply the underlying values and concepts of TQM daily, and they must show by example that the customer is first, that they listen to and respond to employee's ideas, that all employees are respected, that decisions are made and problems are solved based on facts, and that cooperation among everyone is and must continue to be practiced.

Recommended Reading

General Information and Background

Aguayo, Rafael. *Dr. Deming: The American Who Taught the Japanese about Quality*. New York, NY: Lyle Stuart, 1990.

Deming, W. Edwards. *Out of the Crisis*. Cambridge, MA: MIT Center for Advanced Engineering Study, 1986.

Gabor, Andrea. *The Man Who Discovered Quality: How W. Edwards Deming Brought the Quality Revolution to America – The Stories of Ford, Xerox and GM*. New York, NY: Times Books, 1990.

Gitlow, Howard S. and Shelly J. *The Deming Guide to Quality and Competitive Advantage*. Englewood Cliffs, NJ: Prentice-Hall, Inc., 1987.

Kanter, Rosabeth Moss. *When Giants Learn to Dance*. New York, NY: Simon & Schuster, Inc., 1989.

Mizuno, Shigeru. *Company-Wide Total Quality Control*. Tokyo, Japan: Asian Productivity Organization, 1988.

Mizuno, Shigeru. *Management for Quality Improvement, the Seven New QC Tools*. Cambridge, MA: Productivity Press, 1988.

Peters, Tom and Waterman, Robert. *In Search of Excellence*. New York, NY: Random House, 1982.

Peters, Tom and Austin, Nancy. *A Passion for Excellence*. New York, NY: Alfred A. Knopf, 1988.

Walsh, Loren; Wurster, Ralph; Kimber, Raymond J. (Editors). *Quality Management Handbook*. Wheaton, IL: Hitchcock Publishing Co., 1986.

Walton, Mary. *The Deming Management Method*. New York, NY: Dodd, Mead & Company, 1986.

Walton, Mary. *Deming Management at Work*. New York, NY: G.P. Putnam's Sons, 1990.

Japanese Involvement in Quality

Fukuda, Ryuji. *Managerial Engineering: Techniques for Improving Quality and Productivity in the Workplace*. Cambridge, MA: Productivity Press, Inc., 1966.

Imai, Masaaki. *Kaizen – The Key to Japan's Competitive Success*. New York, NY: Random House, 1986.

Ishikawa, Kaoru. *Guide to Quality Control*. Tokyo, Japan: Asian Productivity Organization, 1975.

Ishikawa, Kaoru. *Introduction to Quality Control*. Tokyo, Japan: 3A Corporation, 1990.

Ishikawa, Kaoru. *What Is Total Quality Control? – The Japanese Way*. Englewood Cliffs, NJ: Prentice-Hall, Inc., 1985.

Management Leadership

Deming, W. Edwards. *Quality, Productivity and Competitive Position*. Cambridge, MA: MIT Press, 1982.

Juran, J.M. *Managerial Breakthrough*. New York, NY: McGraw-Hill, Inc., 1964.

Kanter, Rosabeth Moss. *The Change Masters*. New York, NY: Simon & Schuster, Inc., 1989.

Quality in Service Companies and Institutions

Albrecht, Karl and Zemke, Ron. *Service America! Doing Business in the New Economy*. Homewood, IL: Dow Jones-Irwin, 1985.

Hudiburg, John J. *Winning with Quality: The FPL Story*. White Plains, NY: Quality Resources, 1991.

Spechler, Jay W. *When America Does It Right*. Norcross, GA: Industrial Engineering and Management Press, Institute of Industrial Engineers, 1988.

Zeithami, Valarie; Parasuraman, A.; Berry, Leonard. *Delivering Quality Service*. New York, NY: The Free Press, 1990.

Quality in Manufacturing

Hayes, Robert H. and Wheelwright, Steven C. *Restoring Our Competitive Edge: Competing Through Manufacturing*. New York, NY: John Wiley & Sons, Inc., 1984.

Suzaki, Kiyoshi. *The New Manufacturing Challenge*. New York, NY: The Free Press, 1987.

Measuring Quality

Adam, Everett E.; Hershauer, James C.; Ruch, William A. *Productivity and Quality: Measurement as a Basis for Improvement*. Englewood Cliffs, NJ: Prentice-Hall, Inc., 1981.

Amsden, Robert T. and David M., and Butler, Howard E. *SPC Simplified*. New York, NY: UNIPUB/Kraus International Publications, 1986.

Burr, Irving W. *Statistical Quality Control Methods*. New York, NY: Marcel Dekker, Inc., 1976.

Camp, Robert C. *Benchmarking: The Search for Industry Best Practices That Lead to Superior Performance*. Milwaukee, WI: ASQC Quality Press, 1989.

Gitlow & Gitlow, Oppenheimer & Oppenheimer. *Tools and Methods for the Improvement of Quality*. Homewood, IL: Irwin Press, 1989.

Kume, Hitoshi. *Statistical Methods for Quality Improvement*. Japan: Association for Overseas Technical Scholarship, 1987.

Planning for Quality

Cannie, Joan Koob with Caplin, Donald. *Keeping Customers for Life*. New York, NY: American Management Association, 1991.

Juran, J.M. *Juran on Planning for Quality*. New York, NY: The Free Press, 1988.

Juran, J.M, and Gryna Jr., F.M. *Quality Planning and Analysis*. New York, NY: McGraw-Hill, Inc., 1984.

King, Bob. *Better Designs in Half the Time: Implementing QFD Quality Functional Deployment in America*. Methuen, MA: GOAL/QPC, 1987.

Quality and Human Resources

Aubrey II, Charles A. and Felkins, Patricia K. *Teamwork: Involving People in Quality and Productivity Improvement*. White Plains, NY: Quality Resources, 1988.

Dewar, Donald L. *Quality Circle Guide to Participative Management*. Englewood Cliffs, NJ: Prentice-Hall, Inc., 1982.

Olson, Val. *White Collar Waste*. Englewood Cliffs, NJ: Prentice-Hall, Inc., 1983.

Pierce, Richard J. *Involvement Engineering: Engaging Employees in Quality and Productivity*. Milwaukee, WI: ASQC Quality Press, 1986.

Schein, Edgar H. *Organizational Culture and Leadership*. San Francisco, CA: Jossey-Bass Publishers, 1986.

Index